REFORMISM AND REVISIONISM IN AFRICA'S POLITICAL ECONOMY IN THE 1990s

Also by Timothy M. Shaw

AFRICA IN WORLD POLITICS (*editor with Ralph I. Onwuka*)
AFRICA PROJECTED (*editor with Olajide Aluko*)
NEWLY INDUSTRIALIZING COUNTRIES AND THE
    POLITICAL ECONOMY OF SOUTH–SOUTH RELATIONS
    (*editor with Jerker Carlsson*)
NIGERIAN FOREIGN POLICY (*editor with Olajide Aluko*)
PEACE, DEVELOPMENT AND SECURITY IN THE
    CARIBBEAN (*editor with Anthony T. Bryan and J. Edward
    Greene*)
TOWARDS A POLITICAL ECONOMY FOR AFRICA

Reformism and Revisionism in Africa's Political Economy in the 1990s

The Dialectics of Adjustment

Timothy M. Shaw

*Professor of Political Science and
International Development Studies
Dalhousie University, Canada*

St. Martin's Press

First published in Great Britain 1993 by
THE MACMILLAN PRESS LTD
Houndmills, Basingstoke, Hampshire RG21 2XS
and London
Companies and representatives
throughout the world

A catalogue record for this book is available
from the British Library.

ISBN 0–333–57745–0

Printed in Great Britain by
Antony Rowe Ltd, Chippenham, Wiltshire

First published in the United States of America 1993 by
Scholarly and Reference Division,
ST. MARTIN'S PRESS, INC.,
175 Fifth Avenue,
New York, N.Y. 10010

ISBN 0–312–07977–X

Library of Congress Cataloging-in-Publication Data
Shaw, Timothy M.
Reformism and revisionism in Africa's political economy in the
1990s: the dialectics of adjustment / Timothy M. Shaw.
p.   cm.
Includes bibliographical references and index.
ISBN 0–312–07977–X
1. Africa—Economic conditions—1960–   2. Africa—Politics and
government—1960–   I. Title.
HC800.S527   1993
338.96—dc20
                                        92–2904
                                          CIP

To successive generations of African university students who continue courageously to challenge the arbitrary assumptions and assertions of African states

Contents

Contents

List of Maps

List of Tables

List of Boxes

List of Figures

Preface

This text was conceived towards the end of the 1980s, when it became ever more glaringly apparent that the political economy of Africa was in a period of profound transformation, one not yet captured in the established literature. Timely support from the Social Sciences and Humanities Research Council of Canada (SSHRCC) enabled me to spend my 1989 sabbatical year on the continent, based at the University of Zimbabwe, where I was Visiting Professor of Political and Administrative Studies and World University Service of Canada (WUSC) Associate. However, I was diverted there by not unrelated and equally instructive projects on 'liberalisation' in Zimbabwe and 'liberation' in Namibia and South Africa. As it turned out, this was most fortuitous because my overly economy- and policy-centric perspective on structural adjustment has since been transcended by a more comprehensive one which incorporates crucial political conditionalities and popular responses. Happily, the University of Manchester provided me with a perfect opportunity to complete this process of conceptual and editorial revision by giving me a generous Hallsworth Research Fellowship in Political Economy for the first half of 1991, and the UN Research Institute for Social Development (UNRISD) in Geneva facilitated final improvements through a two-month residency in mid-1991. Throughout these 30 months of research and reflection I have been encouraged and challenged by innumerable colleagues in the academy, bureaucracy, and community in Africa, Europe and North America, especially by the new generation of African(ist) scholars who have instructed and supervised me, when they thought I was doing so for them! My Department and University in Nova Scotia have been understanding throughout. And as always, my spouse and critic, Jane Parpart, has been a constant source of support, comment, and diversion. Notwithstanding all this encouragement and input, I alone am responsible for the remaining deficiencies and contradictions.

T.M.S.

List of Abbreviations

ACBI	African Capacity Building Initiative
ACP	African, Caribbean and Pacific (countries associated with the EC)
AIDS	Acquired Immune Deficiency Syndrome
BHN	Basic Human Needs
CFA	*Communauté Financière d'Afrique* (franc zone)
CODESRIA	Council for the Development of Social Research in Africa
COMECON	Council for Mutual Economic Cooperation (Eastern Bloc)
EC	European Community
ECA	UN Economic Commission for Africa
EOI	Export-Oriented Industrialisation
ERP	Economic Recovery Programme
ESAF	Enhanced Structural Adjustment Facility (IBRD)
FLS	Front-Line States (of Southern Africa)
G-7	Group of Seven (industrialised states)
G-14	Group of Fourteen (major developing countries)
HDI	Human Development Index (UNDP)
IBRD	International Bank for Reconstruction and Development (World Bank)
IFIs	International Financial Institutions
IMF	International Monetary Fund
ISI	Import-Substitution Industrialisation
LPA	Lagos Plan of Action
NAM	Non-Aligned Movement
NGO	Non-Governmental Organisation
NICs	Newly Industrialising Countries
NIDL	New International Division of Labour
NIDP	New International Division of Power
NIEO	New International Economic Order
OAU	Organisation of African Unity
ODA	Official Development Assistance
OECD	Organisation for Economic Cooperation and Development
OPEC	Organisation of Petroleum Exporting Countries
PQLI	Physical Quality of Life Index (ODC)

PTA	Preferential Trade Area (for Eastern and Southern Africa)
SADCC	Southern African Development Coordination Conference
SAP	Structural Adjustment Programme
SSA	Sub-Saharan Africa
UN	United Nations
UNDP	UN Development Programme
UNICEF	UN Children's Fund
UNRISD	UN Research Institute for Social Development
US	United States of America
USSR	Union of Soviet Socialist Republics

1 Introduction: Beyond the Dialectics of Dependence

Ex Africa, semper aliquid novi
> Pliny the elder in first century AD and motto of Italian–African Institute

The democratic project or the process of redemocratising African politics is [thus] becoming the hegemonic issue in African studies
> Robert Fatton (1990: 455)

In every crisis there arises an opportunity
> Ancient Chinese proverb

African studies as well as African states and structures were quite transformed in the 1980s: the combined and cumulative impacts of multiple *crises* – debt, drought, devaluation, deregulation and deindustrialisation – have produced new challenges, contradictions and conflicts. Yet, surprisingly, such novel realities have not yet become apparent in analysis even if they have already begun to transform *praxis*.

The new constellations of distinctive relations and prescriptions take place within the context of two novel conditions – *structural adjustments* internally and *strategic agreements* externally – which together have transformed the continent's context: the ideology as well as reality of conditionality and *détente*. Both of these policy directions are advocated and advanced by dominant nations and institutions, notably by the World Bank (IBRD) and International Monetary Fund (IMF) and by the two super-powers, respectively. These conditions have rendered obsolete many of the assumptions and assertions of African regimes, especially 'African socialism' and nonalignment, respectively. Together monetarism and internationalism in the North have transformed the global context for the South: no possibility of the much sought-after New International Economic

1

Order (NIEO); rather the reality of, first, a New International Division of Labour (NIDL) and then, a New International Division of Power (NIDP). These transformations, which climaxed in the last few days of the 1980s, also confirmed the obsolescence of many of the perspectives and policies treated in this volume's predecessor: *Towards a Political Economy for Africa: The Dialectics of Dependence* (Shaw, 1985).

African studies and scenarios for the 1990s and beyond require a new set of approaches and responses which go beyond the established orthodoxies of modernisation and materialist frameworks alike. They require recognition of *revisionist* premises and prescriptions because objective contexts have changed and analytic challenges have emerged. In particular, myriad effects of *economic liberalisation* are beginning to be felt in terms of demands for *political liberalisation*: from privatisation to pluralism. The expansion of the informal sector to supplement the shrinking formal economy is matched in the political sphere by non-governmental organisations (NGOs) replacing diminished state structures. In short, state-society relations are in flux, with informal political economy expanding to fill the space vacated by the contracting formal sectors, economic and political. Yet the African state is diminished not deceased; there continues to be the danger of regressions towards authoritarianism under some variant of military or corporatist rule (Nyang' oro and Shaw, 1989).

The distinctive features of the continent in an era of national adjustments and global transformations need to be recognised and incorporated into both examination and prescription. At the level of *economics* (see Table 1), these include correlates of structural adjustment: rapid devaluation, dramatic desubsidisation, gradual privatisation, expansion of the informal sectors, increased reliance on women etc. And at the level of *politics* (see Table 2), they include: dismantling of the ubiquitous one-party state, recognition of myriad NGOs, expansion of human liberties, and reduced reliance on coercion. To be sure, such measures induce their own reactions, especially among newly 'vulnerable groups' of state functionaries and middle classes (see Boxes 5–7), but the trend is irreversible. Hence the imperative of transcending inherited contemporary orthodoxies in political economy. The recognition and incorporation of the correlates of adjustment and transformation constitute an awesome task for the last decade of the twentieth century but is necessary if appropriate prescriptions are to flow from realistic descriptions.

The twin themes which are emerging from the interrelated processes of economic and political liberalisation are *reform* and *democracy*, respectively: reformation of overly state-centric and stagnant economies and democratisation of excessively centralised and corrupted polities. Together these begin to capture the new dynamic of state-economy and -society relations and have elsewhere been referred to, particularly by rather established American-based investigators and institutions, as adjustment and governance, respectively (cf. Nelson, 1989, 1990).

However, whilst both political economy and *civil society* are in considerable flux it would be misleading to impose extra-African perceptions and expectations on them; unlike Eastern Europe, for example, Africa has a shorter history of modern sovereignty and state hegemony. Only a few countries have resilient 'civil societies', notably Nigeria, Senegal, South Africa and Zimbabwe. So the bases for democratic demands in Africa in the 1990s are different from those in Eastern Europe over the last quarter-century. Rather, the current decade is likely to be characterised by an intense conflict between a diminished state and an empowered society, with the outcome being both unpredictable and variable: an ongoing clash between the claims of *constitutionalism* and the imperatives of *corporatism*. As states become contained by the conditionalities of adjustments so they will possess reduced resources for patronage and cooptation; their only recourse for the perpetuation of order and control will be the typically unreformed forces of coercion – army, police, security and other assorted units – notwithstanding the deservedly unhappy fate of such state functionaries in much of Eastern Europe at the turn of the decade. Conversely, given the shrinkage of state authority, informal economies and parties will continue to expand to fill some of the vacated 'space', so further eroding the established dominance of state actors.

In short, *democratic pressures* from inside and outside the continent will confront regimes whose inherited dominance is already tenuous; such states may react in paranoid rather than progressive ways. The transition from nationalist generation to a post-colonial period will be problematic, with Museveni's Uganda providing some clues (see Box 22): a government which came to power through guerrilla struggle not against a colonial or settler state but rather against a series of oppressive and regressive indigenous regimes.

So both politics and economics are in transition in Africa at the start of the 1990s. The established classic one-party state structure has become discredited and undermined as its tendencies towards

Table 1 Africa: Country Profiles

	Population		GNP per capita ($)		Real GDP growth (annual average % change)		Total debt ($ mn)		Debt service, as % of exports 1989
	(mn) 1990	Growth rate 1985–90	1980	1989	1981–5	1986–90	1980	1989	
Algeria	24.96	2.9	1940	2250	4.46	0.68	19,377	26,067	69
Angola	10.02	2.8	725	620	0.12	4.12	n.a.	6,950	42
Benin	4.63	3.2	320	380	3.72	-0.1	417	1,177	7
Botswana	1.30	3.5	780	1600	11.7	8.44	133	513	4
Burkina Faso	8.99	2.8	240	320	4.92	2.96	334	756	9
Burundi	5.47	2.9	200	220	5.12	1.86	166	867	33
Cameroon	11.83	2.7	960	1000	9.5	-1.7	2,513	4,743	19
Cape Verde	0.37	3.1	520	760	4.82	2.24	20	130	n.a.
CAR	3.03	2.5	320	390	2.4	1.62	20	716	14
Chad	5.67	2.5	160	190	6.54	2.84	218	368	5
Comoros	0.55	3.1	344	450	3.6	1.48	44	176	9
Congo	2.27	2.8	340	940	11.16	1.96	1,496	4,316	27
Côte d'Ivoire	11.99	3.9	850	790	-0.26	-0.96	5,848	15,412	41
Djibouti	0.40	3	n.a.	n.a.	1.52	1.04	32	180	n.a.
Egypt	52.42	2.2	500	630	7.88	2.66	20,384	48,779	22
Eq. Guinea	0.35	2.4	n.a.	430	0.5	2.92	76	228	19
Ethiopia	49.24	2.7	120	120	-0.14	3.88	804	3,013	39
Gabon	1.17	3.3	3900	2960	1.98	0.92	1,513	3,176	12
Gambia	0.86	2.7	350	240	0.96	7.62	137	342	11
Ghana	15.02	3.1	410	390	0	5.36	1,314	3,078	50
Guinea	5.75	2.5	303	430	1.84	3.96	1,117	2,176	15
Guinea-Bissau	0.96	2.3	130	180	7.32	2.04	132	458	4
Kenya	24.03	4.1	420	370	3.62	4.62	3,530	5,690	33
Lesotho	1.77	2.8	410	470	1.38	6.4	71	324	3
Liberia	2.57	3.3	580	n.a.	-0.9	-6.96	686	1,761	n.a.
Libya	4.54	3.6	9741	5310	-3.54	0.44	n.a.	n.a.	n.a.
Madagascar	12.00	3.2	430	230	-0.78	2.4	1,257	3,607	52
Malawi	8.75	3.3	180	180	3.12	2.68	821	1,394	28
Mali	9.21	3	240	270	1.72	6.6	733	2,157	19
Mauritania	2.02	2.8	440	490	-0.34	1.5	845	2,010	20
Mauritius	1.08	1.2	1180	1990	4.46	6.82	467	832	10
Morocco	25.06	2.4	930	880	2.52	4.28	9,678	20,851	32
Mozambique	15.65	2.7	n.a.	80	-7.9	3.64	n.a.	4,737	24
Namibia	1.78	3.2	n.a.	1030	-1.38	2.88	n.a.	n.a.	n.a.
Niger	7.73	3.1	440	290	1.14	2.42	863	1,578	33
Nigeria	108.54	3.5	1030	250	-1.82	3.18	8,934	32,832	21
Rwanda	7.23	3.4	240	320	2.4	-0.56	190	652	19
Sao Tome	0.12	2.4	485	312	-3.88	4.52	24	131	45
Senegal	7.32	2.7	510	650	3.04	2.8	1,468	4,139	29
Seychelles	0.07	1	2000	4170	1.72	5.34	84	169	12
Sierra Leone	4.15	2.6	320	220	-0.6	0.44	430	1,057	n.a.
Somalia	7.49	2.4	140	170	3.5	1.18	660	2,137	34
Sudan	25.20	2.9	430	641	1.06	2	5,163	12,965	8
Swaziland	0.78	3.4	820	900	3.3	5.06	206	281	5
Tanzania	27.31	3.7	280	120	0.44	3.68	2,572	4,918	17
Togo	3.53	3.1	420	390	-1.64	3.18	1,045	1,185	19
Tunisia	8.18	2.4	1410	1260	3.78	3.54	3,527	6,899	23
Uganda	18.79	3.5	280	250	2.22	3	733	1,808	81
Zaire	35.56	3.2	630	260	1.72	1.78	4,860	8,843	22
Zambia	8.45	3.7	600	390	0.74	-0.2	3,266	6,874	12
Zimbabwe	9.70	3.1	710	650	3.44	3.12	786	3,088	26

Aid per capita ($) 1989	Food production per capita (1979–81=100)		Infant mortality (per 1,000 live births)		Life expectancy (years) 1985–90	Adult literacy male/female (%) 1985	Primary school enrolment 1988		Access to safe water (%) 1985–8
	1981–5	1986–9	1980–85	1985–90			Total (%)	Females per 100 males	
6	97	99	88	74	64	63/37	96	80	71
14	93	85	149	137	45	49/33	n.a.	n.a.	35
54	101	114	100	90	46	37/16	63	51	35
133	88	68	76	67	59	73/69	116	107	58
32	101	116	149	138	47	21/6	32	59	67
37	99	98	129	119	48	43/26	70	75	38
41	98	96	103	94	52	68/45	111*	85	32
n.a.	61	84	52	44	66	n.a.	n.a.	n.a.	69
64	94	90	114	104	49	53/29	67	62	12
43	97	101	143	132	46	40/11	51	40	n.a.
n.a.	n.a.	121	109	99	54	n.a.	n.a.	n.a.	n.a.
41	100	97	81	73	53	71/55	n.a.	95	21
35	95	95	105	96	52	53/31	n.a.	70	18
n.a.	n.a.	n.a.	132	122	47	n.a.	n.a.	n.a.	45
31	103	108	115	65	59	59/30	90	75	73
n.a.	n.a.	n.a.	137	127	46	n.a.	n.a.	n.a.	n.a.
14	93	90	159	137	44	n.a.	36	64	19
121	91	81	112	103	52	70/53	n.a.	98	68
n.a.	111	94	154	143	43	n.a.	n.a.	n.a.	75
38	106	108	98	90	54	64/43	73	80	57
62	97	90	157	145	43	40/17	30	45	32
n.a.	116	108	163	151	42	n.a.	n.a.	n.a.	21
41	96	102	80	72	58	70/49	93	94	30
69	85	79	111	100	56	62/84	112	125	48
23	100	95	153	142	53	47/23	35	n.a.	58
3	107	107	97	82	61	81/50	n.a.	n.a.	97
28	98	93	130	120	54	74/62	97	95	32
48	95	85	163	150	47	52/31	72	80	56
57	102	97	180	169	44	23/11	23	59	38
102	91	88	137	127	46	n.a.	52	70	66
54	101	101	28	23	69	89/77	105	88	95
18	100	122	97	82	61	45/22	67	63	61
49	91	84	153	141	47	55/22	68	78	24
26	90	92	116	106	56	n.a.	n.a.	n.a.	n.a.
40	88	86	146	135	45	19/9	30	56	49
3	99	98	114	105	51	54/31	62	82	48
35	97	78	132	122	49	61/63	64	97	64
n.a.	n.a.	85	n.a.	59	67	n.a.	n.a.	n.a.	45
91	102	106	97	87	50	37/19	59	69	54
n.a.	n.a.	n.a.	n.a.	n.a.	47	n.a.	n.a.	n.a.	n.a.
25	99	90	166	154	41	38/21	53	n.a.	42
72	94	97	143	132	45	18/6	52	n.a.	35
31	94	88	118	108	50	33/14	49	n.a.	21
n.a.	100	99	129	118	56	n.a.	n.a.	n.a.	50
39	95	89	115	106	53	93/88	66	99	56
52	91	89	105	94	53	53/28	101	63	71
31	99	96	71	52	65	68/41	116	82	64
24	99	86	112	103	51	70/45	77	82	20
19	98	95	92	83	52	79/45	76	78	34
50	91	96	88	80	53	84/67	97	90	59
28	96	94	76	66	58	81/67	128	95	n.a.

Source: *UN Africa Recovery*, adapted from: (a) FAO, *Production Yearbook*, 1989; (b) UN, *World Population Chart*, 1990; (c) UNCTAD, *The Least Developed Countries 1990 Report*; (d) UNICEF, *The State of the World's Children Report*, 1991; (e) World Bank, *World Debt Tables, 1990–91*, *World Development Report 1990* and *1991*.
NOTE: Figures in current dollars unless stated. [1] Debt servicing figures are for actual payments, not scheduled obligations.
* Figures in italics are for the latest available year.

Table 2 Political Regimes in Sub-Saharan Africa
(South Africa excluded)

Official name	Date of Independence	Head of state	Type of government	Tendencies
People's Republic of Angola	11/10/75	President Jose Eduardo Dos Santos since 1979	Multi-party system since March 1991	Ceasefire anticipated for 30/05/91 and elections before November 1992
Republic of Benin	01/08/60	President Nicéphore Soglo, democratically elected 25/03/91	Multi-party system	
Republic of Botswana	30/09/66	President Quet Ketumile Joni Masire, democratically re-elected 7/10/89	Multi-party system	
Burkina Faso	05/07/60	Blaise Campaoré, by a bloody coup d'état, since 1987	Multi-party system since January 1991: the new constitution limits the type of political parties permitted	Referendum on the new constitution 2/06/91: presidential elections planned for November and legislative ones in December 1991
Republic of Burundi	01/07/62	President Pierre Buyoya, by coup d'état, in 1987	One-party system	A constitutional Commission established in March 1991 is to call a National Conference
Republic of Cameroon	01/01/60	President Paul Biya, chosen by his predecessor	Multi-party system since December 1990	17 officially registered parties; municipal elections in 1992, legislative and presidential ones before the end of 1993

Republic of Cape Verde	05/07/75	President Antonio Mascarenhas Monteiro, democratically elected 17/02/91	Multi-party system	Legislative elections 13/01/91, presidential ones 01/02/91
Central African Republic	13/07/60	President André Kolingba, by *coup d'état*, since 1981	One-party system	End of April 1991, President officially acknowledged multi-party system
Republic of Chad	11/08/60	Idris Deby, by *coup d'état*, since 01/12/90	Interim military regime	New regime promises multi-party system within the next 30 months
Federal Islamic Republic of the Comoros	06/07/75	President Said Mohamed Djobar, elected in March 1990	Multi-party system	
Republic of the Congo	15/07/60	President Denis Sassou N'guesso, since 1979	One-party system evolving towards multi-party system	National Conference taking place end of April 1991
Republic of Djibouti	27/06/77	Hassan Gouled Aptidon, since 1977	One-party system	Strong popular pressure for democratisation
People's Democratic Republic of Ethiopia		President Mengistu Hailé Mariam	One-party system	Principle of multi-party system accepted, but cannot be put in place until end of civil war
Republic of Gabon	17/07/60	President El Hadj Omar Bongo, since 1967	Multi-party system	Legislative elections held October 1990
Republic of Gambia	18/01/65	President Sir Dawda Kairaba Jawara, since 1970, democratically re-elected in 1987	Multi-party system	Presidential elections in 1992

continued on page 8

Table 2 continued

Official name	Date of Independence	Head of state	Type of government	Tendencies
Republic of Ghana	06/03/57	Jerry Rawlings, by *coup d'état*, since 31/12/81	Political activities forbidden	The National Commission for Democracy presented its report 26/03/91; a new constitution to be drafted by a study group to be named in May 1991
Republic of Guinea	02/10/58	President Lansana Conté, by *coup d'état* upon death of Sékou Touré in 1984	Political activities forbidden	In December 1990, a new constitution was approved; it foresees a two-party civilian government for 1996
Republic of Guinea-Bissau	10/09/74	President Joao Bernardo Vieira	One-party system	Multi-party system and free, two-candidate presidential elections approved: new constitution being prepared, transition period until January 1993
Republic of Equatorial Guinea	12/10/68	President Teodoro Obiang N'Guema M'Bassogo, by *coup d'état*, since 1979	One-party system	No indication of change
Republic of the Ivory Coast	07/07/60	President Félix Houphouet Boigny, elected 28/10/90	Multi-party system	Democratic presidential and legislative elections were held in 1990
Republic of Kenya	12/12/63	President Daniel arap Moi, succeeded Jomo Kenyatta	One-party system	Government officially opposed to multi-party system

Country	Date	Head of State	System	Notes
Kingdom of Lesotho	04/10/66	New king enthroned in November 1990	Constitutional monarchy	A constituent assembly was formed in June 1990; the military foresees a return to civilian government after elections planned for June 1992.
Republic of Liberia	26/07/1847	In state of civil war	Interim government not accepted by all parties now in conflict	Elections planned for October 1991, subject to an agreement with Taylor's rebel group
Democratic Republic of Madagascar	26/06/60	President Didier Ratsiraka, elected by referendum in 1989	Since March 1991, multi-party system permitted	In recent weeks, massive popular demonstrations demanding resignation of Ratsiraka were violently repressed. To this day he has refused to step down.
Republic of Malawi	06/07/64	President Hastings Kabundu Banda, since 1963	One-party system	No foreseeable change; the current President, aged 91, is without an apparent successor
Republic of Mali	22/06/60	Zoumana Sako, interim Prime Minister since Moussa Traoré's arrest on 26/03/91	One-party system evolving towards multi-party system	New government committed itself to return power to civilian authorities: elections planned for end of 1991 or early 1992
Islamic Republic of Mauritania	22/11/60	President Maawiya Ould Sid'Ahmed Taya, since 1984	One-party system evolving towards multi-party system	On 14/04/91, President promised free legislative elections and a constitutional referendum in 1991

continued on page 10

Table 2 continued

Official name	Date of Independence	Head of state	Type of government	Tendencies
Mauritius	12/03/65	Executive Prime Minister Aneerood Jugnauth	Multi-party parliamentary democracy	
People's Republic of Mozambique	25/06/75	President Joaquim Alberto Chissano	Multi-party system	Multi-party system and new constitution approved by Parliament: free elections planned for 1992
Republic of Namibia	21/03/90	President Sam Daniel Nujoma, democratically elected	Multi-party system	Parliamentary democracy
Republic of Niger	03/08/60	President Ali Saibou succeeded Seyni Kountche in 1987	Multi-party system since 1990	Free presidential and legislative elections planned for 1991
Republic of Nigeria	01/10/60	President Ibrahim Babaginda, by coup d'état, since 1985	Two-party system, partially in place	Two-party system established in 1990: local elections in October 1990, legislative in October 1991 and presidential in 1992
Republic of Uganda	09/10/62	President Yowéri Kaguta Musévéni, since 1986	Political activities suspended	Period of transition which should have ended in 1990 prolonged for 5 years: new constitution to be put in place between 1992 and 1994

Republic of Rwanda	01/07/62	President Juvenal Habyaramina, since 1973	One-party system evolving towards multi-party system	The National Commission of 21/09/90 proposes multi-party system and free elections: referendum on new constitutional charter planned for 15/06/91
Republic of Sao Tome and Principe	12/07/75	Celestino Rocha da Costa democratically elected 20/01/91	Multi-party system	Presidential elections on 20/01/91, legislative elections 03/04/91
Republic of the Seychelles	29/06/76	President Albert René, by *coup d'état*, since 1977	One-party system	No indications of change
Republic of Senegal	20/06/60	President Abdou Diouf, since 1981, democratically re-elected in 1988	Multi-party system	Multi-party system for past 15 years, but the Socialist Party has been in power since independence
Republic of Sierra Leone	27/04/61	President Joseph Saidou Momoh, since 1985, chosen by his predecessor	One-party system evolving towards multi-party system	In March 1991, the President accepted multi-party system recommended by the Constitutional Review Commission
Democratic Republic of Somalia	01/07/60	President Siad Baré, chased out by civil war	Civil war in progress	Country governed by a coalition of three rebel groups

continued on page 12

Table 2 continued

Official name	Date of Independence	Head of state	Type of government	Tendencies
Republic of Sudan	19/12/55	Omar Hassan Ahmad Al-Bashir, by *coup d'état*, since 30/06/89	Political activities forbidden	The tense political climate and the civil war in the south preclude any sign of change
Kingdom of Swaziland	06/09/68	His Majesty Mswati III, since 1986	Limited constitutional monarchy	In 1973, the constitution concentrated power in the hands of the King; in March 1991 he withdrew his opposition to multi-party system
United Republic of Tanzania	09/12/61	President Al Hassan Mwinyi, since 1985	One-party system	Presidential Reform Commission set up in February 1991, report expected in March 1992; until then, all but those involved with the Commission are forbidden to discuss multi-party system

Republic of Togo	27/04/60	Gnassingbé Eyadéma, by *coup d'état*, since 1963	Single-party system evolving towards multi-party system	Report of round-table conference regarding accession to multi-party system expected in 1991
Republic of Zaire	30/06/60	Mobutu Sese Seko, by *coup d'état*, since 1965	Multi-party system since 06/11/90	Legislative elections in December 1991, presidential elections in January 1992
Republic of Zambia	24/10/64	President Kenneth Kaunda, since 1964	Multi-party system since 03/11/90	Legislative and presidential elections in 1991
Republic of Zimbabwe	18/04/80	President Robert Mugabe, since 1987, re-elected in 1989	Multi-party system evolving towards one-party system	For the last several years, President Mugabe has publicly stated his preference for a one-party system

Source: ICHRDD, *Libertas* 1(3) (June 1991) pp. 4–5; updated September 1991.

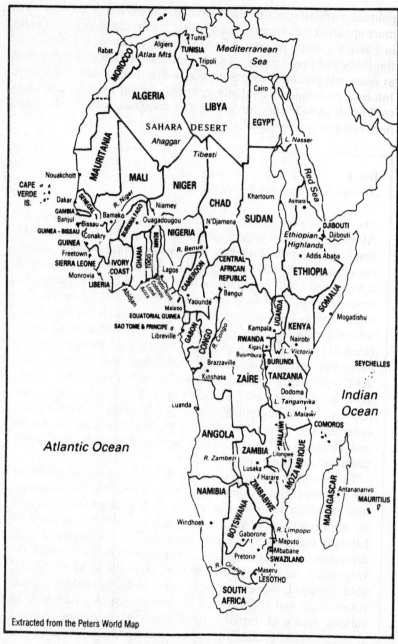

Map 1 Political economies of Africa, 1991
(based on the Peters Projection of Africa)

political authoritarianism and economic inefficiency become ever
more apparent (see Box 1). Even before the dramatic series of events
in Eastern Europe in 1989, throughout the continent the decade of
the 1980s had been one of relentless reconsideration and redirection
as economic pressures increased and political alienation intensified.
Informal economic survival and informal popular participation came
to flourish outside the purview of the increasingly discredited and
impoverished post-colonial state.

Box 1
African Societies and Political Culture

The diverse ecological and economic regions and regimes of
Africa have distinct appearances and aromas. Since pre-colonial
times, the continent's myriad territories have traded across different oceans with only limited intra-African exchange. Multiple
colonial and settler experiences from the eighteenth to twentieth
centuries reinforced such divergent connections. So, today, the
three regions initially identified by Samir Amin (1972: 504) –
'colonial trade economy' (West), 'concession-owning companies'
(Central) and 'labour reserves' (Eastern and Southern) – remain
distinctive, even if subject now to some homogenising pressures:
debt repayments, structural adjustments, international assistance, multinational companies, transnational technologies, taste
transfers etc. Stereotyping about the dynamism of West Africa,
orderliness of Southern Africa, peasantries of Eastern Africa
and aloofness of North Africa has some basis in fact, both
historical and contemporary.

This text is not a travelogue; there are many tourist guides to
the continent. But it is important to recognise that the 'substruc-
ture' on which new states have been built includes values as well
as infrastructures. The early bronzes of Benin, crosses of
Ethiopia and stone shrines of Zimbabwe are illustrative of such
diversities. New technologies and pressures intensified such divergencies: oil plantations and then oil wells in West Africa;
gold, diamond, copper and other mines in Southern Africa; sisal,
cotton, tea, and coffee farms in East Africa etc. Although in
various states of repair, the Portuguese forts and palaces

continued on page 16

Box 1 *continued*
African Societies and Political Culture

concentrated on the Atlantic and Indian Ocean coasts contrast with
Cape Dutch architecture in Southern Africa, Italian legacies in
Ethiopia and the Sahel style in the Western deserts. The hard-
hats and work-boots of Southern Africa's miners contrast with
the hoes of East and West Africa; the fashionableness of cities
like Abidjan, Algiers, Cape Town, Dakar, Harare, and Nairobi
with the timelessness of the continent's extensive rural areas.
And the characteristic acacia trees, evergreens and thorn-bushes
of Eastern and Southern Africa are quite different from the
remaining hard-woods in the rain forests of West and Central
Africa or the sun and dust of the Sahel, Sahara and much of
North Africa. Mounts Kenya and Kilimanjaro are always snow-
tipped, Zimbabwe and South Africa have frosts, and it snows for
the skiers in Lesotho. Not only did the colonialists and settlers
bequeath different architectures, languages and administrative
systems, Africa drives on different sides of the road still: right-
hand in North and West and on the left in Eastern and Southern.
Such is the legacy and diversity of African cultures: social and
historical as well as political and economic (O'Connor, 1991).

Thus, by the end of the 1980s, a few 'second wave' regimes and
structures had begun to appear in response to failings in orthodox
arrangements, notably the National Redemption government in
Uganda. Parallel moves towards two-, three-, or multi-party states in
Algeria, Namibia, Nigeria and Senegal reflect awareness of the need
for popular involvement and support. And original constitutional
provisions – for example, maximum rather than life terms for presidents, reserved seats for women, youth, soldiers, cooperatives and
other recognised interests, and checks on misuse of preventive detention laws in Tanzania – indicate a new consciousness of the negative
developmental impacts of typical one-man life presidencies. Moreover, the first, ageing generation of nationalist leaders, symbolised
now by the remaining survivors – Banda, Hassan, Houphouet-
Boigny, Mobutu and Mugabe – can hardly expect to rule into the next
century. And their successors will be increasingly inclined, encouraged by the example of Eastern Europe, to make clean breaks to

avoid being tainted by such association – for example, Biya after Ahidjo, Chihuba after Kaunda, and Mwinyi after Nyerere. Few direct descendants of the old guard will be permitted in future despite personal and familial accumulation at home and abroad.

African studies and scenarios for the 1990s demand, then, a new set of approaches and responses which go beyond the established orthodoxies of modernisation and materialist frameworks alike. They require recognition of *revisionist* **premises and prescriptions because objective conditions and contexts have changed, generating challenges for both analysis and** *praxis*.

Thus, distinctive features of the continent in an era of adjustment need to be recognised and incorporated into both examination and prescription: especially exponential devaluations, creeping privatisations, ubiquity of informal sectors, recognition of the roles of women, and appreciation of the vulnerability of the ecology. Such incorporation (not just juxtaposition or extension) – correlates of structural adjustment measures – transforms established approaches to explanation and prescription. In particular, it leads to a set of interrelated questions about the definition and composition of crucial institutions such as the state, civil society, informal sectors, social formations, and contradictions and coalitions; in short, development itself. Hence the imperative, for both existential and intellectual reasons, of transcending contemporary orthodoxies (see Box 2).

Of course, such truly '*radical*' analysis, which goes to the roots of current crises and debates cannot ignore theoretical antecedents, notably dependency and materialist *genres*; this is not an appeal to the relativist anarchy advocated by post-modernism. It can, and should, however, go well beyond these particular orthodoxies given changes in the global divisions of labour and power. This imperative should be particularly apparent in the last decade of the twentieth century when new clusters of internal and external forces and factors are present within and around African political economies, from the emergence of the Pacific Rim to the increase in un- and underemployment. This had become clear well before the dramatic transformations in Eastern Europe and the Soviet Union at the turn of the decade, which serve only to underline the essential need for informed revisionism: from definitions of socialism to feasibility of non-alignment (see Box 3).

Yet while there may be some agreement on the list of such issues, particularly as they emerge from research institutes, central banks, NGOs and international consultants if not yet from academe, there is

Box 2
African Authors and Political Decay

Politics is rarely drab or dull in Africa. Rather, it dominates the
news and rumour, and it informs cartoons and songs. Economics
is rarely featured in literatures or lyrics, but personalities and policies frequently are. And no matter how repressive the regime,
humour and rumour persist in diminishing its pretentions.
Wole Soyinka, Nigeria's Nobel Prize winner, Ngugi wa'Thiongo,
abused Kenyan author and playright, Chinua Achebe, voice of
caution about civilian and military excesses are amongst the most
eminent of the many courageous political and social commentators and critics. The songs of Fela in Nigeria or Mapfumo in
Zimbabwe rail against ambition and corruption and the films of
Sembene Osman expose vanities. Despite the threat and reality
of repression, African writers and producers persist in exposing
the pretentions of regimes and personalities: a healthy antidote
to arrogance and adjustment.

African literature is full, then, of African politics and personalities if not political economy. From early classics such as Chinua
Achebe's *Things Fall Apart* and Ngugi's *Petals of Blood* to the
former's *Anthills of the Savannah* and J. M. Coetzee's *Waiting
for the Barbarians*, African writers have commented elegantly
yet profoundly on the foibles and fallacies of their leaders, both
civilian and military. Non-African authors have also contributed
critique and rhetoric about continental realities in sometimes
controversial novels, notably V. S. Naipaul's *Bend in the River*,
Wilbur Smith's *Leopard Hunts in Darkness* and John Updike's
The Coup. And one or two social scientists can even write
elegant prose or poetry such as the novels of Zambian economist
Dominic Mulaisho and verses of Ugandan political scientist
Okello Oculli. The intriguing if inconclusive works of Ali Mazrui
in many mediums including television are, of course, unique.
The popularity, even profitability, of African authors is reflected
in the long-established Heinemann African Writer's Series and
more recent Longman's Drumbeat Series.

Box 3
Plus ça Change: Post-war Planning for Africa

Contemporary planning for the continent by the ECA, IBRD, UN and others has several antecedents in both pre- and post-colonial periods, notably that of 'decolonisation' in the 1960s. The genesis of that process and indeed of current adjustment conditionalities lay in post-World War Two discussions in advance of the Allied victory: the Atlantic Charter and trans-Atlantic negotiations and institutions for the post-war world. The liberal order envisaged was founded on optimistic modernisation assumptions of bourgeois democracy and capitalist economy: from Western-dominated UN and IFIs to civil society and international exchange.

The post-war continent envisaged by the US 'Committee on Africa, the War and Peace Aims' embraced many still-fashionable ideals, including a special relationship between US Blacks and Africans advocated by eminent Committee members like Ralph Bunche and W. E. B. DuBois. The 'contract' proposed anticipated current mutual conditionalities – economic and political liberalisation for external trade, technology and resources. Committee consultations embraced a familiar network of academics, activists, decision-makers, missionaries, and philanthropists from both sides of the North Atlantic and encouraged 'development education'. A significant by-product was Committee member George Haynes' 1950 survey for the YWCA on *Africa: Continent of the Future* in which he anticipated a potential world role based on indigenous capacity and diversity beyond then current colonial and racial tensions.

The US Committee was concerned with the extension of Roosevelt-Churchill's Eight Points to Africa as the foundation for post-war cooperation for development. This legitimised US support for independence – no aggrandisement, consultation, and popular government were the first three terms, while the last three were end of Nazi tyranny, freedom of the seas and travel, and abolition of force, leading to a permanent system of security. Sandwiched between these were two crucial economic conditions – equal access to raw materials and economic collaboration, as

continued on page 20

Box 3 *continued*
Plus ça Change: Post-war Planning for Africa

well as freedom from fear and want. In short, political and
economic conditions were juxtaposed then as now: the liberal
agenda of 'free' trade and markets with 'free' elections and
decisions over global resources, both colonial commodities and
foreign investment. The Committee anticipated an interdepen-
dent world in which sovereignty was expanded yet limited. Independence or control over aggrandisement was a given: 'This
assurance is important and must, of course, be applied in letter
and spirit. The policy is revolutionary in world affairs and especially for Africa' (Committee on Africa, 1942: 32).

On the other hand, newly achieved independence would be
constrained by post-war interdependence as anticipated in func-
tionalist and internationalist plans:

> The new world order will involve more limitations than we
> have had in the past on the scope of national political
> sovereignty everywhere. This should be borne in mind as we
> face the future of African states . . . although . . . Africans
> should be encouraged to look forward to having a much larger
> share in determining their own policy, this must always be
> subject to the general plans for world collective security and
> policing.   (Committee on Africa, 1942: 63)

The US Committee's deliberations in the early 1940s built on a
1926 conference at LeZoute of colonial powers, advisors, missionaries and scholars. Aside from the pervasive liberal modernisation vision, it called for an expanded role for 'voluntary
agencies' in the areas of aid, exchanges, research and understanding. The concern for autonomy and welfare was balanced
by that for cooperation and order. Civil society was to be facilitated but within global and institutional limits. Such pre-
independence scenarios might moderate our enthusiasm for
post-colonial, even post-adjustment, designs and dreams.

no sign of consensus on how to conceive and define them. Notions such as state, civil society, gender, informal sectors, and environment have distinct meanings within different modes of analysis. It is incumbent on concerned African(ist)s to make such differences explicit rather than implicit for reasons of theory and policy as well as debates and politics.

In *Towards a Political Economy for Africa* I had called for a political economy perspective which was radical, historical and interdisciplinary. But, reflective of the times – research for that text was prepared somewhat before the full incidence and impact of continental crises and structural adjustments had become apparent – I advocated a rather orthodox approach which focused on social coalitions as well as contradictions, fractions as well as classes. I was overly optimistic about the prospects for counter-dependence analysis and *praxis* – the antecedents and acceptability of Africa's own *Lagos Plan of Action* – and failed to include or prioritise the range of 'new' forces treated here, from civil society to ecology.

Thus, *Towards a Political Economy for Africa* was ultimately quite cautious and conservative: the state was central yet the dialectic of exclusion and participation was not developed; gender was confined to one confessional footnote (n18 on p. 128); the informal sector merited but one inconclusive sentence (p. 42) (see Box 4); while the environment was not included at all (neither were debt or devaluation let alone democracy or AIDS)! *Mea culpa*! Similarly, the contexts of new global divisions of labour and of power were only tentatively recognised while the proliferation of pressures for structural adjustments and social democracies was hardly anticipated. Finally, the stand-off between alternative perspectives and policies was relatively new, whereas it has now become more entrenched. In short, the African debate has advanced considerably over the last five years, particularly in the spill-over of the dramatic events of 1989 in Eastern Europe, the reverberations of which are only beginning to be felt in the continent itself. African studies thus need to take both structural (e.g. the rise of the Newly Industrialising Countries: NICs) and conjunctural (e.g. the appearance of political pluralism and economic pragmatism in Eastern Europe) changes into account in the last decade of the present century.

In advancing beyond that discourse, I would claim that one of the strengths of the present text is that it not only adopts a compatible revisionist, radical interdisciplinary perspective; it also transcends

Box 4
Informal Sectors: Subsistence and Sustainable?

Aside from debt repayments and military expenditures, the only
continent-wide economic expansion in the 1980s has been in the
informal sectors. These typically small-scale, unrecorded and
untaxed forms of enterprise have grown as the formal, larger-
scale economy has contracted under the impacts of crises and
conditionalities (de Soto, 1989). They have also changed their
characteristics in response to a combination of pressure and
opportunity: no longer just either family labour or small-scale,
and certainly not restricted to internal production and distribution (Maliyamkono and Bagachwa, 1990).

 Some informal trade had always been regional, following patterns of pre-colonial trade across the Sahara as well as across the
Indian Ocean to the Gulf states. In the 1980s, as economic crises
and forex shortages intensified, so the scale of such external
trade multiplied in both legal and illegal goods and currencies.
Most informal sectors remain quite traditional – rural, agricultural and familial connections based on female and child labour –
but new activities have also multiplied – equipment maintenance, second-hand clothes, urban transport and 'informal
finance' in the legitimate, domestic market and forex-dealing
along with gold, diamond, drug and high-tech smuggling in the
illegal, international market. The more risqué and profitable
activities tend to attract men rather than women and adults
rather than minors. Some informal entrepreneurs may create
backwards and forwards linkages which both formal and gov-
ernmental sectors may recognise and exploit without extending
legal recognition; indeed, the former often maintain their informal status through such non-informal connections or protection.

 Regimes, international organisations and NGOs have all come
to recognise such sectors as amongst the few hopeful elements in
Africa, particularly in terms of employment (World Bank,
1990b). But such attention may suffocate their flexibility: once
governments start to legalise, tax or encourage such sectors and
the formal economy attempts to incorporate them, they may lose
their dynamism. In any event, both 'graduation' and accumulation remain problematic.

Despite such dangers and difficulties, however, informal external as well as internal exchange continues to expand in Africa, in part in response to still-artificial exchange rates. Even in Southern Africa, the most structured formal economic region, labour, precious stones or minerals, luxury and stolen goods, and money cross borders, particularly when overland customs posts can be circumvented by tracks, even roads, in the bush, as in East and West Africa. The unemployed take risks of being caught and fined or imprisoned to seek informal work abroad, especially in South Africa and its Homelands. And 'long-distance traders' or 'cash madams' take trains, buses or collective taxis to exchange goods or currencies; and if annual forex allowances and informal banks are insufficient may resort to prostitution to secure monies for informal imports.

Finally, the drug trade has also hit Africa, in addition to historical production and consumption of marijuana, with cocaine, heroin and mandrax being routed from Asia to Europe or North America via some combination or East, Southern and West Africa. And international terrorists sometimes use the relatively relaxed, uninformed and isolated border posts throughout the continent to move into the North. In short, under-financed and -equipped African customs and immigration officials are vulnerable to informal circumvention and gang attack alike. Small wonder that they sometimes resort to connivance to supplement their mediocre incomes and to ensure their own physical survival.

single levels of analysis, attempting to relate adjustment dialectics from global to local levels. On the one hand, it is particularly important when evaluating the developmental and sustainable impacts of structural adjustment to go beyond macro-economics and -politics at the national level to local political economy (cf. Diamond *et al.*, 1988). Conversely, on the other hand, it is crucial to consider the extra-continental context of NIDL and NIDP (cf. Joseph, 1989, 1990). Current issues of 'governance' and 'accountability' cannot be confined to Africa alone but are affected by analysis, criteria and practice outside, especially of international institutions, multinational corporations and transnational civil societies (see next two chapters).

Moreover, I seek here to relate ideology to policy and both to

praxis; the dialectics of the *adjustment paradigm*. Neither policy nor
practice exist in isolation, whether at national or continental levels.
Rather, they are continually interacting under pressure of changing
conditions and coalitions. The hegemony of the structural adjustment
project in the 1980s – hence its claims to the status of a 'paradigm' –
cannot be separated from the *external* resources of the Bank, Fund,
and bilateral donors relative to Africa's vulnerable economies. Conversely, the evolution of adjustment conditions and expectations are
inseparable from *internal* oppositions and defaults.

Furthermore, I seek to treat *repression and regression as well as
economic and political liberalisation*. Unfortunately, the literatures
on the military, police, and other forms of coercion and authoritarianism in Africa have existed in rather splendid isolation from
those on public policy, development administration or political processes, although in fact they are dealing with inseparable phenomena.
I attempt to treat corporatism as well as democratisation, exclusion
as well as participation, accumulation as well as distribution; i.e.
the dialectics of adjustment (Nyang'oro and Shaw, 1989, 1992). As
indicated in the final pair of chapters, the dimensions of and
discourses on adjustment have evolved considerably over the last
decade and are now more realistic and less optimistic about a substantial and sustainable reversal in Africa's (mis)fortunes in the foreseeable future, in part because of the politics as well as economics of
adjustment being quite problematic.

FROM CONSTITUTIONALISM TO CONSERVATISM

While I was less prescient in the early-1980s than I might have been,
fortunately for my reputation but regrettably for the still-fledgling
field, none of the major texts produced within the prevailing modernisation paradigm were any more enlightened or informed. Indeed,
most of them tended to assume that the state of Africa had changed
little over the quarter-century since independence. The mid-1970s
paperback overviews from Christopher Clapham, Richard Hodder-
Williams, Gus Liebenow, and Bill Tordoff were all cast largely within
the modernisation tradition with a predictable emphasis on government, institutions, leaders, policies, regimes and structures. There
was little sense of either external or internal conflicts and constraints:
neither the series of crises of the 1980s nor the structural adjustment

responses were anticipated. The last of these to appear, the Liebenow (1986: 12) text on *African Politics: Crises and Challenges*, in
particular suffered from a time-warp of approach and data: modernisation and nation-building, authority and ethnicity, parties and
militaries – 'even where modernisation is perceived as a positive,
integrative force by the African elites, the pursuit of modernisation
has actually been a significant factor in the instability that plagues
contemporary Africa'. The somewhat more nationalistic and economistic volume by Roger Tangri (1985) was more realistic and critical
yet still superstructural and dated.

And, unhappily, the most current and comprehensive text, prepared over several years by a set of eminent and energetic scholars –
Naomi Chazan, Robert Mortimer, John Ravenhill, and Donald
Rothchild – suffers from similar deficiencies. *Politics and Society in
Contemporary Africa* is full of nice features, including comparative
developmental and political data and regime typology (cf. Table 2),
and it does recognise and distinguish between dependency and
materialist perspectives, but its preferred mode of analysis – political
choice – is quite uncritical and undialectical, even though its focus is
state-society relations. Its inclusion of 'political economy' is welcome
but it remains macro, policy-oriented and non-Marxist overall. It also
refers to gender, informal sector, food and debt, but in a peripheral
and unintegrated manner. The primary concerns of Chazan *et al*.
(1988) are with *political cultures* (cf. Box 1) and relations rather than
with political economy. Likewise, the latest report on the continent
from the World Bank (1989b) on *Sustainable Growth* also covers the
range of current issues, including gender, informal sector, industrialisation, and regionalism, yet its perspective, despite disclaimers
and inconsistencies, remains determinedly traditional. This is particularly serious as the latter, like its predecessor *Berg Report* (World
Bank, 1980), is likely to define the parameters of the paradigm for
African studies in the 1990s (see final chapter and also Box 5).

The initial, optimistic post-colonial period reflected in the above
academic texts came to an end in the early 1980s as the result of a
series of interrelated economic, ecological and political 'shocks'. Yet
the characteristic one-party, even one-man, state structure, with its
extensive bureaucratic, military and parastatal elements, had become
too established and preoccupied to respond promptly, despite forewarning and anticipation in the *Lagos Plan of Action*. By the end of
the 1970s, then, as new ruling classes became jealous of their power,
privilege and property, they also became resistant to opposition.

Box 5
Varieties of Refugees: Economic, Ecological and Professional as well as Political

Africa has more refugees than any other continent, both *per capita* and *in toto*: over 5 million by the late 1980s, half of the global total, at least until the early-1991 Gulf War. Most of these are women, children and the elderly escaping from untenable economic, ecological or political situations: drastic devaluations and adjustments in, say, Ghana, Uganda and Zambia; droughts in the Horn and Sahel; and continuing conflicts in Ethiopia, Liberia, Sahara, Somalia, Sudan and Southern Africa, particularly Angola and Mozambique. The incapacity of already over-stretched African states to cope with such demands has led to considerable NGO involvement in addition to the UNHCR. The continent's insistence that refugee populations be considered an integral aspect of national development was articulated at the International Conference on Assistance to Refugees in Africa (ICARA) in the early 1980s, notwithstanding contrary adjustment conditions. Given continuing crises, 'economic' and 'ecological' refugees have increased in proportion to the 'political'. On-off 'peace' talks in Angola, Ethiopia, Liberia, Mozambique and the Sudan may yet limit the latter. But the number of middle-class 'professional' refugees fleeing to the North as well as to the South will continue to grow as required reforms erode living standards and working conditions in many national administrations, industries and universities, 'capacity-building' notwithstanding. Nevertheless, despite the eruption of civil wars and incidence of unreliable weather, there are some success stories of returning refugees in the 1980s and early 1990s: back to Namibia, South Africa, Uganda and Zimbabwe. Yet the threat and reality of Fourth World migrants into the First are likely to grow as adjustment intensifies: one of the new rationales for continued Northern military capacities in a post-Cold War era, especially in one of protracted recession and associated conservative, even racist, attitudes in some Northern polities and regimes?

Thus, as Cammack, Pool and Tordoff (1988: 4) suggest, African states varied only in 'their capacity to maintain stable rule through combinations of patronage, authoritarianism and repression'. Internal and external changes, along with the transformed policy context symbolised by the *Berg Report*, served to undermine such stability, however, as the direct perquisites of position in the state declined along with national exchequers and currencies. Indirect rewards, such as through 'corruption', might have remained substantial if external capital and aid flows had continued, but discouragement and disincentive served to erode these too. And the overthrow of seemingly well entrenched regimes throughout Eastern Europe in 1989 served as a chilling caution to African leaders who had considered themselves immune to popular pressures; in some instances they lost personal friends and sources of presidential security. *The combination of structural adjustment inside and social transformation outside the continent may yet constitute a heady mixture to embolden a new generation of African organisations for democratic development*.

The state of studies of the African state from a nuanced modernisation perspective was well summarised by Michael Bratton (1989a) in a late-1980s review article for the establishment *World Politics*. His neo-Weberian approach concentrated on more traditional authors and approaches, with only one Zed Press collection (see pp. 44–5 below) being considered. Despite his non-materialist conception of the state, Bratton's (1989a: 409) overview highlighted the new interest in *state–society* relations in Africa as elsewhere, reinforced by economic crises and reforms, pointing to the irony of premature decline:

> The harsh reality of state formation in post-colonial Africa is that, in many countries, the apparatus of governance has begun to crumble before it has been consolidated. *There is a crisis of political authority that is just as severe as the well-known crisis of economic production*. [emphasis added]

Although Bratton (1989a: 411) is here overly concerned with more formal 'interest group' politics and insufficiently concerned with structural adjustments, his concentration on 'associational life that occurs in the political space beyond the state's purview' is welcome. Indeed, as the state shrinks and extra-state organisations and relations expand, so the balance in state–society relations shifts. The state is not totally distinct from civil society, but through myriad

Box 6
The 'New Poor': Demise of the Middle Class

Structural adjustment and related economic difficulties have
served to impoverish the original advocates of independence: the
new middle classes of professionals, especially bureaucrats, doc-
tors, lawyers, soldiers and teachers; but lacking a entrepreneurial fraction in most political economies. The dramatic decline of
real incomes and national currencies since the mid 1970s has
meant that this central social formation has suffered considerable
relative deprivation and distress by contrast to the ruling or
governing class, especially senior politicians and officers in parastatals as well as militaries. To salvage established life-styles, the
former have had to become two-income families in which both
spouses have formal sector employment as well as, typically,
informal sector income. Over time, orthodox professional functions have diminished as the imperative of 'moonlighting',
'black-marketeering', and 'smuggling' has become ever more
apparent in an increasing number of countries (see box 4). Even
so, most middle-class families cannot now expect to replace
elderly cars or trade-up housing let alone travel abroad without
subsidy or assistance from state, company or NGO. Such endangered middle class fractions and communities – whether defined by relation to production and/or power – are increasingly
angry and alienated, as reflected in some elements in civil society. By contrast, the 'new' bourgeoisies retain at least some of the
privileges and perquisites of office and the new peasantries be-
nefit from renewed emphasis on food supplies and the rural
areas.

Meanwhile, the impoverished and endangered professional
cadres seek foreign employment and exchange – typically
through external positions or consultations, respectively – just
to recapture those fruits of independence which had seemed to
be theirs. The 'new poor' or 'newly vulnerable' from the old
petty-bourgeoisie are thus increasingly disillusioned as well as
endangered, with profound implications for socio-economic development in the medium-term: how to sustain adjustment let
alone democracy without the participation of such a crucial class
in any supportive pro-reform coalition (see chapters 3 and 4)?

Finally, middle-aged, urban and educated middle-class African males are statistically the most vulnerable to be infected by the AIDS virus, with profound implications for familial and national development (see box 12). In short, this crucial, stabilising social class is disappearing because of the combination of economic crisis, political change and personal tragedy, so jeopardising both economic and political liberalisation.

ethnic, familial, informal and religious links attempts to both corrupt and contain such associational activities in the context of the global conditions and national conditionalities of the late twentieth century. Whilst Bratton (1989a: 412) pays insufficient attention to the gender and informal aspects of adjustment – production and participation – his support for innovative research at this important interface is helpful and heuristic:

> State–Society relations now stand at a crossroads in Africa. The post-colonial trend to expand political control has peeked, with economic crisis forcing the state to retreat from overambitious commitments . . . because state control of society in Africa has been tentative at best, the retreat of the state will create, willy-nilly, an enlarged political space within which associational life can occur.

The initial, optimistic post-colonial period reflected in the above texts came to a rather abrupt end in the early to mid 1980s (i.e. as they were published!) as the result of a series of economic, ecological and political 'shocks'. Yet the characteristic one-party, even one-man, state structure with its extensive bureaucratic, military and parastatal elements, had become too established and preoccupied to respond promptly, despite forewarning and anticipation in the continent's own *Lagos Plan of Action.* By the end of the 1970s then, as new ruling classes became ever more jealous of their privilege and property, so they became resistant to opposition (see Boxes 14–17). Internal and external changes along with a transformed policy context, symbolised by the turn-of-the-decade *Berg Report* from the World Bank (1981), served to undermine such apparent stability, however, as the prerequisites of state position declined along with national exchequers and currencies (see Box 7).

Box 7
Mobile Elites: Transnational Families

Although representative empirical data are quite elusive for obvious reasons, a significant proportion of Africa's upper classes has some family members either living abroad or able to do so because of residency or nationality rights in either Europe or North America or, less frequently, in South Asia or the Gulf. This ubiquitous transnational connection within elite circles influences values and policies, serving to moderate or complicate dependency realities and nationalist responses. It also prevents overly chauvinist or racist policies in the North during the protracted period of recession (see previous box).

Such elite mobility may be a function of past or present education, or conflict (e.g. the 'Biafra' war or struggles in the Horn or Southern Africa), or opportunity (employment with a multinational corporation or inter- or trans-national organisation), or insecurity (either political or economic, given contemporary conditions). In short, many ruling families, especially their second or third generations, have kin and/or property abroad, especially in ex-metropoles such as Britain or France or the 'new world' such as the US.

Such connections provide a sense of security or choice in the longer term and of opportunity or supplies in the shorter term. These have rarely existed with either the East or the South, despite some expatriate or diasporic African property-owning or job-holding there; neither have they occurred outside the bourgeosie. Most refugees go to neighbouring countries and are non-bourgeois, typically female and either young or old. More middle-class and middle-aged Africans now seek extracontinental connections through which to insulate or insure their life-styles. Work permits or residency rights abroad are even more crucial in an era of policy reforms and forex shortages: rational personal and familial responses to the impacts of market forces!

The orthodox contemporary paradigm for Africa has come, then, to be defined essentially by the World Bank and other extra-continental interests and institutions. In so doing, the structural adjustment project has displaced an indigenous *problématique*, largely conceived as 'state socialism'. The latter had been hegemonic for much of the independence period, developing out of the nationalist movement, which had itself replaced the colonial ideology of the metropolitan powers. By contrast, the adjustment paradigm has now become quite well established and so unlikely to be superceded in the near term, unless the costs and contradictions of national reformation on the one hand and international transformation on the other become too intense (Toye, 1987).

The previous state socialist *problématique* was itself a 'counter-dependence' response to underdevelopment but it led to a seemingly insoluble set of difficulties which adjustment was meant to resolve. The limitations of this nationalist *problématique* became increasingly palpable throughout the 1970s yet many African regimes declined to confront or even consider them. The 'crises' of the late 1970s and early 1980s were at the time predictable and containable if not fully avoidable should political leaderships have been more realistic and courageous. By the time the debt and drought crises became widespread and popularised, however, only strong medicine was sufficient, which essentially meant externally-written and -administered prescription. Hence the historical necessity of such conditionalities although, as noted in the next chapter, these were not so much 'structural' as 'fiscal' or superficial in character.

FROM POLITICAL CULTURE TO POLITICAL ECONOMY

The alternative, more radical and internal, response has consisted of an updated version of sustainable, basic needs ideals: a long term development strategy rather than a supposedly short term economistic reaction. Initially, as *Lagos Plan of Action*, it was a thinly disguised restatement of anti-dependence collective nationalism. But, by the end of the 'lost decade' of the 1980s, it had already been transformed into a more realistic and less rhetorical *Alternative African Framework to Structural Adjustment Programmes*. Although its roots and advocates were essentially African, it came to incorporate elements drawn from compatible agencies, such as UNICEF's

'Adjustment with a Human Face'. Indeed, as the 1990s dawned, reactions against the human costs of adjustment were being widely experienced, as reflected in the South Commission's report *Challenge to the South* and UNDP's *Human Development Report 1990* and *1991* (see Table 3). In response to such sustained criticism in the second half of the decade, the World Bank attempted to incorporate into its increasingly hegemonic paradigm some ameliorative elements. These were revealed in its 1989 report on Sub-Saharan Africa, *From Crisis to Sustainable Growth: A Long-term Perspective Study*, which was the result of a series of consultations with its Council of African Advisors. Yet the rhetoric of an 'enabling environment' was merely a palliative as the essentials of the standard adjustment package remained intact in almost all bilateral negotiations (Martin, 1991; Mosley, Harrigan and Toye, 1991).

Despite some attempts at intellectual synthesis and diplomatic consensus (see Ravenhill, 1990a; Shaw, 1988a), the divide between structural adjustment and self-reliance has remained. Indeed, given the two *genres'* distinct, incompatible roots – in modernisation and dependence theories, respectively – such integration, even juxtaposition, was bound to be elusive. The 1989 stand-off between an ill-advised and -timed joint IBRD–UNDP (1989) tract on *Africa's Adjustment and Growth in the 1980s* and the ECA's (1989c) resilient response, *Statistics and Policies*, was symptomatic of theoretical incompatibility plus divergent definitions, expectations and constituencies. I return to such issues in the concluding chapter.

In brief, the adjustment project does not represent a sustainable development policy; conversely, any viable 'human development' strategy has to respond to changes in continental and global political economies. Africa's states cannot now avoid adjustment conditionalities as they have become the *sine qua non* of short term economic (and regime!) survival. Conversely, African communities cannot sustain adjustment deprivations without opposition and the organisation of local self-help and informal sector institutions. Such dialectics of adjustment will constitute the political and economic dynamic of the continent into the twenty-first century (Callaghy and Ravenhill, 1992).

Probably the only way in which structural adjustment and self-reliance can be rendered compatible is if they occur in *sequence*. Indeed, given the incompatibility between adjustment instructions and directions in the global economy – extroversion despite the disinterest exhibited in the NIDL – some self-reliance would seem to

Table 3   Africa and the South: Regional Aggregates of Human Development Indicators

	Sub-Saharan Africa	Arab States	Asia and Oceania			Latin America and the Caribbean	
			South Asia	All countries	Excl. China	All countries	Excl. Mexico and Brazil
Profile of human development							
Life expectancy at birth total	51.8	62.1	58.4	68.1	63.7	67.4	67.7
female % of male	106.9	104.6	100.4	105.2	106.6	108.7	108.1
Population with access to health services	47	77	56	–	–	70	–
Population with access to safe water	40	71	56	67	51	79	69
Population with access to sanitation	32	–	–	56	–	69	65
Daily calorie supply	91	120	100	112	113	115	109
Adult literacy rate	45	53	42	72	80	82	83
Combined prim. & sec. enrolment ratio	45	71	60	81	79	84	82
GNP per capita	470	1,820	390	530	960	1,830	1,630
Real GNP per capita	1,180	3,290	1,090	2,540	2,720	4,300	3,570
Trends in human development							
Life expectancy at birth 1960	40.0	46.7	43.8	47.0	46.7	56.0	56.6
1990	51.8	62.1	58.4	68.1	63.7	67.4	67.7
Under-five mortality rate 1960	284	271	279	198	189	157	163
1989	179	106	151	57	81	72	72
Population with access 1975–80	27	–	30	–	–	60	58
to safe water 1988	40	–	56	–	–	79	69

continued on page 34

Table 3 continued

		Sub-Saharan Africa	Arab States	South Asia	Asia and Oceania		Latin America and the Caribbean	
					All countries	Excl. China	All countries	Excl. Mexico and Brazil
Daily calorie supply	1965	92	92	88	86	87	100	100
	1985	91	120	100	112	113	115	109
Adult literacy rate	1970	27	34	31	–	–	73	78
	1985	45	53	42	–	–	82	83
Combined primary and secondary enrolment ratio	1970	26	50	45	65	61	68	72
	1987	45	71	60	81	79	84	82
Real GDP per capita	1960	640	1,080	580	700	630	1,760	2,180
	1988	1,180	3,290	1,090	2,540	2,720	4,300	3,570
Human capital formation								
Adult literacy rate	total	45	53	42	72	80	82	83
	male	56	66	55	82	86	84	86
	female	34	39	27	61	73	80	81
Mean years of schooling	total	1.5	2.2	2.2	4.6	4.0	4.4	5.3
	male	2.0	3.0	3.3	5.7	4.7	4.6	5.5
	female	1.0	1.4	1.1	3.5	3.3	4.1	5.0
Scientists and technicians		–	–	3.0	–	–	39.5	52.2
Tertiary graduates		0.2	2.3	0.7	0.9	–	2.5	2.4
Science graduates		24	29	39	–	–	29	28

Employment							
Labour force	38.8	30.7	35.8	54.5	43.9	39.7	38.7
Women in labour force	33.1	15.1	21.3	41.5	37.6	26.2	26.3
Per cent of labour force in agriculture							
1965	79.1	63.0	72.3	77.6	65.7	44.1	41.6
1985-8	67.6	39.2	59.7	68.7	54.1	26.3	29.2
Per cent of labour force in industry							
1965	8.1	13.9	12.1	9.2	13.4	20.9	21.2
1985-8	7.7	14.1	11.3	13.2	11.8	19.0	20.0
Per cent of labour force in services							
1965	12.9	23.2	15.6	13.3	21.4	35.1	37.2
1985-8	24.7	46.7	29.0	18.1	34.0	54.7	50.8
Social security benefits expenditure	–	–	–	–	–	3.1	2.0
Earnings per employee 1970-80	-1.5	–	–	–	–	2.0	0.6
annual growth rate 1980-7	-4.8	–	4.2	–	–	-1.4	-0.7
Military expenditure and resource use imbalances							
Military expenditure 1960	0.7	4.9	2.8	8.2	–	1.8	2.1
1986	3.3	12.6	7.2	5.2	–	1.5	2.1
Ratio of military expenditure to combined education and health expenditure	70	166	164	–	–	29	40
Ratio of ODA received to military expenditure	3.80	0.10	0.46	–	–	0.30	0.45
Arms imports	3,360T	16,740T	6,200T	4,600T	4,220T	3,340T	3,000T
Ratio of ODA for social investment to arms imports	0.38	0.05	0.09	0.36	–	0.15	0.16
Armed forces per 1,000 people	1.7	11.8	2.2	4.0	7.2	3.0	4.5
as % of teachers	90	183	47	66	101	42	67

continued on page 36

Table 3 continued

	Sub-Saharan Africa	Arab States	South Asia	Asia and Oceania		Latin America and the Caribbean	
				All countries	Excl. China	All countries	Excl. Mexico and Brazil
Urban crowding							
Urban population							
1960	15	30	17	19	20	49	52
1990	31	53	27	34	35	72	69
2000	38	60	33	46	42	76	73
Urban population annual growth rate							
1960–90	5.2	4.6	3.9	3.9	4.1	3.7	3.3
1990–2000	5.3	3.9	4.1	4.4	3.5	2.5	2.5
Persons per habitable room	–	–	2.8	–	–	–	–
Houses without electricity	–	–	–	–	–	1.6	1.9
Population in largest city	32	31	11	15	–	46	48
Major city with highest population density	–	–	–	–	35	28	38
Demographic balance sheet							
Estimated population							
1960	210T	120T	600T	930T	270T	210T	100T
1990	500T	270T	1,200T	1,660T	520T	440T	200T
2000	690T	340T	1,500T	1,920T	620T	530T	250T
Annual population growth rate							
1960–90	2.8	2.7	2.3	2.0	2.3	2.4	2.2
1990–2000	3.2	2.6	2.2	1.5	1.8	1.9	1.9
Hypothetical stationary population							
size	2,960T	870T	3,110T	2,840T	1,000T	930T	440T
year reached	2042	2024	2020	2003	2009	2007	2011

Fertility rate		6.5	5.0	4.6	2.6	3.3	3.4	3.6
Crude death rate		15.1	9.1	11.2	7.1	8.1	7.5	8.2
Dependency ratio		97	83	75	53	66	69	71
Population density		245	211	1,876	1,036	779	224	217
Natural resources balance sheet								
Land area		2,040T	1,260T	640T	1,600T	660T	2,010T	970T
Arable land	as % of total land	37	26	50	38	34	37	41
	annual % increase	0.18	0.16	0.10	0.13	0.37	0.82	0.38
Livestock	per capita	0.99	1.10	0.63	0.48	0.31	1.41	1.56
	annual % increase	1.8	2.1	1.9	1.9	3.4	1.6	1.2
Production of fuelwood	per capita	0.84	0.20	0.28	0.29	0.56	0.66	0.45
	annual % increase	2.9	0.2	2.1	2.0	1.8	2.6	2.8
Average annual deforestation		0.5	–	2.1	1.0	–	1.4	0.8
Internal renewable water resources per capita		3.5	1.6	3.4	5.1	12.1	23.0	22.0
Greenhouse index		1.0	0.8	0.4	0.9	1.6	2.1	1.8
National income accounts								
Total GDP		210T	340T	300T	830T	460T	800T	300T
Total GNP		210T	400T	340T	820T	460T	770T	290T
GNP per capita annual growth rate 1965–80		1.5	3.0	1.4	4.0	3.9	3.8	2.0
1980–88		-2.2	0.4	3.0	7.5	–	-0.4	-1.3
Annual rate of inflation		19.6	17.5	7.8	5.6	–	124.5	97.4
Tax revenue		19.7	–	10.7	–	–	16.6	17.6
Overall budget surplus/deficit		-6.1	–	-7.9	–	–	-8.3	-2.8
Gross domestic investment		18	24	22	32	–	22	21
Gross domestic savings		17	21	19	34	–	24	20

continued on page 38

Table 3 continued

	Sub-Saharan Africa	Arab States	South Asia	Asia and Oceania		Latin America and the Caribbean	
				All countries	Excl. China	All countries	Excl. Mexico and Brazil
Child survival and development							
Births attended by health personnel	36	46	30	54	–	77	53
Low birthweight babies	16	7	28	8	15	11	12
Infant mortality rate	108	73	99	41	58	52	51
One-year-olds immunised 1981	30	40	13	48	–	52	37
1988–9	54	72	75	83	–	69	64
Mothers breastfeeding at one year	72	62	76	–	–	38	44
Children suffering from malnutrition underweight	32	20	46	28	–	10	15
wasting	15	–	22	–	–	3	4
stunting	40	–	55	–	–	31	31
Under-five mortality rate	179	106	151	57	81	72	72
Health profile							
Population with access to health services	47	77	56	–	–	70	–
Contraceptive prevalence rate	15	–	31	–	–	57	48
Maternal mortality rate	540	290	410	120	250	110	120
Adult consumption of spirits per capita	3.5	–	–	3.6	–	3.6	5.3
Adults who smoke	–	–	30	–	–	–	–
Population per doctor	22,930	3,720	3,520	2,380	5,830	1,230	1,340
nurse	2,670	960	2,700	1,550	1,160	1,020	900
Nurses per doctor	10.1	4.2	1.5	1.9	5.2	1.3	1.8
Public health expenditure 1960	0.7	0.9	0.5	–	–	1.4	1.5
1986	0.9	1.8	1.0	–	–	2.0	1.7

39

Food security							
Food production per capita index	96	103	103	125	107	100	96
Agricultural production	23	14	32	–	–	10	13
Daily calorie supply per capita	2,150	3,000	2,270	2,600	2,520	2,700	2,530
Daily calorie supply	91	120	100	112	113	115	109
Food import dependency ratio 1969–71	13.1	21.7	4.3	7.1	18.8	31.2	38.5
1986–8	10.0	38.1	5.8	6.7	13.4	14.1	19.8
Cereal imports	7,390T	35,340T	12,500T	33,210T	17,690T	16,670T	9,630T
Food aid in cereals	42	15	35	–	–	18	38
Food aid	590T	540T	510T	120T	110T	410T	410T
Resource flow imbalances							
Total ODA received US$ millions	12,900T	4,290T	6,080T	6,900T	4,680T	3,950T	3,660T
as % of GNP	9.2	1.1	1.7	0.8	0.9	0.4	1.1
ODA for social investment	12.8	14.4	10.0	21.7	24.1	22.0	22.5
ODA for education and health	12.9	2.8	3.2	–	–	1.5	3.4
Total debt	82	61	23	21	32	40	53
Debt service 1970	4.7	–	–	–	–	14.4	11.9
1988	17.3	38.1	21.6	–	–	29.6	24.8
Gross international reserves	1.7	4.5	3.1	3.8	–	2.9	4.0
Workers' remittances	–0.3	0.5	1.8	–	–	0.1	–
Terms of trade	74	68	114	–	–	84	74
Current account balance	–10,570T	–6,750T	–11,190T	8,860T	12,660T	–9,560T	–10,940T

Source: *Human Development Report, 1991* (New York: OUP for UNDP).   T = total.

be inevitable, whether sub-national, national or regional. The proliferation of informal sector activities along with a set of 'second wave'
regional arrangements are indicative of such a possibility (Shaw, 1990b).
In brief, *national and collective self-reliance by default*, given Africa's
exponential marginality in the NIDL and NIDP, would seem to be
inevitable unless either adjustment conditions change or the global economy becomes less competitive and protectionist. Such an unattractive
yet realistic scenario is treated in my concluding chapter.

Given the state of the global political economy and the inadequacy
or inappropriateness of African responses to the decade or more of
'crises', it is pointless to lament from a dependency vantage point the
external source of the prevailing paradigm as do Chinua Achebe *et al.*
in *Beyond Hunger in Africa: Conventional Wisdom and an African
Vision* (1990: 3–4): 'Perhaps the most tragic aspect of this situation is
that the debate about Africa's future is dominated by the international community. Those who are farthest removed from the African realities – who do not feel the pinch or who need not take
responsibility – are the pace-setters.' Nevertheless, their review of
the transition from euphoria to despair in continental affairs is valid
although their long-term projections are overly optimistic and
idealistic.

Conversely, indigenous intellectual reinforcement for ECA, South
Commission, UNICEF and other emphathetic responses is to be
welcomed, especially if it too transcends the old dialectic or debate
between modernisation and dependence. Indeed, given the perilous
place of Africa in the global political economy, the tired stand-off
between modernisation on the one hand and materialism on the other
needs to be overcome. Some creative combination of perspectives
and policies is necessary if the continent's diversity of experiences
and resources is to be mobilised for sustainable development, ideological as well as physical, individual as well as collective (see Tables
1, 2 and 3).

A central feature of the African 'state socialist' structure against
which the World Bank and others have been reacting throughout the
1980s was control over parastatal 'empires', particularly their purch-
ases and employment: the patronage or patrimonial nexus. Rather
than incentives or rewards being distributed through improved services or infrastructures, fidelty was assured through jobs and pay-offs.
As Jeffrey Herbst (1990b) argues, if it is accepted that some of the
cause of the continent's decline was internal, then much of the fault
for it lies in the character of political economy and political logic:

state-determined rather than market-driven. However, overvalued exchange rates, excessive state intervention and inefficient parastatal companies were not irrational 'distortions' for those intent on staying in power, only for the development of the population as a whole. For the political class, such 'bottlenecks' were functional and rational, even essential, in the absence of a strong tax base and alternative, direct incentive structures:

> they make political sense given the political systems that almost all African countries have. Most African leaders operate in political systems where votes do not matter. Instead, rulers try to institu- tionalise their regimes by establishing webs of patron-client rela- tions to garner the support necessary to remain in power. . . . African regimes often rig markets through direct state intervention in order for resources to flow to constituencies important to their continued tenure in office. (Herbst, 1990b: 156)

Such a formulation of the African state socialist *problématique* reinforces the imperative of *political as well as economic liberalisation* if adjustment reforms are to be sustained. For not only do such conditionalities mean economic transitions, they also imply political transformations as well: power through elections rather than corrup- tion, through votes rather than venality. A vibrant 'civil society' outside both state and economy is therefore essential to perpetuate the gains of policy reforms in which accountability rather than auth- ority is the criterion. In short, without attention to 'governance' – introduced in the Bank's own end-decade report – adjustment is unlikely to be either implemented or sustained (Shaw, 1990f).

Whilst Herbst's orthodox approach yields such insights, it also leads to or legitimises unacceptable levels of foreign rather than state interference. For, extending the argument about changing the bases of power, he proceeds to insist that debt reduction should be minimal or conditional lest African regimes backslide on conditionalities: a heightened sustained form of dominance or paternalism. Given their paradigmatic history of patronage, Herbst (1990b: 163) worries that should assorted 'proposals alleviate the debt burden of even the poorest countries, there may be a strong temptation on the part of African leaders to reduce the pace of economic reforms'. Rather than recognising any internal sources of demands for change – from Afri- can civil society – Herbst (1990b: 164) exaggerates their interna- tional origins: 'There is, in fact, every reason to believe that without dramatic external pressure, poor economic policies in African countries will continue'. Such contemporary reflections of the adjustment paradigm stand in stark contrast to previous dependency or materialist approaches which served to support and sustain the dominance of the post-colonial African state.

There remains a danger of projecting Eurocentric trends onto Africa given the new preoccupation of promising East–West relations. And there is a related danger of dismissing the state when in revised form its role remains crucial. Martin Doornbos (1990: 187) has drawn attention to the ironies of current trends in the debate about the state in Africa, notably the switch in orthodox and radical positions:

> global organisations and the donor community have now embraced wholesale the critique of the 'overdeveloped state' which was earlier espoused by radical scholars. . . . In an age of structural adjustment, liberalisation and privatisation, the international community has undergone a major reversal in its appreciation of the role of the African state, and now seems to have opted for . . . an almost anarchistic route. Formerly the exclusive recipient, partner, and rationale of international aid and attention, the African state's 'most favoured' status appears today to have been eclipsed in the donors' eyes by a veil of assumed obsolescence.

Doornbos (1990: 190) laments 'the prolonged withering away of African civil society from academic and policy (in)attention' and cautions that current conditionalities may indeed undermine the state despite its rediscovery by the radicals: '"Policy dialogue", the international donor euphemism, may in the end turn the discussion about the African state into a very academic debate' (Doornbos, 1990: 189). I turn next to an overview of the original radical legacy against which many intellectual as well as institutional adjustment claims are now directed: the continental 'counter-revolution' parallel to the global anti-Keynesian backlash identified by John Toye (1987).

FROM RADICALISM TO REVISIONISM

The optimistic nationalism of the early post-war period led to rather simplistic and uncritical expectations about rapid growth and development in both economy and society (see Boxes 1–3). These were a product of their times, reinforced by modernisation and technocratic ideology: with the defeat of fascism, colonialism was almost dead and equivalence with already industrialised states was all but inevitable. Such misplaced idealism began to be eroded as soon as formal independence was achieved and the realities of underdevelopment began to be appreciated. These were camouflaged for a while by the post-colonial political honeymoon and the post-war economic expansion. However, the relatively heady times of the late 1950s and early 1960s were soon superceded by the unappealing realities of the series of economic 'shocks' of the 1970s, from expensive oil and cheap money to ecological instabilities and vulnerabilities and unstable currencies and exponential debts.

The 'turning point' of the 1970s, symbolised globally by the US decision to stop converting gold at a fixed rate and continentally by the rise to power of Idi Amin in Uganda, led inexorably to the Bank's *Berg Report* and the counter-revolution of structural adjustment. Such anti-Keynesian policies – the Third World equivalent of deregulation and privatisation in the North popularised during the Reagan and Thatcher periods – challenged the foundations of African independent regimes: from state-centric economies to one-party polities. Preoccupations with the series of continental crises diverted attentions from underlying structural and ideological changes which became glaringly apparent by the end of the 1980s. Just as in so many jurisdictions in the North, by 1990 assumptions in the South about state–society and –economy relations were quite transformed: from welfare state to minimum government.

The vulnerability and marginality of Africa are apparent in its scholarship as well as in its insecurity. The derivative nationalisms of the initial post-war period gave way to synthetic studies of dependencies as explanations of underdevelopment. And sub-fields like public administration and international relations also borrowed from both North and South alike; modernisation and realism, respectively. Only a minority of analysts and cases generated truly original, critical insights which dealt with, say, class fractions, gender inequalities, informal sectors, technological changes and ecological costs. Such pluralism within a political economy mode had to await the break-up of the post-colonial paradigm in the 1980s, one of the few positive side-effects of the *Berg Report*, and subsequent shifts in intellectual hegemony (see Conclusion).

So, in addition to the restatement and reinstatement of

modernisation orthodoxies by Bratton, Diamond, Herbst *et al.*, with their emphasis on internal causes and external responses (see next chapter and Shaw, 1992a and b), alternative, radical volumes have also been produced, notably by Zed Press.

Classic within the dated dependence perspective are many titles from Zed, which in the 1980s perpetuated the nationalist tradition originally forged by Penguin. It captured and popularised the 'anti-imperialist' inclinations and frustrations of the new generation of post-independence indigenous scholars who lacked the ideological certainty and professional security of the first generation of nationalist intellectuals. Zed has produced not only individual authors and titles from a variety of 'left' perspectives, mainly of a more nationalist and dependence orientation, but has also published important series on behalf of 'progressive' institutions, notably CODESRIA, the Institute for African Alternatives (IFAA), UN Research Institute for Social Development (UNRISD), and UN University (UNU) Political Economy and Regional Peace and Security Series. From the second, founded in the mid 1980s and now well established in North London, has come major analyses by some of its Council such as Ben Turok: *Africa: What Can Be Done?* (1987), Nzongola-Ntalaja: *Revolution and Counter-Revolution in Africa* (1987), and Bade Onimode: *A Political Economy of the African Crisis* (1988). UNRISD has published Dharam Ghai (ed.), *The IMF and the South* (1991), UNU's Series includes Peter Anyang' Nyong'o (ed.), *Popular Struggles for Democracy in Africa* (1987) while CODESRIA's collections include Ibbo Mandaza (ed.), *Zimbabwe: The Political Economy of Transition, 1980–1986* (1986).

Together, these Zed Press volumes constituted a major attack on and alternative to more established, orthodox approaches, analysts and publishing houses, symbolic of the developmental and intellectual transitions of the 1980s: economic crises and ideological challenges. Not that they are themselves homogeneous. Rather, they constitute a good introduction to some of the differences and debates within the 'left' in such a troubled period: there are varying degrees of materialism and dependency. Both Turok and Nzongola-Ntalaja themselves include revisionist reviews of radical perspectives, seeking to incorporate new ideas and issues into essentially materialist frameworks. The latter introduces and integrates a useful evaluation of francophone contributions to materialist analysis of the continent whilst disagreeing with anglophone figures like Geoffrey Kay (Nzongola-Ntalaja, 1987: 20) and John Saul (Nzongola-Ntalaja,

1987: 17–18). The former refers to Soviet Africanists' analyses as well as to Western Africanists' debates about salient states, especially anglophone ones, and criticises Andre Gunder Frank's simplistic *dependencia* (Turok, 1987: 96 and 108) whilst welcoming Bjorn Beckman's synthetic and dialectical formulation on struggles among rather than around bourgeois fractions (Turok, 1987: 80 and 109–10). These two studies mark the beginning of revisionist tendencies within progressive circles, although their break with previous radical orthodoxies is conditional, as indicated by Turok's unsatisfactory 1989 text on Zambia.

The combination of economic and ecological crises and adjustment conditionalities apparent as the 1980s passed has not only transformed the continent's political economies – in January 1991 the British *Independent on Sunday* warned that 'the Dark Continent is in danger of becoming the Forgotten Continent' (20 January 1991: 24) – it has also changed policy responses and prescriptive analyses. Regretably, it has yet to revolutionise intellectual and theoretical approaches, least of all within Africa itself. Nzongola-Ntalaja suggested a useful periodisation of African Studies up to the independence era of 'neo-colonialism', from colonial anthropology to post-colonial modernisation. However, the interrelated 'revolutions' in global and continental political economies since the 1960s, and particularly since 1980, have yet to be reflected in much African(ist) analysis (Gill and Law, 1988; Murphy and Tooze, 1991) (see final two chapters in this text).

As already indicated, then, the field is still replete with outdated forms of modernisation and materialism, with dependency failing to appreciate the marginality of much of the continent and the centrality of some of the Pacific Rim: NIDL now reinforced by NIDP. The latter was captured in Todd Shields' headline for the report already noted on the great powers' disinterest in current conflicts in West Africa and the Horn: 'The African land the world forgot sinks into anarchy' (*Independent on Sunday*, 20 January 1991: 24). Moreover, the extant field overlooks novel external perspectives, from feminist to discourse analysis, and internal problems, from inqualities to infrastructures. Given the palpable transition of most of Africa's countries and communities because of crises and adjustments, an *appropriate, subtle mode of analysis is required for the 1990s: a neo-materialism which incorporates environment, gender and informal sectors as well as continuing class contradictions and coalitions, popular pressures and regime repression.*

Such **revisionist radicalism** is particularly appropriate to the mood of the times. The externally-induced revisionism insisted on by the Bank and other agencies at the level of economics in the 1980s has been reinforced by a distinctive force at the level of politics at the end of the decade: East European transformations further erode any vestigial legitimacy of the characteristic African state-centric political economy. Together, structural adjustment at the level of the continental economy and strategic détente at the level of the global polity serve to upset orthodox assumptions about the salience of self-reliance and non-alignment, respectively.

Although the intellectual context in the continent remains resiliently traditional, three interrelated and reinforcing sets of pressures towards *revisionist radicalism* are apparent. First, at the *global* level, there is palpable unconfidence within and convergence between both capitalist and socialist systems, from established interventions towards more market forces; neither superpower has the economic clout or capability of either Japan or Germany, let alone the groupings of European Community (EC) or the NICs. Second, at the *continental* level, there is a stampede away from state intervention and towards reform packages, with profound implications for development policies and projections: from one-party states towards pragmatism and pluralism. And third, at the *regional* level, there is exponential revisionism, not only about national strategies but also about formal negotiation and informal exchange. Indeed, in the somewhat heady atmosphere of the new decade in Eastern Europe and elsewhere, there is a danger of a reversion to the indefensible optimism of the post-independence period: misplaced triumphalism. In both East and South, just as in the West, there is likely to be a prolonged period of readjustment and digestion through the 1990s. Indeed, regression and recession remain possible despite high hopes.

Nowhere is the mood of optimistic revisionism more apparent than in *Southern Africa* where peace talks, in association with structural adjustments and multi-party arrangements, have proliferated in Angola, Mozambique and Namibia, as well as in South Africa itself. In the latter, the mixture of ANC and United Democratic Front/Mass Democratic Movement pressures along with debt and inflationary imperatives compelled the relatively 'liberal' de Klerk regime to move towards negotiations, with profound implications for the region as a whole (see Box 23 and Swatuk and Shaw, 1991).

In short, the turn of the decade is characterised by a remarkable and unanticipated degree of revisionism, whether radical or sustainable. Somewhat surprisingly, perhaps, the continent can now contemplate another decade of economic and social difficulties yet within a global system digesting a set of transformations, both economic and strategic. The reformist preoccupations of both East and West constitute a transformed environment for African development. The troubled decade of the 1980s provides a cautionary backdrop for a range of unanticipated choices in the 1990s, some of which are hardly appreciated yet in the continent itself.

This revised text represents, then, one attempt to recognise and evaluate such revisionist inclinations, taking into account both structural adjustment and Eastern Europe as salient factors. This new trail has already been blazed by creative colleagues like Claude Ake, Yusuf Bangura, Peter Anyang' Nyong'o, Tom Callaghy, Bonnie Campbell, Eboe Hutchful, Julius Ihonvbere, Richard Joseph, John Loxley, Thandika Mkandawire, Ruth Meena, Julius Nyang'oro, Maria Nzomo, Richard Sandbrook, Jane Parpart, and Issa Shivji *et al.*, who have raised issues of adjustment, corporatism, democracy, ecology, gender, informal sector, militarism, etc. Yet it is important not to be too current or extremist as such revisionist strands are inseparable from historical and contemporaneous elements. Thus, on the one hand, the overly optimistic Warrenite rhetoric of Gavin Kitching, John Sender and Sheila Smith has to be treated with the utmost caution. Yet, on the other hand, the 'old' socialism of Dan Nabudere and Bade Onimode should now be discarded as overly structurist. And finally, none of these new factors, and the social forces which they reflect and generate, can be treated in isolation. It is not enough to 'add gender and stir', or to inject a dash of some other spicy ingredient, like social ecology, informal sector or popular participation (see Peet, 1991), because such features are inseparable from the continuing contexts of class and culture. Any such grand synthesis in likely to be quite elusive or meaningless: *distinct historical periods and political economies must be carefully distinguished*. Yet the revisionist mood does need to be recognised and sustained during the 1990s as without novel, radical analyses and policies, Africa's structural and exponential difficulties will not be identified let alone treated and, hopefully, resolved (see concluding chapter).

FROM PARADIGM TO PLURALISM

The overly slow genesis of this monograph is inseparable from such historical changes and concerns. Initially, towards the end of the 1980s, I had sought to reflect on the profound impacts of adjustment conditionalities on the continent's political economy, notably the rearrangement of social relations given devaluation, desubsidisation etc. I had already intended to treat the ecological, gender and informal sector implications of such reforms. However, as the 1980s yielded to the 1990s, it was apparent that an inflammatory mixture of domestic resistance and external transformation was percolating throughout the continent. In large part, this constituted a belated response to or recognition of the profundity and irreversibility of the adjustment project, particularly reflected in female and non-governmental reactions. But in part it was also an expression of surprise at the intense changes in Eastern Europe and their implications for state socialism everywhere (Shaw and Inegbedion, 1991, 1992).

Thus external reformations, including the end of the Cold War, have reinforced and emboldened smouldering internal resentments, leading to the proliferation of movements for formal multi-party systems in 1990 and after: 'new' internal as well as international divisions of power. Such directions have been reinforced by structural adjustment policies which undermined the established state and were legitimised by democratic pressures at a global as well as local level. 1990/1 thus constituted more of a symbolic conjuncture for Africa than merely the start of the UN's Fourth Development Decade or the Lome IV Convention with the EC. It was a watershed because of the coincidence of interrelated internal and international transformations, many of which were hardly anticipated, particularly not by African(ist) scholars: the end of both 'lost' and 'adjustment' decades.

There is, to be sure, even now a danger of overreacting: some regimes, such as that of Banda in Malawi, have not been really disturbed by either economic adjustment or political advocacy. And many are seeking to arrange cosmetic rather than substantive reforms, sufficient to meet the increasingly interventive 'political' conditionalities of Western donors. Yet in others, perhaps suprisingly including the hitherto more hard-line 'Afro-Marxist' states such as Angola, Benin, Ethiopia, both Guineas, and Mozambique (see Table 2), the mix of adjustment and pluralism is heady. Hence the excuse for my own procrastination: *social and political adjustments on the continent became irrefutable and irreversible by the start of the 1990s,* as suggested in this text (Shaw, 1991a, 1992a).

The new acceptability in both analysis and praxis of *pluralism* in Africa has led to attention to 'governance', especially by the World Bank, Carter Center (see Map 3), and Hoover Institution (World Bank, 1990b; Joseph, 1989, 1990; Diamond, 1988, respectively). But such national and formal levels of institutionalisation and investigation need to be joined by local and informal concentrations, as suggested above by Bratton. In particular, the notion of civil society or 'informal politics' must be emphasised to balance any excessive focus on formal institutional competition over the state: 'popular participation'. To be sure, non-state actors, especially national and international NGOs, have always been present on the continent, even in pre-colonial times (see Shaw, 1990f). Companies and churches were particularly important in the transitions both to and from colonialism, and have become so again in the era of adjustment, which facilitates private sector production and non-state sector welfare (see Box 19 and next chapter).

As the state has shrunk under exponential conditionalities, so NGO and quasi-NGO roles have expanded, in both local and national, grassroots and top-down structures. These have drawn legitimacy from a similar pattern of rejuvenation of civil societies in Eastern Europe and have attracted resources from foreign donors anxious to decentralise and/or privatise their aid delivery whether it be for emergency or programme assistance. In short, informal political organisations have been able to take advantage of the contemporary conjuncture to advance both institutional and national agendas, with fascinating implications for the future of state and development. Roger Simon (1982: 69) has provided a useful formulation of the concept 'civil society' from a Gramscian perspective, although his final, incorporative sentence may be controversial:

> It comprises all the 'so-called private' organisations such as churches, trade unions, political parties, and cultural associations which are distinct from the process of production and from the coercive apparatuses of the state. . . . Civil society is the sphere where capitalists, workers and others engage in political and ideological struggles and where political parties, trade unions, religious bodies and a great variety of other organisations come into existence. It is not only the sphere of class struggles; it is also the sphere of all the popular-democratic struggles which arise out

of the different ways in which people are grouped together – by sex, race, generation, local community, region, nation and so on . . . . Since civil society includes all the organisations and institutions outside of production and the state, it includes the family.

In the African case, the revival of civil society or political liberalisation has tended to succeed rather than precede economic liberalisation, whereas in the now classic case of Eastern Europe the sequence was reversed. Popular pressures incited by the human costs and consequences of adjustment have led to necessary self-sufficiency in the provision of basic needs. In turn, these constitute the organisational basis of a reinvigorated democratic community with links to burgeoning informal sectors and non-state actors. I treat the adjustment genesis of many such groups in the next chapter, from rural and female credit cooperatives to small-scale agribusiness industries. Here, I simply note, unhappily, that much current analysis of democratisation in Africa overlooks its pre-colonial antecedents and its post-colonial popular roots (see also Box 1).

Civil society, especially its NGO component, may then constitute the 'third' force or level between state and economy or official and private sectors. Yet the degree to which it is autonomous is problematic given the authority and capacity of the government and the resources and energy of the private sector. We should also be careful about allowing any one perspective to define and 'capture' such concepts as their locations and implications vary among modernisation, dependence and materialist genres. In particular, the excessive populist claims for the informal sector by Hernando de Soto (1989) and his backers in USAID should be resisted. Civil society has its own deficiencies and dialectics in Africa as elsewhere (Bratton, 1989a and b).

The 1990s opened, then, with an apparent, unanticipated proliferation of African regimes willing to abandon their single-party format in favour of formal two-, three- or multi-party systems (see Table 2 and Map 3). In some cases, these declarations were the result of considerable pressure (Ethiopia or Zambia) or planning (Nigeria or Tanzania); in others, they appeared to be mostly ploys (Malagasy or Zaire). Just as most African economies have agreed to a series of reforms, so many polities are now committed to a set of elections. To be sure, some of these African 'democracies' may change little (e.g. Houphouet-Boigny's *Côte d'Ivoire* or Mobutu's Zaire) and others may extend established patterns of corporatism centred on the military (Nigeria) or party (Tanzania) (see Conclusion and table 2). Furthermore, some one-party states are still quite resistant towards pluralism (e.g. Moi's Kenya or Banda's Malawi). However, such moves have made it somewhat more difficult for Mugabe's United ZANU(PF) or Nujoma's SWAPO to declare one-party states in Zimbabwe or Namibia, respectively. And South Africa under majority rule will likely be multi-party with an ANC-dominated multi-racial government. The pattern of institutionalisation of such pluralism remains to be seen – will it be reflected in multiple interest groups and a larger, legitimate civil society? But at least the list of formally democratising states has continued to grow in the early 1990s.

'Politics' in Africa at the start of the 1990s is, then, in something of a transition. The established paradigmatic single-party 'state socialist' structure has become quite discredited and undermined as its tendencies towards political authoritarianism and economic inefficiency become ever more apparent. The decade of the 1980s became one of relentless reconsideration and redirection as economic pressures intensified and political alienation spread. Informal economic survival and informal popular participation came to flourish outside the purview of the discredited and impoverished state.

Given the remarkable, if not entirely unanticipated, conjuncture of the turn of the last decade, the present text is eclectic and tentative as well as radical. The proposed juxtaposition of internal and international forces make such a position judicious. Continuing changes in political economy and development policy are suggestive of exponential revisionism for the decade. I am not concerned to construct a new framework but, rather, to outline an approach which can best explain Africa at the end of the twentieth century, a task made more urgent by the transformations in Eastern Europe with their impact on an already adjusting continent. Just as apparent 'revolutions' in Eastern Europe can be exaggerated so there is a danger in seeming to go beyond radical orthodoxies in Africa. Regretably, most supposedly 'Marxist' studies of African political economy have been peculiarly non-materialist in content. In general, they have been characterised by uncritical adoption of received Northern stereotypes and unquestioned assumptions of Southern homogeneity. In fact, African political economies are quite distinctive and variable; *distinctive* because of a range of bourgeois and peasant factions, and *variable* because of a range of country sizes, statuses and structures, from would-be NICs to the least-developed and debt-affected 'Fourth World' (see Tables

1, 3 and 5). Just as the histories and economies of colonial Africa varied so too do the inheritances and politics of post-colonial Africa; such inequalities are increasing in a period of structural adjustments. Thus the need for 'defensive radicalism' (Ake, 1981) varies among regimes and periods: more necessary in the most impoverished states, less necessary in those in which a degree of state cooptation and depoliticisation remain possible.

Similarly, given the distinctive character of (dependent and state) socialisms(s) and capitalism(s) in Africa it would be quite unmaterialist to expect that its social relations and directions would be either homogenous or at all similar to those in advanced industrialised countries at the end of either nineteenth or twentieth centuries. Rather, a dialectical approach requires a sensitive perspective on the character of social forces, their contradictions and coalitions. In particular, this means being realistic about the constraints confronting 'revolutionary pressures' in the continent, from the spectre of state repression to the imperative of survival strategies. Indeed, 'repressive' or 'reactionary' pressures have been more ubiquitous than revolutionary. In short, workers displaced through 'deindustrialisation' may be expected to become active in the informal sectors rather than in radical politics (see Box 4). Likewise, most petty-bourgeois or bourgeois factions outside the state system concentrate on how to articulate with rather than overthrow it. Hence the need for a revisionist if not new perspective.

Likewise, all too many materialist and modernisation, as well as structuralist or Weberian, analysts have spent disproportionate amounts of time and effort in characterising the 'African' *state*: overdeveloped? underdeveloped? hard? weak? soft? developmental? autonomous? etc. (Beckman, 1988, 1989). The definition and nature of the state in Africa varies between countries, periods and regimes. In an era of structural adjustment it may have become somewhat diminished but it never disappears. Moreover, even at the turn of the decade, some states retained considerable resources for interventions, strategic as well as economic (e.g. Nigeria in Liberia, Zimbabwe in Mozambique), but also remained vulnerable to social pressures, both bourgeois and non-bourgeois. Given the variety of political economies as well as theoretical approaches, it is fanciful to expect agreement on the definition of the state let alone its hard or soft character (cf. Rothchild and Chazan, 1988), especially if its conception within the dominant paradigm is in flux; i.e. from intervention to governance. Yet the retreat to 'ambiguity' or 'enigma'

Box 8
Private Wealth: Public Squalor

The gap between private affluence and public poverty has always
been considerable in Africa both in some pre-colonial kingdoms
and in some post-colonial 'empires'. Colonial elites reinforced
the natural proclivities of indigenous successors. The chasm
between tyrants and subjects has been greatest in, say, Bokassa's
Central African Empire and Mobutu's Zaire, and least in Nyerere's Tanzania or Khama's Botswana. Nigerian tendencies towards aggrandisement and excess were most apparent at the
height of the Shagari oil boom at the start of the 1980s when
private jets superceded Mercedes-Benz as status symbols. Then,
out of necessity, private generators, wells and radio networks
replaced collective electrical, water and communications systems; the rich in both state (civilian and military) and private
sectors could afford exclusive facilities while the poor had to
endure run-down communal infrastructures. Whilst the decline
of national systems has been most dramatic in Amin's Uganda,
JJ's Ghana and Mobutu's Zaire, it has also become apparent,
albeit for less malign reasons, in Nyerere's Tanzania and Kaunda's Zambia. The causes and consequences of breakdowns in
public structures vary but the tendency is a corollary of reforms
like deregulation and desubsidisation. As the World Bank
(1989a: 24) proudly proclaims, with profound developmental
implications:

> The efforts to contain spending in Sub-Saharan Africa have
> significantly changed expenditure patterns in the 1980s. The
> share of interest payments, the only category taking a progres-
> sively larger share of government spending tripled during
> 1980–87. . . . This increase has forced a relative compression
> in wages and salaries, other purchases of goods and services,
> and capital spending.

of Herbst (1990: 1–12) is a form of camouflage even cowardice within
the modernisation paradigm.

As Ian Roxborough suggested in a recent review article, there
has been a certain circularity in much 'development studies' in the

post-independence period, with the 'modernisation' perspective showing remarkable resilience, especially in terms of the NICs and of structural adjustments. Given the new diversity in the 'Third World', Roxborough (1988: 756) calls for an emphasis on comparative history and a deemphasis on paradigmatic theory:

> no sensible theory of historical change can entirely dispense with the core propositions of modernisation theory. That modernisation theory appears to be making a comeback is therefore hardly surprising. Indeed, like the poor, it has always been with us, in Marxist and non-Marxist variants.

Roxborough's (1988: 753) revisionist lament about the deficiencies of all extant perspectives is relevant to Africa as well as to the rest of the South and to policy as well as theory:

> Neither dependency theory nor neo-Marxism turned out to be the panacea for which many were searching. The result has been a widespread pessimism and disenchantment with all theoretical approaches . . . modernisation, dependency and world systems theory . . . do not represent separate and competing bodies of thought.

Nevertheless, I would oppose throwing the radical baby out with the theoretical water as continental crises and global changes have forced dramatic reevaluations of policy as well as perspective. Moreover, there is considerable danger in abandoning the field to supposedly pragmatic and technocratic 'fixes' which have no sense of or scepticism about history and political economy. The latest, contradictory World Bank report devoted to the continent, *From Crisis to Sustainable Growth*, should reinforce such fears, especially given simplistic explanations of and comparisons with the one-party states of Eastern Europe in their transitions; hence the preliminary effort here to be both critical and creative given Africa's challenges in the 1990s: *radical revisionism.*

The new decade should reinforce scepticism at the levels of both theory and policy given the continent's precarious place in the new international divisions of labour and power. Yet revival of simplistic dependence and self-reliance is inappropriate given transformations in national and global political economy and political culture. Moreover, misgivings are beginning to proliferate about the orthodox structural adjustment project, while the niches secured by the NICs are foreclosed to late-comers. As even *The Economist* suggested on 10 March 1990:

> In their increasingly desperate search for an African success story, the World Bank and the IMF paint Ghana's economic reforms as brightly as they can. They too are eager for Mr Rawling's programme to succeed; it was, after all, meant to be a model for the continent. . . . Unfortunately, the military rulers keep arbitrarily interfering. Neither donors nor private investors will play along with an authoritarian regime for much longer. To build on the fragile gains of the Rawling years, Ghana needs democracy all the more. With Eastern Europe in line for both aid and investment, it will have an even harder time attracting either.

In short, African states will have to define their own paths, hopefully in association with their own peoples: the democratic imperative. There is considerable danger in continent-wide explanations and prescriptions given its diversities, just as there is in generalising from either NICs or Eastern Europe. Cautionary insights derived from 'The Limitations of the Special Case', Dudley Seers' (1989) initial seminal contribution to the industry (Hancock, 1991) now called 'development economics', can still be carefully noted for post-adjustment Africa. It is quite apparent that historical limitations of distinctive national political economies and of the global context of international inequalities now have to be augmented by contemporary conditions – notably, the continued centrality of the ('developmental'?) state and the 'new' international divisions of labour and power.

No simple set of reforms or conditions can ensure the revival of development throughout the continent whether it be based on orthodox NIC or EOI or ISI 'models'. The inherited differences have after some twenty-five to forty years of independence (twelve in the case of Zimbabwe; two in the case of Namibia) become a rich range of (changeable) inequalities. Hence the imperative of appropriate nuance in policies and conditionalities for the 1990s which transcend both IBRD and ECA orthodoxies. Each African political economy has become its own special, yet comparable, case! This is the intellectual and political challenge to which radical revisionism is intended as a tentative response (Shaw, 1990a and e).

CONCLUSIONS

Following the two 'oil shocks' of the 1970s, a series of 'adjustment shocks' in the 1980s, and 'environmental shocks' in both decades, Africa could have benefited from a period of sustained expansion in the early 1990s, preferably reinforced by a North–South 'peace dividend'. Instead, in addition to the diversions of Eastern Europe, it has had to deal with (a) the prospects of a 'third oil shock' related to the set of events around the Gulf War; (b) a recession in much of the North leading to lower levels of both external demand and foreign investment; (c) the danger of further protectionism because of the prolonged stalemate in GATT's Uruguay Round; and (d) the rush towards regionalisation of the world economy, intensified by the prospects of Europe 1992, necessitating the continent's own 1991 Abuja Declaration of an 'African Economic Community' (see Appendix: pp. 179–98). Together, these unhelpful or unsettling factors will both delay recovery, exacerbate inequalities and complicate adjustment contexts; hardly auspicious auguries for the new decade! Indeed, such negative and unstable global conditions may further encourage tendencies towards self-reliance as both necessary and inevitable in the circumstances; this is treated in chapter three below.

The *agenda* of African political economy has changed dramatically, then, from the late-1970s' and early-1980s' optimistic certainties about one-party state socialism to the mid- and late-1980s' pessimistic scepticism about such received wisdom. Moreover, the dogmatic responses of Bank and Fund – the ubiquitous structural adjustment project – had by then also resulted in cautions as well as reactions, revisionism and opposition. In short, the essentially externally determined conditionalities led not only to internal responses of implementation with alienation; but they also coincided with related struggles of civil society for popular participation, gender equality and sustainable development. Thus the context or dialectic by 1990 for African political economy was quite transformed. The question remained, however: which, if any, of these new issues would come to dominate the political agenda during at least some of the decade?

The *integration or incorporation* of this set of 'new' factors into African political economy is, of course, complex and problematic. However, to avoid or abandon the attempt is inexcusable when it is apparent that these will impact upon both short- and long-term development performances and prospects. Moreover, the process may be assisted by the new pragmatism already apparent in much of the 'new' generic political economy, which has shed its dogmatic structuralist framework to adopt a more flexible Gramscian-type approach in which ideologies are treated as well as institutions (Gill and Law, 1988; Murphy and Tooze, 1991). Yet this is *not* to advocate any premature retreat into post-modernism: the end of history, or at least of orthodoxy. Rather, it is to recognise that legacy and specificity both affect the salience, status and sequence of such novel forces over time and between territories. Hence, as noted already, I shy away from a fully developed 'theory' for Africa. Instead, as a corrective to misleading orthodoxies, I simply suggest the imperative of *recognising and respecting a range of 'new' forces on the continent in the 1990s* (see Box 9).

Such new pluralism in perspective balances the new pragmatism in policy. However, this does not constitute the abandonment of materialist analysis; merely its refinement to incorporate Gramscian-type notions like hegemony. The emphasis in radical revisionism for

---

Box 9
The Essentials of Luxuries: from Stereos to Satellite Dishes

Colonisation brought with it a cargo-cult. The new elite of independent Africa insisted, understandably, on a similar if not superior life-style to that of the departing Europeans. Initially, these expectations included subsidised luxury housing, access to a quality car, and a stereo system. In the 1960s, a TV became *de rigueur*; in the 1970s, a VCR and/or micro-wave; and, in the 1980s, a compact disc player and/or satellite dish. Depending on how far South one lives, these may vary in size from some 10 to 50 feet in diameter, and so cost less than $1,000 to more than $5,000.

Such contemporary taste-transfer not only exhausts national treasuries in the short term, it also sets up inappropriate expectations and role models in the longer term. How can devalued, devastated African economies sustain such consumption patterns unless continental commodities are revalued dramatically or unless black-marketeering becomes ever more ubiquitous? And if elites demand satellite TV, the masses will at least insist on transistor radios, from 'walkmans' to 'ghetto blasters'.

Africa is on nuance – changes and comparisons over time – not the abandonment of political economy inherent in the fad of post-modernism. To help capture some of the new complexity, I have adopted for this academic text the form but not the content used by the World Bank and related international agencies: 'boxes' which highlight issues, cases and contradictions. These are intended to illustrate how the new pluralism/pragmatism works out in practice: some salient examples of novel situations and reactions. These help to reinforce the appeal and promise of the new political economy by contrast to the conservatism and caution of both traditional modernisation and orthodox adjustment approaches. Some of the more salient elements of such reformism – political as well as economic liberalisation – are indicated in the following chapters.

2 The African Condition: From Crisis to Conjuncture

The gravest development problems are in Sub-Saharan Africa. Unfavourable external conditions (including a prolonged fall in the terms of trade of primary goods exporters) and inadequate domestic policies have caused economic, social, and environmental decline. After reasonable growth in the 1960s and early 1970s, the region's economic performance deteriorated. . . . Saving and investment rates fell sharply in the early 1980s.

IBRD, *World Development Report 1989*: 12

'the debt problem' (in Africa) is to a considerable extent a symptom of a balance of payments weakened by adverse world economic forces and domestic policy shortcomings, as well as of reduced access to new capital inflows.

SCF/ODI, *Prospects for Africa*: 64

Despite the widespread adoption of adjustment programmes, African countries paid back more – a total of $1.5 billion – to the IMF from 1986 to 1989 than they gained in new borrowing.

Ravenhill, 1990: 714

The structural adjustment project of the Bank and Fund has transformed the actualities if not yet the analyses of Africa's political economy. And this transformation – from devaluations and privatisations to deregulation and user-pay – has taken place not only at the level of policies but also in terms of politics and economics. Initial post-independence assumptions about the centrality of the state and the inevitability of development have been superseded by the erosion of the state and concentration only on growth, which nevertheless remains problematic. As reflected in most contemporary analysis, the mood has changed from one of cautious optimism to continuous pessimism: how to recapture the idealism and dynamism of the early independence period?

STRUCTURAL ADJUSTMENT POLICIES AND *PROBLÉMATIQUES*

In retrospect, the decade of the 1960s now looks like an aberration – expansion with development – followed by exponential crisis in the 1970s and contradictions and conditionalities in the 1980s. Yet despite the visible and palpable transformations, most analyses are stuck in an apparent time-warp: the paradigmatic state-centrism of one-party, military and/or one-man rule characteristic of the late 1960s and early 1970s. This is so despite the set of dramatic responses to drought and adjustment: food riots, informal sectors and women's assertions. Moreover, although Bank and Fund conditionalities may in theory be short term palliatives, in practice they have long term implications; they have transformed not only internal and external terms of trade but also both of these sets of social relations. Indeed, the political economy of Africa – definitions and relations of state, class and community – has changed for the foreseeable future (Shaw, 1992a and b).

The structural adjustment programmes emanating from the Bank are themselves in evolution as policy results and debates are continuously evaluated and incorporated. At the start of the 1990s, they appear to have become both more comprehensive and more flexible as they move away from initial stabilisation responses characteristic of the Fund and begin to address some of the unwelcome negative social consequences of fiscal 'reform'. The priority and intensity of the range of elements – devaluation, deregulation, desubsidisation, liberalisation, privatisation etc. – also vary as some are more fundamental in one set of political economies than in others. Nevertheless, despite some welcome flexibility from the late 1980s – back to some educational assistance reminiscent of the 1960s but now redesignated 'human resource development', for example (World Bank, 1991a) – the character of most national packages tend to be quite homogeneous, leading to 'defaults' or backsliding on some conditionalities as political opposition or other unforeseen consequences arise (Mosley, Harrigan and Toye, 1991). And, just as in Eastern

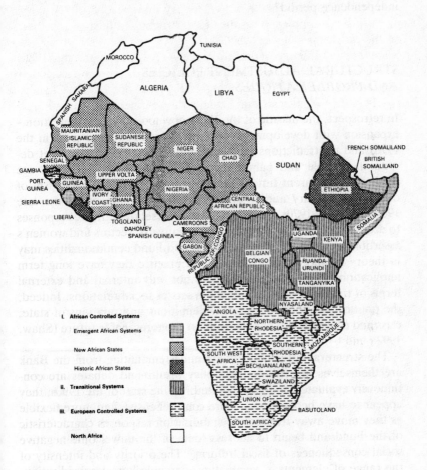

Map 2 Political systems in Sub-Saharan Africa, 1960

SOURCE: Almond and Coleman (1960) p. 263.

Europe, African states and social forces tend to learn from each other: how to subvert unacceptable consequences and costs. In short, a strengthened and enlarged civil society may be one of the more promising yet unplanned results of the structural adjustment project on the continent (see next section).

Unhappily, though, it is now widely recognised that the 1980s constituted a 'lost decade' for Africa in terms of per capita incomes and rates of national development (see Figures 1 and 2). Yet Chandra Hardy (1990: 3) suggests that actually the continent has suffered *two decades of stagnation in real incomes*. Of course, it has to be appreciated that national accounts data for most African countries are quite unreliable (cf. Table 1). In reality, given the ubiquity of informal sectors, national and personal incomes may be twice as high as suggested; more so in less structured economies, like those of Angola, Nigeria, Sierra Leone, Uganda and Zaire, less so in more organised states like Malawi, Senegal, South Africa and Zimbabwe (see Tables 4 and 5). Such recognition may serve to reduce the apparent inequalities on the continent somewhat, although ubiquitous cross-border trade may flow in alternate directions depending on market, especially exchange rate, conditions on either side. Indeed, the Zambia–Malawi or *Côte d'Ivoire*–Ghana trade may be illustrative in this regard: the former benefitted when their economies were strong and their currencies were overvalued whereas the latter gained as their relative situations improved.

It is also crucial to recall that Africa was not always so marginal or informal. In the post-war period, several of its economies boomed, particularly those producing and exporting commodities or minerals like cotton and copper. Thus, in the late 1950s, Ghana's per capita income of just below $500 p.a. was the same as that of South Korea yet by the late 1980s the latter's was over six times that of the former (Pickett and Singer, 1990) (see Figures 3 and 4).

Africa had somewhat naively tried to anticipate and divert the veritable 'counter-revolution' posed by structural adjustment through its prior development of the *Lagos Plan of Action* (*LPA*) in the early 1980s. In retrospect, this constituted the final version of traditional dependency responses: economic nationalism that advances self-reliance through state-managed programmes. But, in part because it was not in tune with the new times, this was insufficiently supported in either political or financial terms to be effective. Moreover, its counter-dependency orientation was incompatible with the new logic of liberalisation: monetarism in the North and capitalisms in

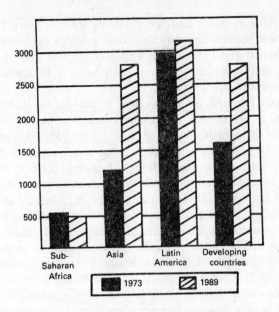

Figure 1   Real GDP per capita
(1980 dollars)

SOURCE: United Nations (1991).

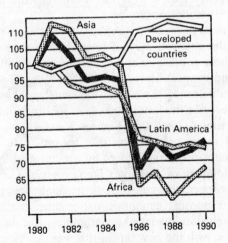

Figure 2   Terms of trade
(1980 = 100)

SOURCE: United Nations (1991).

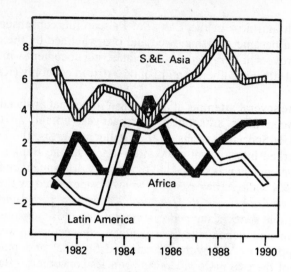

Figure 3   Africa's growth record
(annual % change of real GDP)

SOURCE: United Nations (1991).

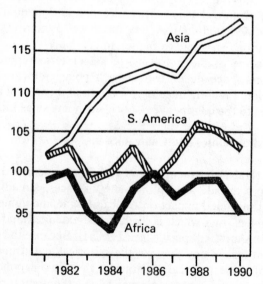

Figure 4   Per capita food production
(1979–80 = 100)

SOURCE: United Nations (1991).

the South and now in the East. So, the careful, consensual *Lagos Plan* soon became overshadowed and overwhelmed by the contrary and controversial *Berg Report*: the pioneering document which advocated and advanced liberalisation of the African economy (Ravenhill, 1986).

Despite several attempts at achieving a somewhat artificial consensus between these antagonistic perspectives, notably in the mid-decade UN Special Sessions on the continental crisis, the late 1980s were marked by a revival of counter-attacks as the Bank's *Accelerated Development* was succeeded by *Africa's Adjustment and Growth in the 1980s* while Africa's *Lagos Plan* was superceded by the *African Alternative Framework to Structural Adjustment Programmes*. The incompatible geneses and *genres*, orientations and assertions of modernisation and dependency perspectives, respectively, were never more apparent. And with the unequal financial and political resources of the two pairs of central agencies concerned – Bank/Fund cross-conditionalities versus ECA/OAU insolvency – it was and is inevitable that Washington's prescriptions will be more authoritative and effective at least in the short term than those from Addis Ababa. Unhappily, this is likely to be the case also for the comprehensive, yet idealistic and state-centric, African Economic Community agreed at the OAU's 1991 summit at Abuja, which was primarily a response to regionalisation elsewhere in the world economy.

I treat some of the unfortunate, longer term repercussions for Africa from a decade or two of such policy reforms in the next chapter. Here I merely trace the evolution of theoretical and political approaches to the continent's political economy since independence.

Bank Conditionalities and Contradictions

The structural adjustment dictates of Bank and Fund have, after more than a decade already in some instances, already had a profound and sustained impact on Africa's fragile and vulnerable political economies, one which is likely to be extended and exponential rather than short and specific (see Table 4). Because the advocates of adjustment lacked any sense of the historical and structural characteristics of these political economies, their initial policy responses were both superficial and controversial. Neither debt repayments nor policy reformulations could overlook the essentially extroverted dualisms of Africa, dualisms especially of class, sector and space, and sometimes of gender and generation. To be sure, *structural change*

Table 4 Total External Public and Private Debt and Debt Service Ratios

	Total long-term debt disbursed and outstanding						Total interest payments on long-term debt (millions of dollars)			Total long-term debt service as a percentage of					
	Millions of dollars			As a percentage of GNP						GNP			Exports of goods and services		
	1970	1980	1987	1970	1980	1987	1970	1980	1987	1970	1980	1987	1970	1980	1987
Low-income economies															
Excluding Nigeria															
1 Ethiopia	169	701	2,434	10	17	46	6	17	51	1.2	0.8	3.4	11.4	5.8	28.4
2 Chad	33	201	270	10	28	28	0	0	3	0.9	0.4	0.7	4.2	3.6	3.9
3 Zaire	311	4,294	7,334	9	43	140	9	197	119	1.1	3.6	4.7	4.4	15.2	12.8
4 Guinea-Bissau	–	125	391	–	119	321	–	1	4	–	3.8	7.2	–	–	37.0
5 Malawi	122	644	1,155	43	56	98	4	35	26	2.3	5.9	6.0	7.8	21.5	23.3
6 Mozambique	–	–	–	–	–	–	–	–	–	–	–	–	–	–	–
7 Tanzania	265	2,137	4,079	21	42	144	–	–	–	–	–	–	–	–	–
8 Burkina Faso	21	299	794	7	21	44	0	6	14	0.7	1.2	1.7	6.8	7.5	–
9 Madagascar	89	956	3,113	10	30	163	2	27	83	0.8	1.8	7.7	3.7	11.1	35.3
10 Mali	238	685	1,847	71	42	96	0	3	13	0.2	0.6	1.7	1.4	3.6	9.9
11 Gambia, The	5	106	273	10	44	151	0	0	5	0.2	0.3	8.2	0.5	1.2	12.9
12 Burundi	7	141	718	3	16	60	0	2	15	0.3	0.7	3.6	2.3	6.7	38.5
13 Zambia	653	2,274	4,354	38	63	228	–	–	–	–	–	–	–	–	–
14 Niger	–	704	1,513	–	28	73	–	65	73	–	4.9	7.2	–	19.0	46.9
15 Uganda	138	603	1,116	7	35	30	5	2	24	0.5	1.3	1.9	2.9	6.7	19.5
16 São Tomé and Principe	–	23	84	–	51	337	0	0	2	–	2.2	15.3	–	4.4	41.5
17 Somalia	77	601	1,719	24	111	237	1	2	4	0.3	1.4	0.9	2.1	4.4	8.3
18 Togo	40	913	1,042	16	82	91	1	19	29	1.0	4.2	5.5	3.1	8.1	14.2
19 Rwanda	2	164	544	1	14	26	0	2	7	0.1	0.4	1.0	1.2	2.4	11.3
20 Sierra Leone	59	351	513	1	22	65	0		1						

21 Benin	41	348	929	15	30	57	0	3	15	0.6	0.8	2.0	2.4	2.9	15.9
22 Central African Republic	24	160	520	14	20	49	1	0	9	1.7	0.2	2.1	5.1	0.8	12.1
23 Kenya	406	2,675	4,978	26	39	64	17	173	244	3.0	5.5	7.6	9.1	18.5	33.8
24 Sudan	–	4,130	8,429	–	61	102	–	–	–	0.4	0.2	0.6	–	–	–
25 Comoros	1	43	188	5	36	95	0	0	1	0.4	0.2	0.6	–	2.1	5.2
26 Lesotho	8	63	237	8	10	37	0	2	5	0.5	0.7	2.3	4.5	1.3	4.4
27 Nigeria	567	5,301	28,121	4	5	111	28	551	569	0.7	0.8	3.9	7.1	2.8	11.7
28 Ghana	497	1,138	2,237	23	26	45	0	–	58	1.2	2.3	3.7	5.5	8.3	20.3
29 Mauritania	27	734	1,868	14	109	215	0	13	28	1.8	4.5	9.9	3.4	11.1	18.2
30 Liberia	158	573	1,152	39	53	108	6	23	6	4.3	3.5	1.0	8.1	6.3	2.5
31 Equatorial Guinea	5	58	175	8	–	–	0	0	3	0.0	–	–	0.0	13.6	23.1
32 Guinea	312	1,032	2,010	47	63	78	4	23	37	2.2	5.8	5.4	–	17.2	–
Middle-income economies															
33 Cape Verde	–	20	121	–	15	69	–	0	3	–	0.2	4.0	–	–	–
34 Senegal	131	967	3,109	16	34	69	2	57	116	1.1	6.4	6.4	4.0	22.1	22.3
35 Zimbabwe	–	–	2,095	–	–	37	–	–	–	–	–	–	–	–	–
36 Swaziland	37	166	273	33	31	46	2	7	12	3.1	2.3	5.2	–	2.7	6.1
37 Côte d'Ivoire	266	4,742	11,714	20	48	124	12	385	597	3.1	9.5	15.6	7.5	25.9	40.8
38 Congo, People's Republic	124	1,427	3,679	47	90	195	3	42	45	3.4	5.7	10.3	11.5	8.8	18.6
39 Cameroon	140	2,227	3,306	13	33	27	5	119	176	1.0	3.4	4.8	4.0	12.8	27.9
40 Botswana	17	152	514	21	18	38	0	7	32	0.7	1.5	5.2	1.0	1.7	3.7
41 Mauritius	32	320	591	14	29	34	2	22	31	1.4	3.6	4.6	3.2	7.0	6.5
42 Gabon	91	1,308	1,605	29	34	53	3	123	57	3.8	10.8	2.3	5.7	16.8	5.1
43 Seychelles	–	25	124	–	18	35	–	0	3	–	0.2	4.2	–	0.3	–
44 Angola	–	–	–	–	–	–	–	–	–	–	–	–	–	–	–
45 Djibouti	–	26	152	–	8	–	–	1	3	–	1.0	–	–	–	–

Source: World Bank, 1991b.

rather than adjustment had become an imperative because of state-determined stagnation: neither internal nor external indebtedness could be sustained indefinitely. And the continental discussions before and after the first continental economic summit in 1980 indicated growing awareness of such necessity. Yet it was the combinations of *Berg Report* and multiple famines which concentrated minds both on and off the continent at the opening of the 1980s, just as the end of the Cold War and another oil shock did at the start of the 1990s (Adedeji and Shaw, 1985; Ravenhill, 1990b).

Symbolic of profound divergencies but also of pressures for convergence were Bank attempts, intensified in the second half of the 1980s, for 'policy dialogue' and donor support; the latter was the other, external side of the conditionality contract. As already noted above, there have been essentially two, quite similar rounds in the Bank-Commission stand-off: the initial *Berg* versus *LPA* conflict, which led eventually to the mid-decade UN sessions and compromises, to be followed in the late 1980s by the parallel *Sustainable Growth* versus *African Alternative* dispute (World Bank, 1989). This, likewise, led to a formal yet tenuous stalemate: 'Joint Statement on Africa's Long-Term Development' (May 1989). It was the Bank's preoccupation with maintaining donor support for structural adjustment, notwithstanding the demands and diversions of Eastern Europe and no matter how problematic, controversial or expensive the programmes, which culminated in the politically disastrous *Africa's Adjustment and Growth* (World Bank and UNDP, 1989). This tract's adversorial message had already been foreshadowed in superficial, glossy publications like *African Update* (1988/9) and *Africa: Heading for Tomorrow* (1988), the latter formally from the Bretton Woods Committee, a US advocacy group for Bank, Fund and related regional development banks. The Committee's special report on 'Economic Reform in Sub-Saharan Africa' echoed and anticipated the familiar refrain of necessary adjustment, noting the human dimension difficulties and highlighting then-'success stories' – the Gambia and Tanzania, Niger and Malawi – along with the difficulty of sustained implementation in cases like Zambia. Yet glossy public relations and changeable lists of 'strong' and 'weak' reformers are not enough. Adjustment remains problematic in impact because it is improbable in content (see Figure 5).

It is inexcusable to fall into the same trap as the Bank and Fund and over-generalise about the incidence and impact of reforms. Nevertheless, although the intensity and sequence of adjustments

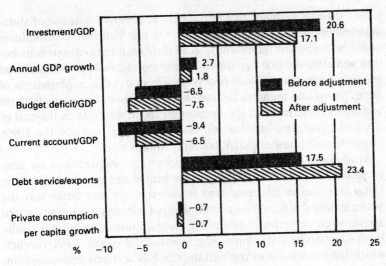

Figure 5 Sustainability of adjustment
(annual average % change in indicators
for 15 sub-Saharan countries with SAPs)

SOURCE: United Nations (1991).

have varied, especially between externally- and internally-induced changes, there are a set of some half a dozen commonalities which can be identified as results which are quite distinct from Bank and Fund expectations and claims. These have tended to appear across the spectrum of reformers – maximum and minimum, ex- and non-, even self-designed, like the 1991 Zimbabwe programme (Shaw and Davies, 1992; Davies, Sanders and Shaw, 1991).

First, the intense and incomplete structural adjustment process has diverted just about all African political economies away from *longer term issues of development* – ecology, industry, infrastructure, technology – and has instead focused attention on short term questions of debt and trade – how Africa relates to the rest of the global economy. African regimes, especially their economic and financial components, have become quite preoccupied over the last decade by the relentless round of Bank and Fund missions and related bilateral donor and commercial bank consultative groups in Paris and London: external financial agencies and agendas determine internal processes and priorities (Martin, 1991). In short, the policy environment, reflective of the *de facto* paradigm, is hardly propitious for alternative, innovative, indigenous directions.

Second, the adjustment project has led to new continental as well as internal *inequalities* (see Box 9). The old distinctions between larger and smaller, more and less industrialised, more and less self-sufficient countries – i.e. Third versus Fourth Worlds – have been superceded by the divide between 'strong' and 'weak' reformers. This novel yet fundamental distinction is, of course, determined by Bank indicators and interests; i.e. whether African regimes have succumbed to its pressures and effected its terms or not. Thus, whether or not Bank conditionalities are efficacious, this new dichotomy will further complicate and retard attempts at regional cooperation, as treated in the penultimate chapter. It will also provide opportunities for creative informal sector responses just as the presence of the not yet devalued CFA zone has done already. As noted above, patterns of informal commodity, currency and labour flows shift in response to the rise and fall of national economies and structural adjustments. Indeed, they may constitute more reliable and sensitive indicators of adjustment impacts than rather rhetorical and changeable Bank categories, especially given the high rate of slippage in effecting conditionalities.

Third, even in the short term, adjustment reforms have *transformed political economies* leading to intense domestic changes and debates. Beyond the most visible resistance to unacceptable, often impossible conditionalities – so-called 'food riots' – there is an ongoing shift in social relations, notable in the decline of the middle and lower classes and revival of some peasant and other rural interests (see related boxes). The prospects for the un- and under-employed are worse than ever. Only the very rich, well connected, and internationally mobile can survive. The combination of devaluation, deindustrialisation, downsizing (of the bureaucracy as well as industry) and desubsidisation means that the middle-class, is particularly hard hit, resorting to 'moon-lighting', informal sectors, and almost any form of access to foreign exchange or 'forex'. Indeed, the continent is preoccupied with a form of forex 'fetishism' given its enhanced buying power. Meanwhile, the majority opposed to the unacceptable social costs of adjustment – the undermining of established political cultures and norms – has grown as the relentless, exponential impacts of conditionalities have become apparent.

Fourth, then, the correlate of such opposition is the *dwindling of support for reform*, both internally and externally. The naive innocence of the Bank in its advocacy of the adjustment project was first apparent in its initial expectation that social groups or 'coalitions' in the Third World would respond positively to its initiatives. When it became apparent that resistance was more likely than acquiescence or acceptance, it consulted with scholars and commentators on how to popularise its conditionalities. Clearly, some social groups have benefited from adjustment, notably some fractions of capital, larger peasant farmers and smaller informal traders. In their review of the sequencing and selling of adjustment, Mosley and Toye (1988: 405) argue realistically that:

> first, that the design of structural adjustment packages is a matter of political calculation rather than simply of economic analysis, and secondly, that what has to be designed is not simply a list of measures to be implemented or not implemented, but a strategy for strengthening the groups which stand to gain by reform.

The schism over adjustment divides regimes as well as societies: a few senior economic agencies support it, notably Bank and Fund associates such as Ministers of Finance and Governors of Central Banks, while the majority oppose it, especially activists or populists in development and welfare ministries. In brief, most cabinet members are decision-takers rather than -makers on crucial adjustment features.

Fifth, then, *adjustment serves not only to divert attention from development in the short term but also to undermine the resilience of the state in the longer term.* Whilst the Bank and Fund may claim that 'market forces' can lead to growth, the history of industrial development, including the post-war period, indicates otherwise, as Manfred Bienfeld, Nigel Harris and others prove in their increasingly persuasive revisionist response: the NICs are characterised by strong rather than weak states. Paradoxically, then, so-called 'strong' reformers of necessity erode their inherited structures; so as 'weak' regimes they will be less likely to develop over time in a sustainable manner, notwithstanding the flow of external resources and approvals. To be sure, overdeveloped, corrupt and inefficient states are contrary to development. But few weak governments have achieved and sustained development, and then only in special circumstances, such as Hong Kong pre-1990s. By eroding African structures, no matter what their deficiencies, adjustment may permanently damage the continent's prospects for long term development, confining it forever to a basket-case status. Hence the irony and irrelevance of the Bank's highly touted 'African Capacity Building Initiative': special training and facilities for a new indigenous elite who are to effect adjustment into the next century (World Bank, 1991a).

Sixth, *at best adjustment may lead in the short term to recaptured growth*. But despite claims from Bank and Fund to this effect, the results to date are, frankly, ambiguous, even disappointing (see Table 5). Contrary reports emerging from Washington and Addis Ababa in the first half of 1989 pointed to the inconclusiveness of the data. *Africa's Adjustment* from the World Bank and UNDP (1989: ii) claims to show 'emerging signs of economic improvement since the mid 1980s' while the ECA's (1989: i) *Economic Report on Africa 1989* for the same three-year period of the mid-decade asserts that 'the deterioration in the overall economic situation in Africa continued unabated as economic performance during the period was generally disappointing'. These distinct counterpoints are reinforced in divergent introductions to this pair of reports. Edward Jaycox, Bank Vice-President for Africa, argues in *Africa's Adjustment* that 'an important feature of the movement toward policy reform and orderly structural adjustment is that Africans accepted the principal responsibility for their economic decisions and destiny . . . data in this report suggest that a strategy of adjustment with growth is viable in Africa' (World Bank and UNDP, 1989: iii). By contrast, ECA (1989a: iii) Executive-Secretary, Adebayo Adedeji, responds in *Economic Report* that

> Any attempt to portray the economic situation currently prevailing in Africa in rosy terms, to minimise the impact of an adverse external environment and to depict the effects of structural adjustment programmes as having been always positive, does not only detract from the reality of the situation, but is also cynical in the extreme.

Symbolic of such profound divergencies, but also of endless pressure for convergence, were Bank attempts, intensified in the second half of the decade, for 'policy dialogue' and donor support. As noted already, there have been essentially two rounds (thus far at least!) in the Bank-Commission standoff.

In reality, of course, adjustment policies and evaluations have always been more political than economic. As Martin (1991) and others recognise, adjustment terms have *not* all been the same, even if they reflect a common ideological orthodoxy. Rather, some

Table 5 Balance of Payments and Reserves

| | Current account balance (million of dollars) | | | | | | Net direct private investment (millions of dollars) | | | Gross international reserves | | | | |
| | After official transfers | | | Before official transfers | | | | | | Millions of dollars | | | Months of import coverage |
	1970	1980	1987	1970	1980	1987	1970	1980	1987	1970	1980	1987	1987
Sub-Saharan Africa													
Total										2,028 t	15,056 t	8,030 t	2.1 w
Excluding Nigeria										1,804 t	4,416 t	6,532 t	2.0 w
Low-income economies										1,677 t	13,481 t	4,821 t	2.0 w
Excluding Nigeria										1,454 t	2,841 t	3,323 t	1.8 w
1 Ethiopia	-32	-126	-264[a]	-43	-186	-475	4	0	-	72	262	245	2.3
2 Chad	2	12	-83	-33	-16	-324	1	0	4	2	12	57	1.4
3 Zaire	-64	-292	-705	-141	-559	-851	42	6	10	189	380	417	1.8
4 Guinea-Bissau	-	-	-26	-	-	-66	-	9	-	-	-	-	-
5 Malawi	-35	-264	-24	-46	-315	-53	9	9	-	29	76	58	1.8
6 Mozambique	-	-367	-372[a]	-	-423	-676	-	0	0	-	-	-	-
7 Tanzania	-36	-502	-128[a]	-37	-606	-605	-	0	-	65	20	32	0.3
8 Burkina Faso	9	-49	-124	-21	-259	-124	0	0	-	36	75	328	4.4
9 Madagascar	10	-568	-135[a]	-42	-635	-241	10	-7	0	37	9	185	3.1
10 Mali	-2	-124	-111	-22	-234	-313	-1	2	4	1	26	25	0.5
11 Gambia, The	0	-74	6	0	-112	-40	0	12	3	8	6	14	1.6
12 Burundi	2[a]	-84	-132[a]	-8[a]	-129	-185	0[a]	1	2[a]	15	105	69	2.8
13 Zambia	108	-537	21	107	-545	-12	-297	62	0	515	206	111	1.4
14 Niger	0	-276	-67	-32	-429	-201	4	44	-	19	132	254	6.4
15 Uganda	20	-83	-107	19	-121	-200	4	2	1	57	3	55	1.0

continued on page 74

Table 5 continued

#	Country	Current account balance (million of dollars) After official transfers 1970	1980	1987	Before official transfers 1970	1980	1987	Net direct private investment (millions of dollars) 1970	1980	1987	Gross international reserves — Millions of dollars 1970	1980	1987	Months of import coverage 1987
16	São Tomé and Príncipe	–	1	-17	–	1	-28	–	–	–	–	–	–	–
17	Somalia	-6	-136	248[a]	-18	-279	-59	5	–	0	21	26	17	0.4
18	Togo	3	-95	-73	-14	-181	-147	0	42	12	35	85	361	7.3
19	Rwanda	7	-48	-131	-12	-155	-250	0	16	23	8	187	164	4.6
20	Sierra Leone	-16	-165	-5	-20	-209	-9	8	-19	-6	39	31	6	1.0
21	Benin	-3	-197	-208[a]	-23	-261	-223	7	4	–	16	15	9	0.2
22	Central African Republic	-12	-43	-96[a]	-24	-141	-214	–	–	20[a]	1	62	102	3.2
23	Kenya	-49	-886	-497	-86	-1,006	-639	1	5	0	220	539	294	1.4
24	Sudan	-42	-564	-422[a]	-43	-648	-702	14	78	–	22	49	12	0.1
25	Comoros	–	-9	-23	–	-20	-61	-1	0	–	–	6	31	4.3
26	Lesotho	18[a]	-11	-12	-1[a]	-117	-16	–	–	8	–	50	68	1.9
27	Nigeria	-368	5,131	-380	-412	5,299	-380	205	-740	2	223	10,640	1,498	2.3
28	Ghana	-68	29	-275	-76	-54	-275	68	16	386	43	330	332	3.0
29	Mauritania	-5	-134	-73[a]	-13	-251	-164	1	27	5	3	146	77	1.5
30	Liberia	-16[a]	46	-118	-27[a]	10	-163	28[a]	–	5[a]	–	5	1	0.0
31	Equatorial Guinea	-6	–	-8	-6	–	-36	–	–	–	–	–	1	0.1
32	Guinea	–	-9	-53[a]	–	-26	-114	–	34	39	–	–	–	–

Middle-income economies									351 t	1,574 t	3,209 t	2.2 w
33 Cape Verde	–	–25	–	–	–25	–	–	–	–	36	57	–
34 Senegal	–16	–386	–316a	–66	–526	–608	5	13	–50a	22	25	23	0.1
35 Zimbabwe	–14a	–244	50	–13a	–302	–22	–	2	–24	59	419	370	2.7
36 Swaziland	–	–135	40	–	–211	–2	–	17	10	–	159	127	3.0
37 Côte d'Ivoire	–38	–1,826	–624a	73	–1,836	–641	31	95	0	119	46	30	0.1
38 Congo, People's Republic	–45a	–166	–245	–53a	–230	–298	30a	40	–40	9	93	9	0.1
39 Cameroon	–30	–395	–1,112a	–47	–499	–1,112	16	105	31a	81	206	78	0.3
40 Botswana	–30a	–75	597	–35a	–207	458	6a	109	125	–	344	2,057	17.6
41 Mauritius	8	–119	72	5	–130	47	2	1	44	46	113	362	3.5
42 Gabon	–3	384	–210	–15	350	–231	–1	24	121	15	115	18	0.1
43 Seychelles	0	–16	–31	0	–30	–48	–	6	8	–	18	14	0.5
44 Angola	–	–	–	–	–	–	–	–	–	–	–	–	–
45 Djibouti	–	–	–	–	–	–	–	–	–	–	–	64	–

Source: World Bank (1991b).

a World Bank estimates.　　　t = total.　　　w = weighted average.

countries (read regimes or leaders) have been treated better than others, either because their economies were in such an advanced state of decay (e.g. Uganda) or because they were seen to be of 'strategic' significance (e.g. Sudan and Zaire, at least before the demise of the Cold War's extension into Africa) or because they were considered to be 'models' (e.g. Ghana in the 1980s and Mauritius in the 1990s?) (see Ravenhill, 1990a: 715–27). The very special treatment accorded to Egypt by the US in early 1991 in recognition of its crucial role in the anti-Saddam Hussein 'coalition' confirms this point! Given both NIDL and NIDP, such calculations may diminish or disappear, and certainly the salience of the continent has continued to decline as both Eastern Europe and the Middle East have come to demand heightened attention.

Furthermore, ironically, although adjustment criteria in general are intended to contain the state and liberate the market, some of them strengthen the former by extracting more from the latter. In a somewhat revisionist mood, reflecting some shifts in Bank and donor preferences by the late 1980s, Herbst (1990a: 8) argues that

> It is important that the state actually became stronger and larger during a structural adjustment exercise because further economic growth is dependent on the state doing what only it can do: build and maintain infrastructure, provide social services and support a viable legal system. . . .
>
> Economic reform in Africa does not mean simplistically removing the state from the economy and letting the 'magic of the market' work its wonders. Rather, economic reform means redirecting state activities so that the state does what only it can do and avoids doing the things (like setting price controls) that it does disastrously.

To ensure an acceptable division of responsibilities between state and market over time, a strong domestic civil society is an imperative rather than the continuous external monitoring of adjustment conditionalities demanded under Bank terms.

Finally, seventh, the apparent, belated (re)discovery of *basic needs and infrastructures* by the Bank and others would be laughable had not millions of Africans had to suffer through the 'adjustment decade' of policy dialogues (see Table 6). Given the undeniable human dimensions and costs of adjustment, some measures to ameliorate them are now being included at the margins of national programmes:

Table 6 Human Development Index, 1991

	Life expectancy at birth (years) 1990	Adult literacy rate (%) 1985	Mean years of schooling 1980	Educational attainment	Real GDP per capita (PPP$) 1985–88	Adjusted real GDP	Human development index	GNP rank minus HDI rank[a]
Medium human development								
South Africa	61.7	85.0	3.7	57.9	5,480	4,880	0.766	0
Seychelles	70.0	88.0	4.6	60.2	3,430	3,430	0.752	−22
Libyan Arab Jamahiriya	61.8	56.5	2.7	38.6	7,250	4,927	0.665	−41
Tunisia	66.7	57.6	1.8	39.0	3,170	3,170	0.588	−11
Botswana	59.8	70.0	2.0	47.3	2,510	2,510	0.524	−8
Gabon	52.5	56.1	2.5	38.2	3,960	3,960	0.510	−49
Algeria	65.1	48.6	1.3	32.8	2,470	2,470	0.490	−46
Swaziland	56.8	68.0	3.0	46.3	2,110	2,110	0.462	−5
Namibia	57.5	73.0	1.7	49.2	1,500	1,500	0.440	−28
Lesotho	57.3	72.6	2.7	49.3	1,390	1,390	0.432	14
Morocco	62.0	41.7	1.8	28.4	2,380	2,380	0.431	−10
Cape Verde	67.0	47.0	2.0	32.0	1,410	1,410	0.428	−6
Zimbabwe	59.6	62.3	2.0	42.2	1,370	1,370	0.413	−6
São Tomé and Principe	65.5	58.0	2.3	39.4	620	620	0.399	0
Kenya	59.7	65.0	2.0	44.0	1,010	1,010	0.399	17
Egypt	60.3	44.6	1.7	30.3	1,930	1,930	0.394	−10
Congo	53.7	51.7	2.0	35.1	2,120	2,120	0.374	−25
Madagascar	54.5	76.9	2.0	51.9	670	670	0.371	31
Zambia	54.4	67.4	2.6	45.8	870	870	0.351	19

continued on page 78

Table 6 continued

	Life expectancy at birth (years) 1990	Adult literacy rate (%) 1985	Mean years of schooling 1980	Educational attainment	Real GDP per capita (PPP$) 1985–88	Adjusted real GDP	Human development index	GNP rank minus HDI rank[a]
Cameroon	53.7	48.0	1.4	32.5	1,670	1,670	0.328	-33
Ghana	55.0	52.8	3.3	36.3	970	970	0.311	4
Côte d'Ivoire	53.4	48.7	1.7	33.0	1,430	1,430	0.311	-21
Zaire	53.0	65.9	1.5	44.4	430	430	0.299	28
Comoros	55.0	48.0	1.0	32.3	760	760	0.274	-8
Tanzania, U. Rep. of	54.0	52.0	2.0	35.3	570	570	0.266	29
Nigeria	51.5	42.7	1.0	28.8	1,030	1,030	0.242	9
Togo	54.0	37.9	1.5	25.8	700	700	0.225	-2
Liberia	54.2	32.3	1.6	22.1	890	890	0.220	-16
Rwanda	49.5	45.4	1.0	30.6	730	730	0.213	1
Uganda	52.0	42.8	1.0	28.9	410	410	0.204	5
Senegal	48.3	32.1	0.7	21.6	1,250	1,250	0.189	-29
Equatorial Guinea	47.0	44.9	0.8	30.2	700	700	0.186	-13
Malawi	48.1	41.7	1.7	28.4	620	620	0.179	16
Burundi	48.5	42.1	0.3	28.2	550	550	0.177	1
Ethiopia	45.5	50.0	1.0	33.7	350	350	0.166	18
Central African Rep.	49.5	31.5	1.0	21.3	780	780	0.166	-14
Sudan	50.8	24.4	0.7	16.5	970	970	0.164	-30
Mozambique	47.5	27.6	1.6	18.9	1,070	1,070	0.155	14
Angola	45.5	35.7	1.5	24.3	840	840	0.150	-53
Mauritania	47.0	27.5	0.3	18.4	960	960	0.140	-34
Somalia	46.1	16.9	0.2	11.3	1,330	1,330	0.118	4

Benin	47.0	18.7	0.6	12.7	1,050	1,050	0.114	−24
Guinea-Bissau	42.5	30.2	0.3	20.2	670	670	0.088	−3
Chad	46.5	23.0	0.2	15.4	510	510	0.087	5
Djibouti	48.0	14.0	0.3	9.4	730	730	0.083	−38
Burkina Faso	48.2	14.5	0.1	9.7	650	650	0.081	−11
	45.5	21.5	0.1	14.4	610	610	0.079	−19
Niger	45.0	22.7	0.3	15.2	500	500	0.072	−15
Mali	43.5	16.8	0.8	11.5	910	910	0.066	−39
Guinea	44.0	20.3	0.5	13.7	650	650	0.064	−14
Gambia								
Sierra Leone	42.0	13.3	0.8	9.1	1,030	1,030	0.048	−25

Source: UNDP, *Human Development Report, 1991*, pp. 119–21.

a A positive figure shows that the HDI rank is higher than the GNP rank, a negative the opposite.

so-called 'social dimensions of adjustment'. Moreover, the Bank has created its own social dimension mechanisms and evaluations, especially the 'African Capacity Building Initiative' which seeks to rebuild, albeit on Bank and donor terms, some of the institutions and skills destroyed in the 1980s by the theological advocacy of 'market' responses. These, along with semi-private adjuncts like the African Economic Research Consortium, seek to reconstruct intellectual and organisational resources at national and regional levels to provide the bases for sustainable adjustment, the Consortium seeking to create 'networks' of economic research and 'centres' of graduate training, mainly in the positivist, behaviouralist paradigm; one which is quite compatible with that of adjustment, by contrast to other genres.

Commission Advocacy and Constraints

The ongoing critique emanating from the ECA and related African and international institutions, notably UNICEF and the majority of NGOs, has been integrated into the *African Alternative*, itself a derivative from the *Lagos Plan* and subsequent continental and UN proposals. The central features of this indigenous and sympathetic response include the following.

First, the African framework insists that the crucial intention of any adjustment programme should be *development rather than growth*. It asserts that while stabilisation responses may be necessary in the short term, they should take into account established historical contexts and conditions, especially the genesis and character of underdevelopment. In short, renewed growth is not enough; more sustainable, structural change remains an imperative for the majority of the people.

Second, it claims that the difficulties and deficiencies of current conditionalities result from a *mistaken premise: inattention to underlying characteristics*: 'The structures of Africa's political economy demonstrates convincingly why policy reforms aimed merely at improvements in financial balances and price structures are unlikely to succeed in bringing about economic transformation and sustained development' (ECA, 1989b: 1–9). Orthodox IMF-style adjustments cannot be efficacious in a set of largely non-industrial, non-monetary economies dominated by dependence and underdevelopment in which short term flexibility is minimal.

Third, *Africa has lamented the disinterest of Bank and Fund in the social costs or dimensions of adjustment*, especially education and health: 'Successive structural adjustment programmes are rending the fabric of the African society' (ECA, 1989b: 1–7). The exponential decline of BHN satisfaction makes future development problematic until the 'lost generation' has been replaced and neglect of human resources, technological capacities and communal welfare ended. The cumulative, 'hidden' costs of a decade of adjustment are incalculable (see Box 10).

Box 10
Decline in Basic Human Needs (BHN) Satisfaction

Structural adjustment conditions, combined with inflation and population expansion, have led to a precipitous and exponential decline in BHN satisfaction throughout the continent, especially in education and health. Contractions in government budgets for such services combined with devaluation (i.e. higher local prices for imported inputs) have produced a dramatic increase in opportunities and facilities and a parallel increase in user-pay costs (Cornia *et al.*, 1987, 1988, 1992). These have been advocated and authorised by the World Bank (1988) in its companion educational policy volume to the decade-long series of financial reports. Aside from declines in literacy and well-being in the short term (UNDP, 1990), in the longer term, structural adjustments will affect the generation and utilisation of technologies and skills (see concluding chapter). Meanwhile, many underpaid professionals have their attentions diverted by the imperatives of incomes and inputs from informal sectors – from chicken-rearing and taxi-driving to drug-running and international consultancies (see Boxes 4 to 7) – and institutional morale and productivity are in serious decline. African case studies (Malawi, Nigeria and Zambia) of 'Adjusting Education to Economic Crisis' are presented in the January 1989 issue of *IDS Bulletin* (20 (1)) while UNICEF's *State of the World's Children 1989* (1989: 18) laments that 'a decade of achievement is threatened' as the preoccupation with debt diverts attention away from 'adjustment with a human face'. It cautions 'that policies which lead to rising malnutrition, declining health services, and falling school enrollment

---

continued on page 82

Box 10 *continued*
Decline in Basic Human Needs (BHN) Satisfaction

rates are inhuman, unnecessary, and ultimately inefficient'.
UNICEF advocates a transnational 'alliance for children', building on its well-attended but overshadowed (by Gulf War then
Eastern Europe, especially USSR) children's summit in the fall
of 1990, to mobilise concerned groups against the unacceptabil-
ity of the current 'human costs' of adjustment; a humanitarian
and partisan position compatible with that of the ECA and other
opponents of orthodox conditionalities. Bread for the World
Institute's *Hunger 1990* (1990: 40–65) report contains devastat-
ing critiques on the impacts of crises and adjustments in several
parts of the continent (see Tables 1, 3 and 4). The World Bank
(1991a) has responded, with characteristic belatedness, through
its African Capacity-Building Initiative (ACBI); but this is too
little, too late and too elitist to correct continuing continental
declines in literacy, numeracy and energy. Meanwhile, UNDP
(1991: 84) in its second *Human Development Report 1991* has
called for a 'global compact for human development', by contrast to World Bank attempts to encourage a 'reform' coalition in
each adjusting country (Gulhati, 1990).

Fourth, *African Alternative* claims that *current conditionalities have
neglected several crucial issues and forces*, such as the informal sector,
environmental protection, regional cooperation, women's roles,
popular participation, and adequate institutional and infrastructural
resources. Such factors are the focus of much of this text as they have
also been largely overlooked by orthodox scholars as well as policy-
makers, primarily because they are not salient within the dominant
paradigm. The end-decade *Long-Term Perspective Study* from the
Bank did respond to some of these lacunae yet in a superficial and
contradictory manner as 'add-ons' rather than core features. Such
treatment parallels that of the hegemonic perspective and confirms
the narrow, short term character of the adjustment project.

Fifth, the African opposition recognises the *profound changes of
technologies and sectors occurring in the NIDL*. It accepts the 'fallacy
of composition' argument; i.e. that more production and devaluation
of colonial commodities will only lead to lower prices and incomes

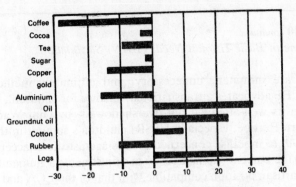

Figure 6   Africa's commodity prices
(% change, 1990 over 1989 average)

SOURCE: United Nations (1991).

(see Figures 6 and 7). The continental crisis is not only short term and economic. Rather, it is also long term, structural and ecological: the place of commodity-producing political economies in an era of high-tech micro-chips and bio-engineering whose centre lies in the Pacific Rim rather than the North Atlantic.

Sixth, African leaders have come, albeit reluctantly, to recognise the *limitation of top-down change and now call for 'democratic development'*; i.e., popular participation not only in production and consumption but also in planning and implementing. The apparent lack of support for adjustment provides an opportunity for local, consensual decision-making not only about ideology and policy but also about resources and accountability. The continent needs strong, popular states to survive rather than weak, unpopular regimes. Many of its communities may be more able and willing to meet such political rather than economic conditionalities, so posing a dilemma for at least some donors: the ranking of these two sets of conditionalities, given that strong rather than weak states may be best able to sustain adjustment terms, at least in the immediate future.

And finally, seventh, Africa resents the *insensitive homogeneity of most adjustment packages* which fail to take into account histories, ecologies, resources and performances, let alone interests and demands: the excessive reliance on a singular orthodox set of mechanisms – devaluation, deregulation, liberalisation, deflation, deficits etc. Notwithstanding occasional flexibility in the face of defaults or demands (Martin, 1991; Mosley and Toye, 1991), adjustment

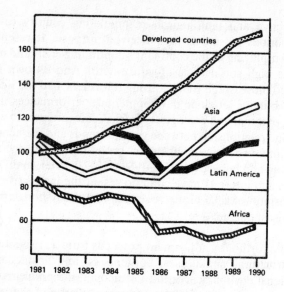

Figure 7   Purchasing power of exports
(1980 = 100)

SOURCE: United Nations (1991).

conditions in general are still 'inappropriate for the process of adjustment in African countries given the structural rigidities and the
desired goals of transformation and sustained development in the
African continent' (ECA, 1989b).

(On the intensity of this debate, especially the unanticipated and
unproductive IBRD report which further undermined global consensus and African support, see Melvyn Westlake, 'Digest With a Pinch
of Salt', *South*, 103 (May 1989) 19, and 'African Economies: Reform
on Trial', *Economist*, 311 (29 April 1989) 53–4. Given the unilateral
and tendentious character of *Africa's Adjustment with Growth* even
The Economist sided with *African Alternative*.)

These and other criticisms were contained in a rigorous and resilient riposte from the Commission, an unattractively titled but well
produced rejoinder: *Statistics and Policies: ECA Preliminary Observations on the World Bank Report 'Africa's Adjustment & Growth
in the 1980s'*. These exposed the methodological and empirical deficiencies and deceptions of the Bank, which contradicted other Bank
reports and other sections of *Africa's Adjustment*. The Commission
asserted that the Bank's report was one-dimensional, non-replicable,

highly selective and tautological, manipulating country categories and time-periods to suit its preconceived purpose. It resented the latter's down-playing of the continent's continuing crisis and its disregard of the high social costs of adjustment. And its own findings contradicted those of the Bank: 'strong reformers' had the worst, not the best, economic let alone developmental, performances. Because of ongoing external and ecological 'shocks', 'any attempt to establish a one-on-one relationship between growth trends and the adoption or non-adoption of structural adjustment programmes is prone to over-simplification and fallacies' (ECA, 1989c: 10). In brief, many African institutions and interests have come to resent the insensitive, doctrinaire imposition of such terms, asserting that their short term shock effect is unsustainable:

> the path of orthodox adjustment proceeds from a crisis situation in which structural weaknesses, bottlenecks, and hostile economic international environment tend to compound the problems of economic decline, rising capital dependence, collapse of the rural economy, capital flight and brain-drain, mass poverty and increased immiseration to a situation of temporary relief from problems of financial disequilibria but without improving the structural weaknesses of the economy.

Instead of theoretical adjustments, *African Alternative* expected that 'national packages and programmes of adjustment with transformation will have to be much less dogmatic and much more pragmatic than orthodox programmes' if the African state is to advance development into the twenty-first century.

Thus, as the decade of the 1990s opens, the development debate in Africa is once again at a stalemate or crossroads, notwithstanding the paradigmatic status of the modernisation approach. The mid-decade moves towards consensus floundered again at end-decade on a combination of national diversities and international divergencies, now reinforced by the diversions of Eastern Europe for IFIs and national ideologies alike. It is quite unlikely, given IBRD/IMF assertiveness and ECA/OAU resistance, that a continent-wide consensus can be reassembled before the end of the century, except through the imperatives of conditionality: the external, regional, national and social interests are too diffuse given the incidence and impacts of adjustments, conflicts and windfalls. It is only agreement of reform frameworks that gives the continent an appearance of homogeneity;

in reality, impacts and implementations vary widely, giving rise to further differences. So country and class inequalities are likely to intensify, with profound implications for cohesion and cooperation. Unless the economic, political and social implications of crises and conditionalities are sustained only a few states, sectors and social groups will be better off in the year 2000 than they were at independence. This unpromising condition will require continued innovative political and intellectual responses, from a rather dispirited and devalued leadership.

The ubiquitous policy environment at the turn of the decade at least draws attention to internal as well as external contradictions and limitations. The dependence logic of the previous decade – NIEO demands – encouraged the identification of foreign 'scapegoats' in which it was 'easy for domestic ruling classes to attribute economic failures to the machinations of external ("Northern") forces'. Whilst there are many deficiencies and difficulties with the Sender and Smith thesis on capitalism on the continent, their lament for the 'externalisation' of contradictions and criticisms remains all too poignant, serving to explain why the Bank's *Berg Report* was able so rapidly to achieve hegemony at the interrelated levels of policy and praxis:

> This 'scapegoatism', supported by a majority of intellectuals and academics within Africa, and by activists within the aid lobby of the advanced capitalist economies, prevents the formulations of practical domestic political interventions which strengthen progressive domestic class forces.
>
> By denying the existence of a domestic bourgeoisie and a domestic proletariat, or by stressing the privileged, 'aristocratic' nature of the African working class, the political agenda becomes dominated by rhetorical condemnation of the World Bank, the IMF, multinationals etc., leaving very little space for the more mundane and immediate issues of trade union rights, wages and working conditions. The political agenda also precludes the construction of economic strategies and specific proposals for state interventions which are rooted in 'effective reality'.
>
> (Sender and Smith, 1986: 132)

In response, as indicated already, 'old' state-socialists like Bienefeld have resisted such 'new' left acceptance even advocacy of growth through 'market forces', lumping them together with orthodox monetarists. Although Bienefeld's effort to revive dependency concerns along with the African state focuses on the legacy of Bill Warren, surprisingly he does not treat the latter's Africanist disciples, Sender and Smith. Rather, he asserts that a continued role for the 'developmental' state is still imperative on the continent, as in the NICs and now Eastern Europe, if more popular and sustainable forms of policy and production are to be devised in response to the crisis:

> the new orthodoxy of the Bank, as well as the Chicago Marxism of the Warrenite school, both represent the ideological rationale for a 'solution' of this problem that puts the interest of capital first and leaves the human consequences of this process as an unfortunate 'problem' to be solved by some token assistance and a lot of hand wringing. (Bienefeld, 1988: 86)

However, despite all such confounding discourse and compelling evidence to the contrary, the study of 'politics' in Africa has remained preoccupied by the analysis of formal institutions, relations and ideologies: no-, one-, two-, or multi-party states, with or without federal elements; Afro-Marxist, African socialist, or African capitalist regimes; or various kinds of military governments, whether praetorian or direct. Yet, even before the crisis of the 1980s, it was apparent that African politics was no longer just official 'high' politics but included myriad links of patrimonialism: patron–client connections to organise power and property. Thus, pre- and post-independence coalitions incorporated a variety of interest groups as well as parties and ideologies which were gradually restructured as the state became more exclusive and exploitative. And in the 1980s as it became diminished in financial and organisational terms so its control over social forces was eroded further.

A corollary of such restructuring has been that 'interest groups' have had or been able to expand to fill the gaps left by the decline in the quantity and quality of state services. Hence, as recognised below, the new vitality of 'civil society' as 'liberalisation' is transmitted and translated into a proliferation of non-state organisations concentrated in the areas of agriculture, education, environment, health, rural development and women. Well-established, 'old-fashioned' cooperative movements, labour unions, professional associations and women's institutes have now been joined by 'new wave' 'non-governmental organisations' (NGOs), with a focus on current issues such as AIDS, children, informal sectors, unemployment, women etc. In turn, NGOs have often established national coordinating committees and transnational cooperative connections, both of which serve to advance and protect their interests (Clark, 1991; Fowler, 1991).

The pressures on as well as opportunities for such NGOs in a period of structural adjustment are intense: supplementing shrinking state resources in educational, health, rural and women's sectors as fiscal restraint eliminates supplementary budgets for such services. If NGOs, including missions, had not stepped in to salvage some welfare institutions then recent increases in African child mortality, adult illiteracy and national unemployment would have been even higher than they have been. However, whether such NGOs can sustain such expanded roles throughout the 1990s remains quite problematic despite extra-African private donations and official assistance. Moreover, as in the West, there is a continuous dilemma, that successful NGOs will become the target of official attentions even cooptation or coercion.

I turn next, in the final part of this chapter, to some of the social dialectics or dimensions of orthodox adjustment, treating a crucial element of any political economy – class formations and relations – before looking at the primary structures in which they are located and over which they are in struggle: the state and its economy. I then conclude by looking at that social sector which lies more or less outside both of the latter: civil society.

SOCIAL DIALECTICS OF ADJUSTMENT

Class

> Compared to the advanced capitalist states, the identification of classes and their alliances in Africa is a much more speculative matter.
>
> Turok (1987: 67)

Analyses of class structures in Africa are both problematic and controversial, particularly after a decade of adjustment impacts and ideologies: problematic because of the coexistence of capitalist and non-capitalist relations of production and controversial because of the popular claim from within and without that classes do not exist on the continent. If the latter draws support from orthodox modernisation analysis of internal structures – *there are no classes* – then the overly-external perspective draws support from dependence assertions: *there is no bourgeoisie*. Whilst both of these extremes can find some historical, empirical support for their claims – ethnic, racial, regional or religious conflicts in, say, Sudan and the absence of an indigenous bourgeoisie in, say, Djibouti – almost all African political economies are characterised by complex and fluid social relations in which class is central, although other factors are, of course, present (cf. Boxes 5–8).

However, such relations must be periodised and personalised so that changes and characters can thereby be incorporated. The hierarchy of classes and fractions is dynamic – different bourgeois fractions have different degrees of dominance at different times – so that typologies of distinctive political economies are required, which go well beyond formal distinctions of national party rule. And class analysis should expand to include the colourful idiosyncracies of, say, Sese-Sese Mobutu or Kamuzu Banda on the one hand and Fela or Mapfumo on the other: the state bourgeoisie and cultural petty-bourgeoisie, respectively. Property and personality, let alone ideology, are intertwined in Africa as elsewhere: conspicuous consumption and survival strategies coexist in unequal political economies (cf. Box 9).

Except for ultra-modernisation and -materialist positions, there is grudging recognition in both analytic and policy circles of salient class differences – bourgeoisie, petty-bourgeoisie, proletariat, peasantry and the un- and under-employed. There is less consensus on the nature of fractions within such classes but I would insist on the following being recognised in most political economies, albeit in varying proportions:

bourgeois fractions – bureaucratic and parastatal, comprador, military, national and state (political and party);
petty-bourgeois fractions – academic, cultural, entrepreneurial, technological and professional;
proletariat – artisanal and 'unskilled', 'labour aristocracy' and non-unionised;
peasantry – large, middle and small; and
un- or under-employed – informal, criminal and highly marginal or vulnerable.

In all of these distinct fractions, there may also be a variety of ethnic, gender, ideological, institutional, personality, racial, regional, religious and other tensions which moderate or mitigate 'class' contradictions. Within such a framework there are endless possibilities of conflict and cooperation, especially when these other variables are incorporated.

Amongst the most important *coalitions* have been the initial broad, inclusive 'nationalist' *inter*-class alliance and the subsequent, increasingly exclusive post-independence *intra*-class 'triple alliance' of national, state and transnational bourgeoisies. And amongst the more controversial notions have been those of 'labour aristocracy' and 'graduation' from, say, big peasant to petty-bourgeois farmer and from informal sector to, say, petty-bourgeois entrepreneur. It is particularly important in contemporary Africa to also recognise that *downward* mobility is as, or more, likely than upward: the continuing crisis and adjustment process have undermined the life-styles of the petty-bourgeoisie and proletariat in particular (see Boxes 6–10). Depending on analytic perspective, these social forces are in struggle over economy and state, now civil society also, particularly over access to foreign exchange and commodities.

Finally, it is important to relate distinctive patterns of class and fractional relations to particular *periods of time* and to *types of state*. The classic broad nationalist coalition at independence fragmented everywhere into various forms of bourgeois dominance, usually state (initially political then bureaucratic and finally parastatal) and comprador at first, then military and, finally, encouraged now by structural adjustment, the national fraction. As indicated in the first chapter, state socialist regimes tended to be dominated by other jealous political and parastatal fractions, state capitalist by bureaucratic and comprador fractions, and capitalist by national fractions. In turn, these had distinctive associations with petty-bourgeois and proletarian forces, especially right after independence when expansion was commonplace; hence notions of upward-mobility and labour aristocracy. However, once the post-colonial honeymoon of the 1960s was over, contraction became ubiquitous, leading to a less generous era in which class alliances became more exclusive; hence the state versus military tension and alienation of petty-bourgeois and proletarian fractions. And the 1990s structural adjustment project has tended to marginalise hitherto central state fractions to the advantage of the national bourgeoisie whilst also advancing the visibility and profitability of a previously ignored class – the peasantry, especially its more 'progressive' or expansive 'bigger' elements.

State

> no political economy is intelligible without the analysis of the crucial role the state plays in the economy.
>
>   Nzongola-Ntalaja (1987: 20)

> The state in Africa may be incompletely formed, weak and retreating, but it is not going to wither away.
>
>   Bratton (1989a: 425)

Structural adjustment reforms in Africa have sought to shrink the state to advance market forces and regain economic growth. Although they represent the single most substantial and sustained attack on the African state since independence, they constitute but the most recent stage in the cyclical rise and fall, expansion and contraction of this state. Both pre-colonial and colonial states endured such sequences, growing in the post-World War II period as colonial 'welfare' schemes led onto independence and as Keynesian economics encouraged intervention. Such unlineal expansion continued throughout the early period of post-colonial rule, to be criticised if not always contained under the pressures of external shocks from the early 1970s onwards. The conditionalities of reduced state expenditures and personnel in the 1980s have undermined most established assumptions about the African state. However, as Bratton (1989a: 410) cautions, 'The African state is weak by any conventional measure of institutional capacity; yet it remains the most prominent landmark on the African institutional landscape.'

The state in the Third World has everywhere been a controversial and elusive concept as recognised above, from modernisation definitions of governments, rules and regimes to dependence assumptions of external domination and domestic agents. Even more materialist perspectives on its class bases and correlates have had to be revised as bourgeois fractions and coalitions have multiplied. And the palpable hijacking of so many states by narrow and self-serving interests, along with transformations in the global economy, has compelled revisionism within each mode. As Turok (1987: 99) notes:

access to the state has been the central political issue in two decades of post-independence politics.

This view of the disastrous consequences of bourgeois manipulation of the state is widespread in contemporary analyses of Africa. It expresses the distress so frequently articulated in private by many Africans at the horrendous conditions now prevalent in many African countries and which are laid at the door of contemporary bourgeois forces inside and outside the state.

The manipulation of constitutions and the corruption of institutions are not peculiarly or exclusively African phenomena. But on the continent, these processes may proceed relatively unchecked as countervailing forces are, or have been to date, underdeveloped: media, interest groups and other forms of transparency and accountability in civil society may themselves yet be repressed. Pressures for democracy are themselves dialectical, of course. But, as recognised below, the late 1980s has witnessed an explosion of demands for participation and democracy both from outside – human rights and democratic development – and inside – populist, nationalist, feminist and green movements in addition to NGOs (Clark, 1991).

The rather diminished and discredited condition of the African state from the mid 1980s onwards has changed the salience of some on-going debates, particularly over its dependence and development. First, simplistic and homogeneous notions of such states' external determination and orientation have to be challenged: African regimes are not just 'agents' or 'puppets', especially not so a quarter-century or more after independence at a time when only a few political economies remain attractive to external interests whilst many never were so. As Turok (1987: 108) cautions:

We ought to be rather more careful about the way we talk about dependency, compradorism and underdevelopment. Are these conditions so overwhelming and so given to over-determination that African states and societies are externally captive, the bourgeoisies inevitably compradorist and their economies blocked?

Notions of overdeveloped, small and weak states along with various class alliances and arrangements need now to be situated in the structural adjustment context: how authoritarian, how autonomous, how effective, how interventive and how strong in the 1990s? Such issues need to be situated in the environments of a) global trends towards more conservative and constrained states and b) Bank/Fund pressures for 'strong reformers' which leads to 'weak states'. These are particularly poignant when the strong states of the South have become the NICs whereas Africa and other 'Fourth World' regions are being compelled, at least by orthodox reform policies, to become ever more weak.

Thus, in the late 1980s and early 1990s not only has the class composition of the African state been in transition – more national and less state (bureaucratic and parastatal if not political or military) and comprador fractions? – but also its size, scope and status have been progressively diminished. No doubt, this is not an irreversible direction, but it does have profound implications for development prospects in the medium term if contemporary, comparative history has anything to tell us. Two immediate questions arise. First, if the African state has fewer resources and positions will there be less or more competition for access to them? And second, will the trend towards more participation and accountability, at least in more marginal areas and issues, be generalised to central institutions and questions? Advocates of the structural adjustment project with its modernisation antecedents would claim that private and informal sector expansions would also facilitate democratic processes. Yet both adjustment and modernisation are permissive of coercive interventions to maintain order, which may become more necessary than ever if economic contraction generates intensified opposition and competition (see below). Such are the contradictions of structural adjustment: market and/or military forces?

Thus, despite its apparent diminution, the debate about the *state* in Africa may yet realise an enhanced level of sophistication by the mid 1990s for two reasons in particular. First, revisionist awareness of the ahistorical character of Bank/Fund assertions of the need to shrink the state; as Bienefeld and others insist, the lesson to be drawn from the NICs is the centrality not superfluity of the developmental state. And second, the appearance of 'second wave' post-colonial regimes like that in Uganda means that distinctive forms of state structure are beginning to become apparent, no longer inherited legacies but more appropriate to the times and needs. Thus Museveni is himself adamant about the imperative of a strong state to treat current adjustment problems: a benign authoritarianism in which the state secures order so that subsistence and saving can occur with safety and sustainability (see Box 22).

Unhappily, one of the indications of Africa's *marginality* is that there is insufficient awareness or consciousness of it in the continent itself. Despite the ubiquity of the adjustment syndrome and the preoccupations of some central bankers and development administrators, there is reluctance to admit the vulnerability of the continent: that capital and resources, including human, are flowing *out of* Africa, which lacks both OECD and NIC members or aspirants (cf. Box 7). As much of the world enters a post-industrial, high-tech era, most of Africa is moving back towards either the production and consumption of basic agricultural needs or the exportation of unprocessed primary production as consequences of the logics of devaluation and liberalisation. The continent characterised by least industrial production now suffers from fewer micro-computers, facsimiles and other forms of rapid information and communication: deindustrialisation.

Economy

> the reality of capitalist development in many African countries can no longer be ignored.
>
> Sender and Smith (1986: 130)

> Economic restructuring has become high politics in Sub-Saharan Africa. . . . The IMF model has almost never worked in Sub-Saharan Africa.
>
> Lancaster (1989: 213)

Notwithstanding the new orthodoxy about the desirability even inevitability of intense adjustment, much of Africa's debt is, despite Bank allegations and the assertions of Herbst *et al.*, not a function of either bad policies or bad terms of trade; rather it is a consequence of personal acquisitiveness and agressiveness, including massive presidential and military expenditures. Naylor in *Hot Money*, for example, points to the individual accumulation of Mobutu in Zaire: 'by 1982, Mobutu had stashed in Swiss, Belgian, and French bank accounts about $4 billion. Others put the current total at $5 billion, the rough equivalent of Zaire's total foreign debt', while Shehu Shagari's right-hand man and brother-in-law, Alhaji Usman Dikko, is alleged to have accumulated $1.7 to $5 billion during the brief half-decade civilian interregnum in Nigeria (Naylor, 1987: 243). The latter's collapse resulted in the collapse of the Indian Sethia and Sudanese Gaon financial empires, along with the technical default of Britain's hitherto respectable Johnson Matthey Bank (Naylor, 1987:

242). But, according to Naylor (1987: 241), by 1983 'estimates of the amount looted by phony invoicing and exchange fraud ran as high as $7.5 billion, a sum equal to about 40% of the Nigerian foreign debt'. The successor Buhari regime estimated that one unscrupulous Nigerian-expatriate 'mafia' alone smuggled up to 100,000 barrels per day out of the country, worth $1 billion annually. Such allegations have bedeviled debt calculations and negotiations as Martin (1991) notes, in addition to the military component of the continent's debt: the costs of presidential or regime security and coup deterrence.

Not all African regimes comply over time with all the myriad conditionalities insisted upon by the IFIs. Moreover, in fact, the latter only insist on the strict terms of national Policy Framework Papers in particular instances, displaying most leniency when 'strategic' or 'model' countries or leaders are involved, as indicated by permissive responses to, say, Zaire and Rawlings on the one hand or Zambia or Banda on the other. In the case of Zaire, the IMF's Erwin Blumenthal attempted to create some order in the country's chaotic finances, where *circa* 15% of the national budget constituted Mobutu's 'pocket-money'; but he eventually retired in disgust (Naylor, 1987: 239). Likewise, Kaunda's appointment of a Canadian central banker to bring the Bank of Zambia under control is indicative of the pressures, given allegations of KK's $4 billion overseas accounts. Symbolically, Jacques Bussiere had previously served a similar role in neighbouring Zaire!

But the more significant, substantive form of backsliding has lain in the failure of many, probably most, regimes to meet Bank/Fund deadlines as agreed in the proliferating, yet essentially homogeneous, Policy Framework Papers: an under-researched plethora of missed deadlines and conditionalities (Brown, 1992; Martin, 1991; Mosley, Harrigan and Toye, 1991)! Therefore, African administrations face an endless round of explanations and renegotiations lest default occur and forex dry up. In such dire straits, conditionalities and cross-conditionalities – now stretching from economic reform to political pluralism and military down-sizing – constitute powerful pressures: neo-dependency for the late twentieth century?

Adjustment Coalitions and Civil Society

The combination of adjustment conditionalities inside Africa and democratic transformations outside it has served to refocus attention on *politics* in the continent. The characteristic post-colonial one-party state had assumed, based on its nationalist origins, that its 'commandist' style could last forever. Its centralised, statist structures were classically top-down with ideological declarations, regime reshuffles and foreign policy directions all coming from state houses rather than even cabinet offices, party headquarters or national assemblies. The incumbents thus became isolated and authoritarian even if on coming to power they had had more open and democratic inclinations, even intentions. Although occasionally overthrown by military coups and sometimes eliminated through death, the real downfall of many of Africa's initial roster of presidents was a function of economic decline reinforced by civil wars and ecological decay.

The apparent ossification of many post-colonial regimes in Africa in response to exponential crisis – political brokers have fewer resources and results in a period of reduced budgets and contracts – has led to novel and increasingly salient forms of opposition. Thus in addition to the five types of internal conflict identified by Chazan *et al.* (1988: 183) – 'elite, factional, communal, mass, and popular' – sustained structural adjustments are leading to new varieties of resistance – anomic, ecological, female, generational, and religious. These unanticipated responses to 'reform' projects are harder to contain because of their resilient social bases and organisational forms: anarchic, cooperative, 'green', fundamentalist, informal sector, rural and women's groups tend to reflect and reinforce authentic social roots and structures so that state control or cooptation are problematic. The relative autonomy of such contemporary NGOs serves to enhance their capacity for opposition and offers alternative bases for organisation and action.

Such social correlates of reform projects have profound and protracted consequences for the continent's political economies and confirm the irreversible character of structural adjustments (read structural *change*) of a type not really anticipated by even its strongest advocates. The reappearance and redefinition of these 'social movements' towards the end of the 1980s constitute the bases of positive responses to current political conditionalities. They expand the arena of civil society and enhance its resistance to state subversion or repression, so advancing human needs and rights.

Yet we should be cautious about claiming too much originality and spontaneity for contemporary forms of civil society. Colonial officers and missionaries had recognised its potentials as well as its limitations early on to advance efficient governance and evangelism. As part of the post-war focus on development and self-government, NGOs and related voluntary agencies were encouraged, within limits. In particular, post-war 'colonial' development coincided with 'workers' education', together reinforcing the rise of the nationalist middle class of professionals and entrepreneurs. Thus, George Haynes' (1950: 13) survey of *Africa: Continent of the Future* identified the 'need for building-up voluntary, self-directed groups and discovering leaders for them' – the continuing dialectic of how non- or semi- or quasi-governmental many such agencies are in reality (Clark, 1991; Fowler, 1991).

Dramatic changes in regime policy if not personnel because of economic and ecological difficulties have been particularly apparent in Angola, Ethiopia, Ghana, Mozambique, Zambia and Uganda. By the mid 1980s, however, most governments, whether long-standing or recent, were under structural adjustment terms which serve to transform state–society relations for the foreseeable future. Both remaining presidents-for-life and populist successors have had to concur, at least formally, with an essentially common set of conditionalities, initially economic now political as well.

One aspect of the hegemony of structural adjustment was a mistaken assumption at the start of the 1980s that its economistic logic founded on market forces would lead to *political support*. Indeed, such was the misplaced confidence of the Bank and its associates in the project that its officials were bemused at the exclusiveness (i.e. smallness!) of supportive 'coalitions' advancing reform. Of course, the very idea that already impoverished people would welcome reformation let alone further deprivation was quite remarkable, reflective perhaps of the over-confidence of neo-classical economists at the time. Indeed, the opposite was the case: mass opposition to orthodox adjustment terms expressed as 'food riots' or protests against rising prices of education, foods, habitat, health, transportation and other basic needs.

In short, both the number and the temper of so-called 'vulnerable groups' (Cornia *et al.*, 1987, 1988, 1992) became worse over the adjustment decade for obvious reasons. To be sure, a small minority of social groups did gain through deregulation, desubsidisation, devaluation etc., notably remaining senior state functionaries, the few large- and medium-scale farmers, and major informal sector entrepreneurs. But the great majority of peasants, workers, un- and underemployed, and hitherto middle classes suffered rapid deprivations. Indeed, as indicated in Box 6, African states may have lost their middle classes through adjustment because their real incomes declined precipitously so that they have become unable to replace precious cars, stereos, TVs and other equipment. They also tend to be the most vulnerable to the AIDS virus (see Box 13). And their professional frustrations of under-funding and -equipping have also led to white-collar brain drains, mainly to Europe and North America, but also to less devastated countries and cities on the continent, such as Abidjan, Dakar, Gaborone, Harare, Nairobi and now Cape Town and Johannesburg. In short, the dominant reaction everywhere in Africa to adjustment has been negative rather than positive at the level of political opinion and expression, but more creative in terms of social organisation. As Ravenhill (1990a: 717) admits, 'if programmes are to succeed, governments need to assemble a new coalition in favour of adjustment': a decidedly herculean task for the 1990s!

Economic liberalisation has served, then, to erode the scope and status of the hitherto unassailable post-colonial African state, leading by the late 1980s to both internal and external pressures for parallel *political liberalisation*. The latter has been advanced by the tacit domestic devolution of responsibilities for some services and roles because of deficit reductions and user-pay rationalisations to NGOs, whether transnational or national. Thus, as the cost and availability of basic goods and services through the state became problematic, NGOs became expected to fill the gap by being either augmented or even created: Christian and Moslem missions, cooperative movements, community groups, credit unions, small-scale industrial federations, unemployed associations, youth and women's groups, even informal and criminal associations. Such self-help or -reliance institutions as well as self-defence associations proliferated in burgeoning poor neighbourhoods around major cities, but also in the rural areas, particularly those close to border areas (see Box 4). International NGOs became especially active in related 'emergency' situations, such as Ethiopia, Mozambique and the Sudan, but also in the more 'open' or capitalist countries, such as Kenya, Senegal and Zimbabwe. And the resilience of both indigenous and international NGOs was reinforced not only by the demands inherent in adjustment reforms but also those in the opportunities occasioned by donor policies: the spread amongst Western agencies of notions of decentralisation, efficiency, institution-building, 'private' sector, etc.

In short, there was something of a convergence of interest among adjustment problems, donor priorities and NGO opportunities, all within the ubiquitous neo-classical context of the 1980s. Yet, regrettably, most mainstream restatements of African politics still fail to treat such informal, popular forms of participation, reverting to old-fashioned notions of national constitutions, elections, parties etc. This is particularly unfortunate as the definition and implementation of novel political conditionalities are being determined by such traditional political scientists from the reinstated, if not fully rehabilitated, modernisation paradigm. It is especially ironic as the very policy reforms which have been demanded for Africa are among the causes of the revival of civil society. Thus orthodox typologies (see Maps and Table 2) fail to go beyond formal political structures to treat the bases of any sustainable redemocratisation, which really lie in local communities and processes (cf. the symbolic reissue of a set of classical essays by Sklar and Whitaker, 1991). They also fail to appreciate the prospects for regression from as well as progression towards democratic patterns, notwithstanding the apparent extension of conditionalities to include reductions in military expenditures. This becomes especially salient given the relentless resistance to adjustment programmes by most social groups and the recourse to the threat or exertion of coercion by insecure regimes, despite the latest, external demand for capped or reduced military (and police and intelligence?) costs. This emerging tension between democratic aspirations and conditionalities on the one hand and authoritarian imperatives on the other hand is likely to animate African political economies for the foreseeable future, leading back in the the next century towards some form of welfare policies and practices, if for no other reasons than regimes' survival and flows of debt repayments (see conclusion).

Yet although both internal pressures and international conditionalities may together be advancing the prospects for democracy on the continent, my overall conclusion would be that the former are more salient than the latter, whilst drawing some legitimacy from changing external conditions. Indeed, it is the shift in the global context away from both bipolarity and state socialisms which has facilitated the revival and resilience of 'domestic forces'.

Nevertheless, despite the reassertion of civil society, in part through Bank/Fund conditionalities and correlates, the preconditions for sustained democracy may not yet exist on the continent: a *political fallacy of composition* parallel to the more familiar economic one! Liberal bourgeois democracy developed in some parts of Europe in a specific period, when capitalism and colonialism were in formation. Although democratic forms have survived in some parts of the Third

World such as Botswana, Costa Rica, India, and Malaysia, the absence of a strong bourgeoisie and the decline of the middle classes means that in most African states the social bases are either absent or insufficient (see Box 6). Moreover, the SAP project may be contradictory – undermining prospects of strong bourgeois and petty-bourgeois forces whilst insisting on democratic forms. Until such a contradiction is resolved – strong not weak bourgeois fractions or weak not strong democratic terms – democracy will be a superficial, superstructural concept, fostered by external interests rather than internal imperatives. In such circumstances, corporatist arrangements are more likely: to contain the contradictions and limitations of adjustments.

Thus it is vitally important to note that to date many African NGOs are, in reality, like many in the North, quasi- or semi-nongovernmental, or 'quangos': of necessity, they had continuous, albeit pervasive and problematic, relations with the state, especially the 'home' regime but also the 'host'. Most NGOs are coordinated within some national confederation or council and have to seek and receive official approval if not support. Like elements within informal sectors, NGOs have somewhat ambivalent attitudes towards the bureaucracy, party, even military with which they have to deal, sometimes being 'fronts' for competitive interests within incumbent regimes. Such complexities are found within female as well as other non-official movements, notably when the 'first lady' has ambitions to lead the nation's women on behalf of the president or party (see Box 16).

None the less, contemporary political as well as economic liberalisation has served to revive and reinforce *civil society* in much of the continent at the start of the 1990s. NGOs moved into some of the space vacated by the shrinking state, providing services to meet at least some of the basic needs no longer satisfied through official welfare agencies. The political orientation of education, employment, health and other non-state actors vary but in general are cautious, particularly if they treat sensitive issues like AIDS, communication, gender and population. Nevertheless, they have come increasingly to provide alternative avenues of expression to the hitherto jealous and ubiquitous one-party state, with its hierarchy of levels and organisations, such as those for women and youth. Indeed, in a few countries at specific times, the NGO world has come to rival that of the state in its complexity and controversy, with powerful queens and kings or 'Lords of Poverty' (Hancock, 1991).

In general, the incremental openness and opportunities represented by the NGO community have been further enhanced and legitimised by the social transformation of Eastern Europe at the turn of the decade. It is possible to exaggerate the consistency and inevitability of the dramatic changes which led to the rending of the iron curtain; the digestion of such profound social reformations will take years, even decades. However, coming on top of a now-established concern for human rights in the Third World, they offer further strength to embryonic changes in Africa. The World Bank and other external agencies had already become concerned about 'governance' by the end of the 1980s, in part because of the related issues of corruption and accountability. Such questions of democratic development became more visible and acceptable with the global trend, albeit not a unilineal one, towards *perestroika*.

Fortuitously, the ECA had already made preparations for a further conference in its series on the continental crisis, to follow those in Abuja (June 1987) and Khartoum (March 1988) (see *African Development Perspectives Yearbook 1989*), which had progressed from 'Economic Recovery and Accelerated Development' to the 'Human Dimension'. Appropriately, the third, in Arusha, Tanzania in February 1990, was on 'Popular Participation'. The timing could not have been better, coming right after the dramatic series of events in Eastern Europe and just before their spill-over into the continent itself. On this occasion, indigenous interests seized the initiative, calling in the 'African Charter for Popular Participation' for sustainable democratic development which provided for freedom of expression and organisation for NGOs, students, trade unions, youth, women etc. The Tanzanian conference happily coincided with Nelson Mandela's release from imprisonment in South Africa. Sadly, however, Robert Ouko's murder in neighbouring Kenya was revealed as the conference was dispersing. Both of these coincidences pointed to the imperative of continuous popular participation if developmental directions are to be decided and evaluated in an open manner in the foreseeable future.

The continental conjuncture of the late 1980s has thus opened up the possibility even probability of a creative period of ideology and hegemony for African political economies, symbolised by dramatic changes in Angola, Mozambique, Namibia and South Africa. In all of these Southern African states, some mixture of structural adjustment, popular participation and political struggle has resulted in a chance for both economic and political liberalisation (Swatuk and

Shaw, 1991). Given the combination of NIDL and NIDP as well as continental changes, the elusive pro-adjustment coalition anticipated by the Bank may be superceded by popular forces favouring greater degrees of self-reliance. Indeed, if a combination of national elections and local NGOs can seize the political stage for long enough, then a new hegemonic bloc may be installed which would institutionalise accountability, participation and transparency. Such a prospect, which remains idealistic, would have been inconceivable a decade ago when pessimism and stagnation prevailed. To be sure, more open and dynamic political economies will not arise simultaneously throughout the continent. But if several examples of comprehensive liberalisation survive and flourish then the old *problématique* of one-party state socialism will have been displaced.

There is as yet no clear correlation between economic reform and political change or even between economic revival and constitutional reorganisation. Moreover, local, popular forces and movements are more important for democratic development than formal, national structures. Nevertheless, the unintended consequence of structural adjustment has been *political as well as economic liberalisation*. Drawing some inspiration from extra-continental transformations, civil society in Africa has risen Phoenix-like from the ashes of discredited and depressed single-party political economies. The issue for the 1990s is whether, given external contradictions and internal reluctance, progress towards democratic development can be sustained in a sufficient number of states or whether authoritarian and corporatist reactions will overwhelm the tender shoots of non-state organisations: the unanticipated dialectic of adjustment indeed!

3 The Continent in the 1990s: New Factors and Forces

The African crisis cannot be resolved without a full-scale democratisation of the African society.

CODESRIA Bulletin (1988: 7)

The struggle for democracy in Africa will doubtless take many forms and directions.

'Democracy & Development', *ROAPE* (1990: 5)

It is now clear that the main cause of the wave of political change sweeping Africa is not the aspirations of African intellectuals, much as they long for liberty; nor is it a union of the political opposition and the masses. . . .

No. The principal cause of Africa's wind of change is the World Bank and the donor countries. They are explicitly demanding political change as a condition for further loans to Africa.

Africa Confidential, 31(15), 27 July 1990: 3

Analysis of and advocacy on the African crisis in the decade of the 1980s have tended to be concerned either with macro development policy or with micro social reality. All too few analysts or activists have treated both macro explanation and micro prescription or projection. Hence the imperative of a comprehensive political economy of the continental condition in which these concerns are not only identified and juxtaposed but also integrated. For the causes and consequences of Africa's continuing economic difficulties and declines lie in both external and internal, macro- and micro-level relations: the dialectics of national and personal responses to adjustments constitute the core of the continent's contemporary features and the base of its foreseeable futures.

The ongoing social discourse – the 'politics' of adjustment – is as important as and inseparable from the endless policy dialogue yet it is rarely treated in either texts or declarations despite its ubiquitous character. Whilst it is problematic to identify the changing patterns of social relations in such a context, it is incumbent at least to attempt to do so. For such relations define the parameters of choice and constraint, expectation and realisation, for both international and internal actors alike. Treatment of them also constitutes whatever claim the present text has to originality.

Notwithstanding the ravages of debt, drought and structural adjustment, the orthodox 'political sociology' perspective on the continent remains resilient. It has always been hegemonic in the post-colonial era, an adjunct of modernisation theory, and is most recently reflected in texts like Jackson and Rosberg (1982) and Chazan *et al.* (1988). It always offered some insights, such as the conclusion to Coleman and Rosberg's 1964 text (672): 'The one-party syndrome . . . does not necessarily represent the end of the line in the political evolution of the new African states.' And it is being revived and restated in the early 1990s by Patrick Chabal's *Power in Africa: An Essay in Interpretation* which rejects dependency or substructural approaches in favour of political discourse reflective of the French Africanist school. If Chabal is still interested in the comparativeness and specificities of African politics, Colin Leys (1991) has recently returned to African, especially Kenyan, political economy, inquiring into the character of the indigenous capitalist class and its state. Thus, rather than aberrations and insecurities, Leys can focus on longer term social changes in which the interests of capital come to transcend apparent political instability and incomparability. The tensions within the Kenyan capitalist class – ethnic, national, personal, political, regional and religious – may complicate unilineal Warrenite progression towards capitalist development along the lines which Sender and Smith suggest; but they do not deter production and accumulation, although they may reduce efficiency and predictability. Moreover, the left does not always get it right, as revealed by Donald Ray's useful yet untimely *Dictionary of the African Left* (1989: 32–3) in which he rather over-enthusiastically argued:

First, that the growing significance of the African left demands that we pay greater attention to its nature and evolution. Second, the left is now an indigenous and integral part of African life. Third, the growing complexity of the African left is often manifested in

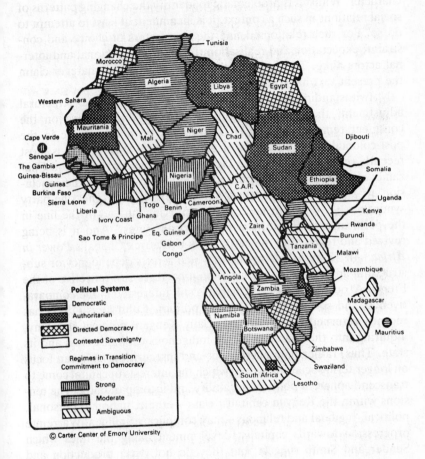

Map 3   Political systems in Africa, 1991

SOURCE: Carter Center of Emory University.

unexpected forms: contrary to certain preconceptions, the Soviet model has not yet proven dominant.

Reflective of continued continental dependency and vulnerability is the quest for comparative analyses and policies; external models or indicators. Africa itself is very rarely the target for comparison or emulation. The most frequent and fanciful focus for comparison is the NICs: how can Africa emulate the four Asian tigers and two or three Latin cases? Occasionally there are further comparisons with Asia, including India and China. And Gerald Helleiner (1989: 19) has recently contrasted it with Latin America as a whole in terms of history, industry, policy and society:

> There are many issue areas in which African policymakers might usefully draw broad lessons from Latin America. Among these one can include appropriate incentive structures, industrialisation strategies, responses to external shocks, anti-inflation policies, policies for foreign direct investment, and economic integration . . . there may be a lot to be gained from more detailed analysis of the relevance of the recent historical experiences of Colombia and Peru for such countries as Kenya, Ivory Coast, Cameroon and Senegal. Similarly, countries like Zambia and Zimbabwe might learn from comparisons with the experiences of Chile in the 1950s and Bolivia, Ecuador and Uruguay in the 1980s.

Whilst such cross-national and -decade comparisons may be illustrative and instructive, African states are also competitive with others in the Third World for markets, investments and technologies: another *Challenge to the South*!

Indeed, the revival, almost popularisation, of an export-oriented (EOI) strategy under structural adjustment conditionalities constitutes a central feature of the macro-level political economy of the continent. But this gives rise to the fallacy of composition: if all African economies produce more of similar 'colonial' commodities then the demand and price for these will fall even further, so eliminating any gains from devaluation, deregulation etc. As indicated below, the inherent limitations of the prescription are leading to a new rank-ordering of countries which analytic typologies have yet to capture; i.e. the same medicine has differential results, in part because patients differ in terms of their size, metabolism etc. and in part because they also vary in terms of adherence to the instructions.

Furthermore, shifts in ideology as well as *praxis* have led to a new attentiveness towards a range of novel factors, including ecology, gender and informal sectors. As insisted by Richard Peet (1991: 141), however, these should not be either divorced from or supercede materialist analysis. Rather, he calls for 're-examining gender and environmental relations in one region'. Such a responsive, incorporative perspective is compatible with the revisionism advocated here: to expand not discard structuralist, materialist analysis by responding positively to a variety of ecological and feminist critiques. Conversely, of course, such discourses should come to recognise that they are not complete by themselves as they lack a broader sense of historical contexts and conjunctures. Notwithstanding extravagant, even 'extremist', claims to the contrary, these do not constitute new 'great traditions', merely correctives to established and continuing *problématiques*. Conversely, the 'post-modernist' rejection of all established frameworks has likewise to be denied as over-reaction.

The post-colonial 'nationalist' regimes were typically determined and dominated in their early years by a *political-bureaucratic* fractional alliance which had constituted the core of the anti-imperial coalition. As the independent states evolved so two further bourgeois fractions emerged to challenge the political and bureaucratic elements – *military* and *technocratic* – reflective of expanding and indigenising armies and universities. Hence the wave of coup attempts and spread of alienation, leading to regime defensiveness and coerciveness. The one indigenous fraction less extensive and influential in Africa than in most of the South was the *national* bourgeoisie, much of which was European, Indian or Lebanese in Southern, Eastern and West Africa, respectively. Conversely, particularly in the immediate post-independence period, the *comprador* fraction was extensive and important, at least until Africanisation, indigenisation and nationalisation pressures and policies proliferated. These policy orientations and directions have subsequently been reversed in the 1980s under adjustment strictures.

In short, the post-independence history of Africa can be reinterpreted through the lenses of nuanced materialism in which fractions and genders as well as classes are recognised. In general, fractional conflict has been gender-exclusive: few women were involved in either state centrism or *coups d'état*. Likewise, the primary cause of the rise of one-party states was the nationalist elites' fears of losing power and property to alternative classes and fractions. As the African economy slowed in the 1970s so 'state capitalism' flourished, ostensibly because of its developmental superiority but in reality because of its acquisitive potentiality. Some entrenched political and bureaucratic fractions were displaced by coups, but their hegemony and legitimacy were only really undermined by structural adjustment, with its 'counter-revolutionary' ideology of market forces rather than state dominance.

Two crucial and competing elements in any revisionist analysis of the continent are, then, the often incompatible roles of *state* and *market*. Both have been redefined and reconsidered in a somewhat dialectical manner through the crisis decade of the 1980s, informed by the adjustment paradigm: less state and more market. But as the evident deficiencies of the latter have become more apparent so the former has been somewhat rehabilitated, a moderating influence informed by the less acerbic post-Reagan/Thatcher environment: if the state continues to play a crucial role in the OECD and NICs, why not in Africa? James Pickett's (1989: 80 and 83) recent review of theoretical, historical and comparative literatures is reflective of the prospects for a new revisionist balance in the mid 1990s:

> interventionist policies in Africa are probably largely to blame for the continent's disappointing lack of economic progress. . . .
> It is consequently now appropriate to caution against expecting too much from the market in Sub-Saharan Africa.

As I anticipate in the concluding chapter, disillusionment with market forces may yet come to relegitimise the place of the state, especially if it is simultaneously made more responsive and accountable to democratic expressions and organisations.

PROPERTY AND POWER: PRODUCTION AND REPRODUCTION

> The notion that the bourgeoisie, the state bourgeoisie and the petit-bourgeoisie are simply intermediaries for imperialism with no interests or agenda of their own is both inaccurate and unhelpful.
>
> Turok (1987: 80)

It may appear trite to say so, but the ruling class in Africa has not been able to sustain either its rule or its class without continuous access to the state. However, the degree to which it has been able to maintain and maximise such privileged access varies because of other internal and external pressures and claims on the state. Clearly, no African political economy is either completely independent or dependent, autonomous or captured. The balance between these two extremes varies between territories and over time. Likewise, some fractions are more autonomous of (e.g. comprador, national and technocratic) and others more associated with (e.g. bureaucratic, military and political) the state, at least with the 'old' pre-adjustment and -contraction state. Power in the classic African state has tended to lead until recently to power over property: the state bourgeoisie has benefited from its bureaucratic or political status. Likewise, its ability to reproduce itself may depend as much on access to power as to property. The structural adjustment project may erode such assumptions and compel aspirants to follow a more orthodox non-state path; such is the intention of the Bank/Fund project.

However, even until the end of the 1980s, relation to the state still affected, even determined, access to power and property. Except in the few, more *laisser faire* political economies, relation to production or distribution alone has been less efficacious, again at least until current reform conditions have become more effective. As the state has shrunk in the last decade, so control over it has become less profitable and more competitive, except for the exclusive but dangerous presidential entourage. Increasingly, non- or semi-state fractions have had to respond to 'new' market forces and opportunities, such as in the informal sector, rather than concentrating only on access to and position within the state.

Meanwhile, symptomatic of alternative analyses of the political economy of Africa in this transitional period are divergent definitions and expectations of *the state and its patrimonialism*. First, ironically, both radical and conservative analysts consider the *state* to be part of the problem – it is either too bourgeois or too interventive, respectively – whereas the pragmatic modernisation advocates, particularly in their Weberian guise, still consider it to be essential as well as reformable. Of late, even progressive scholars have leapt to its defence, notably Fred Bienefeld's end-decade pleas in *Monthly Review* and *Review of African Political Economy* for relearning some of the lessons of history: no sustainable development without a truly 'developmental state'. But as indicated in the conclusion below, the 'developmental' characteristics of most African regimes have been quite deficient. So any rehabilitation of the characteristic 'African' state would have to include notions of accountability and responsibility otherwise corruption would again become its dominant feature rather than dynamism.

Likewise, secondly, on the questions of *patrimonialism*, the Weberians consider such links to be functional as well as inevitable whereas the radicals treat them as subversive of both development and change. The optimism of the modernisation majority is most apparent in the 'American' school of Callaghy, Chazan, Rothchild, Young *et al.*, especially in the curious case of Zaire, as reflected in an uncritical review article on clientalism in Kenya by Joel Barkan and Frank Holmquist. They argue that the 'harambee' state's connections with small- and middle-peasantry through 'self-help' schemes ensures stability and development; this as Moi's regime becomes ever more coercive and oppressive. Such institutionalisation, according to Barkan and Holmquist (1989: 380), leads to predictable as well as positive outcomes though ongoing bargaining:

> The relationship between the state and self-help is reciprocal and mutually supportive. . . . Because of this relationship, which would not exist without the broad social base on which self-help rests, a lot more rides on self-help than the pace of rural social-service development. The legitimacy of the state – indeed, the viability of the political system in the rural areas – may also turn on its continued dynamism.

Barkan and Holmquist thus overlook central features of the Kenyan political economy – its landed aristocrats, national and international capitals, informal sectors etc. – but do conclude by relating clientalism to structural adjustment: will such supposedly institutionalised self-help permit the state to disengage from the costs of rural development without losing support? Here budget rationalisation and administrative decentralisation may be in contradiction and so reinforce peasant ambiguity as 'The result is the risk of overregulation of self-help and the choking off of peasant initiative at the very time when the state wishes to shift a greater proportion of the cost of rural social services back to the peasantry' (Barkan and Holmquist, 1989: 378).

By contrast, one policy proposal to emerge from the analysis of *The African Debt Crisis* by Trevor Parfitt and Stephen Riley in advance of current espousal of political liberalisations is that structural adjustment conditionalities should include the inclusive democratisation of the hitherto exclusive patrimonial state. For them, clientalism is part of the problem rather than a solution. So they advocate democratic development to ensure both BHN and accountability, encouraged by national and international NGOs and ODA agencies, otherwise increased financial flows might serve to reinforce tendencies towards corruption and corporatism. Thus Parfitt and Riley (1989: 182) advocate:

> reform of the state so that it will represent the interests of the majority of the people rather than the sectional, largely urban based clientalist groups. And democratic reform of the African states must entail the political mobilisation of the large mass of rural producers who provide the bulk of the resources that are seized and redistributed by such states . . . the establishment of legitimate democratic states would obviate the danger of a relapse into patrimonialism after the departure of the IMF.

To be sure, despite the demise of the Cold War and the West's declining interest in the continent, the Bank and Fund may never leave Africa! The most marginal of all the Southern regions, consisting of the largest number of Fourth World states, may no longer warrant diplomatic, political or strategic interest, as revealed in the West's callous disregard for destructive civil strife in Liberia and Somalia in the early 1990s, and clearly its economic attractions are very limited. As HRH The Princess Royal, lamented in her 'Plan to rescue the forgotten continent':

> the real reason . . . is that Africa has been driven off the world's agenda by neglect . . . any attempts to put Africa back on the agenda are to be welcomed . . . we are, as a human race, inter-dependent. Africa is part of that interdependency. For our own economic, social and other interests, we need to maintain an investment in Africa. (*Observer*, 28 April 1991: 22)

Indeed, it was confidence in the then novel context of 'interdependence' which emboldened the post-war planners to consider "independence" for the continent in the late 1940s, as treated in Box 3.

Yet, like formal independence, the adjustment 'contract' is two- rather than one-way, so the intensive and extensive *interventionism of conditionalities* will be perpetuated: sustained involvement of aid agencies rather than companies, diplomats or soldiers. Indeed, Bank, Fund and the bilaterals are more entwined and entrenched at the start of the 1990s than a decade before, notwithstanding their anti-state and -dependence rhetoric. Some of their conditionalities and criteria may have evolved marginally during the 'lost decade', towards more flexible yet more comprehensive terms. But in general they continue to reward 'strong' rather than 'weak' reformers, other than in situations where vestigial diplomatic or strategic interests displace straightforward economic and financial ones.

In brief, the combination of crises and debts, adjustments and conditionalities, has *transformed Africa's political economies*: issues of environment, gender, informal sector etc. can no longer be excluded or separated from more orthodox approaches, whether they be modernisation or materialism. These factors, when combined with the new divergence of states – weak or strong, reformist or otherwise – have generated a new diversity of coalitions as well as conflicts. The most extensive alliance tends, of course, to be one which opposes adjustment, while dominant interests tend to acquiesce for a variety of reasons. But others have emerged in response to these and other new issues – green, feminist and populist lobbies, respectively. In association with more formal, national movements for multi-party democracy, they constitute a rather irrepressible force for popular participation and human rights, notwithstanding regimes' continued tendency to revert to coercion to contain such opposition. But such pressures constitute unanticipated and unintended consequences of adjustment and other changes over the last decade or so.

SOCIAL CONTRADICTIONS AND COALITIONS

Structural adjustment conditionalities have resulted in profound social changes in Africa through the decade of the 1980s in both 'strong' and 'weak' reforming states: most academic analyses have yet to capture these even if much policy dialogue already takes them for granted. Such changes have not been direct; neither have they been homogeneous or unilinear. Rather, as they occur within the context of heterogeneous political economies, their characteristics differ although their catalyst may be a common set of policy dictates. Furthermore, they are not simply the direct results of IBRD and IMF terms. Instead, social constraints impose some limits on the scope, scale and speed of conditionalities; *sequence* is crucial to success and sustainability, and may consist of slippage, even regression. Hence the focus here on the continuous dialectic of adjustment, with its social as well as economic and ecological implications.

To be sure, there may also be some commonalties in adjustment impacts: the bureaucratic and professional bourgeois fractions have been affected negatively everywhere and there are more un- and under-employed throughout the continent. But the ability of political and military, comprador and national bourgeois fractions to survive is a function of their organisational power and the pragmatism of many regimes. Likewise, whether improved internal terms of trade in the rural areas advance large-scale 'commercial' and plantation agriculture, or medium-size 'master farmers', or traditional peasants depends on each specific combination of history and policy.

Nevertheless, it is axiomatic that adjustment intensifies *social inequalities* and tensions and encourages exceptional levels of corruption among the more bourgeois elements, whilst simultaneously generating an escalation of crime amongst the proletariat (see Boxes 14–16). In such circumstances it is quite surprising that the Bank and Fund should have ever anticipated supportive coalitions. The most active socio-political alliances in the 1980s, both domestic and external, have been to oppose or undermine conditionalities. Pro-adjustment alliances have been limited to rather narrow and conservative groups concentrated in official and financial circles who believe that a more capitalist strategy is not only inevitable but also desirable and feasible: African variety of monetarist advocates located in central banks and finance ministries, with their own bureaucratic interests, versus service and welfare divisions.

By the end of the 1980s, however, the Bank had come to realise that some direct *incentives* were needed both to popularise adjustment (or at least reduce its alienating effects) and to maximise support (or minimise opposition). It had already recognised this in some national negotiations; hence the 'special', relatively generous deals for Rawlings' Ghana, Numeiri's Sudan or Mobutu's Zaire. These were in addition to the pre-1992 elections terms for Nigeria arranged in London as well as Paris and the debt forgiveness extended to Mubarak's Egypt as compensation for its participation in the anti-Iraq 'coalition' in the 1991 Gulf War.

In response to both the realities and complaints of so-called 'vulnerable groups' to adjustment contractions and deprivations, particularly reduced availability of already scarce and expensive commodities and services, the Bank came to concur with targetted *ameliorative measures* in a series of countries from Ghana to Zimbabwe. But any such injections of new resources for education, health and infrastructure were not 'free': states and consumers have to pay for them through proliferating user-fees. In any case, they are wholly inadequate given the decline and decay in such basic services over the previous decade or two. Nevertheless, even limited recognition of and reaction to at least some of the social costs or dimensions of adjustment is an indication that the political, institutional and diplomatic pressures from a wide variety of sources have had an impact (Mosley, Harrigan and Toye, 1991; Nelson, 1989, 1990). Yet, in some senses, the Bank has now reverted to its 'nationalist' role reminiscent of the 1960s of developing 'capacities', infrastructural, intellectual and institutional. Whether it can sustain such an 'old' role in Africa in the transformed world of the 1990s remains problematic, mainly because it has internalised so much of the neo-conservative counter-revolution that any return to neo-Keynesianism would be rather dangerous.

In the post-adjustment era, the character of any domestic coalition for *sustainable African development* would have to be reflective of popular, not just dominant, interests; peasants and workers could no longer be excluded, neither could women and the un- and underemployed. The balance of bourgeois and petty-bourgeois fractions would also vary depending on political economy and political culture: what balance in the classic 'triple alliance' of national, international and state capitals as well as in the racial, ethnic, religious and gender compositions of professional and entrepreneurial groups? Novel political conditionalities seek to set some of the terms for such 'new' politics by insisting on basic democratic forms but they can hardly predetermine or predict the actual pattern of social relations. Nevertheless, 'political science' in its orthodox and radical guises is back in fashion in a way that it has not been since the heyday of 'modernisation' optimism in the late-nationalist, early-independence period.

Notwithstanding the restitution of this discipline, the crucial feature of any sustainable programme lies in the recognition and rehabilitation of both state *and* market as neither are sufficient by themselves. This entails going beyond the orthodoxies of left and right, socialists and monetarists, to accept the necessity of *both* state involvement and market forces: a truly revisionist synthesis or compromise! Certainly, the lesson to be derived from the (economic) success stories of the NICs is that state-supported structures are essential for the mobilisation of resources in cooperation with corporatist capital and social labour. Thus Bienefeld (1988: 77) cautions against blind acceptance of current conditionalities which would further retard the continent's ability to revive and redefine its development in the NIDL:

> In effect the adoption of the market-oriented policies offered by the new orthodoxy would tend to reinforce the status of the African economies as relatively passive appendages of the international economy. In some cases this could be beneficial, reducing the damage that could otherwise be inflicted by certain internal interest groups. However, it would also probably undermine Africa's ability to build those political coalitions that will ultimately have to develop their capacity to sustain coherent national development strategies that are both economically dynamic and sensitive to that particular society's long-term social and political needs.

Such rejoinders to the counter-revolution have become more articulate and acceptable as it became apparent in the second half of the 1980s that orthodox adjustment could not work for all African states either simultaneously or rapidly. So at least some parts of the IFIs have come to display a new readiness or pragmatism to heed revisionist voices on debt repayments and policy reforms. Given the further 'external' shocks of Eastern Europe and the Gulf War, no mechanistic implementation of orthodox conditionalities can be successful throughout the continent; bureaucratic, investment, trade and technological resources are insufficient.

Any sensible, sustainable response to the African crisis at the end of the twentieth century has to accept, then, a continued *role for the state* (redefined as both democratic and developmental) as well as a *focus on people's development rather than on debt or deregulation.* Thus the definition and direction of the 'new' post-adjustment state is crucial: neither corporatist nor patrimonial but rather a truly developmental state, which means one that is democratic as well as *dirigiste.* The structures of accountability as well as activism will, of course, vary among countries, regions and periods but all would entail respect for human rights and regard for human needs. Moreover, all would advance local as well as national organisation and articulation to further development everywhere; i.e. NGOs in a dynamic and recognised civil society.

TYPES AND PERIODS OF POLITICAL ECONOMIES

Despite continentalist analyses and aspirations, Africa has never been either homogeneous or cohesive. In the long sweep of pre-colonial history, indigenous empires rose and fell in different regions depending on ecological, economic, strategic and technological conditions – from the Ashanti to the Zulus, Benin to the Shona. The incidences and impacts of company, colonial and settler rule exacerbated pre-colonial legacies and intensified regional distinctions. Thus, Amin (1975) identified three regions in the period of formal integration, as noted in the first box – Africas of the 'colonial trade economy' (West), 'concession-owning companies' (Central), and 'labour reserves' (Eastern and Southern) – which followed upon the pre-mercantilist and mercantilist periods. But in the subsequent independence periods – nationalist (1960–80) and structural adjustment (1980 onwards) – differentiation and regionalisation have proceeded apace.

The heurism of Amin's formulation has declined as states have moved away from independence whilst still constituting an invaluable basic framework for further analysis given its recognition of continental diversity within an unequal global system. In particular, his centre–periphery dichotomy is rather formal and structural; this now needs to be transcended to explain subsequent and continuing dynamics and divergencies. In light of dramatic changes in the last two decades, Amin's (1975: 524) conclusion now appears to be overly simplistic: 'there are no traditional societies in modern Africa, only dependent peripheral societies'.

As the continent has entered the 1990s, adjustment has compelled many communities to rediscover their traditional roots – structures and skills – and scholars to revise orthodox typologies of African states and societies (cf. Crook, 1990). Moreover, the series of economic shocks – high and then low prices of energy and money, series of drastic devaluations plus deindustrialisation, and almost lineal declines of commodities' prices and demands – has transformed regional and social relations. The new realities of ecological pressures, informal sectors, forex shortages, and endless conditionalities have caused significant shifts within and among political economies. And the dramatic implications of the NIDL have now been joined and intensified by those of the NIDP.

Although the Bank and Fund have essentially defined the contemporary paradigm for the continent's policies and politics, neither their assumptions nor their typologies should go uncontested. To be sure, the orthodox modernisation framework of the comparative politics *genre* has needed to be discarded – party states, military regimes, and presidential styles – as both outmoded and superstructural. Likewise, realist distinctions of the international relations school among major, small and micro-states have typically treated only superficial national attributes. And the policy-derived dichotomy of 'strong' and 'weak' reformers is pejorative and unidimensional. Instead, we need to treat contemporary political economy, which captures class and other forces along with adjustment and foreign policies: some mixture of varieties of *corporatisms and capitalisms* – i.e. modes and relations of production, reproduction and accumulation, recognising that democratic voices as well as developmental demands can no longer be ignored. In short, Africa in the 1990s contains a variety of semi-democratic and -capitalist systems in which several types of corporatism – authoritarian, bureaucratic, military and populist – and capitalism – agrarian, informal, industrial and state – can be abstracted. The challenge of the Fourth UN Development Decade and beyond is for each political economy both to aspire to and to achieve an appropriate and sustainable style and structure for both politics and economics.

MEDIUM-TERM IMPACTS OF STRUCTURAL ADJUSTMENT ON POLITICAL ECONOMY

The proliferation of structural adjustment programmes throughout Africa in the 1980s and since means that the political economy of the continent by the middle of the 1990s is quite transformed. Economic liberalisation, even if inconsistent and incomplete, has encouraged political liberalisation which, in turn, has affected the sequences and impacts of economic reforms. Old assumptions about the centrality of the state are being superceded by new awareness of its marginality: classic structures of single parties, interest groups and parastatals are being undermined by notions of multi-parties, civil society and deregulation. Yet as such conditionalities multiply so inequalities intensify.

In treating the African 'conjuncture' in the early 1980s, I suggested that new inequalities were inevitable both within and between states given the continental crisis. I indicated then that African political economies could be divided into three categories – state capitalist, state socialist and socialist – with most falling into the first (Third World) or second (Fourth World) categories. Despite many claims to the contrary, few ever reached the last, 'socialist' stage, let alone becoming 'communist', as indicated by rapid events in recent years. Given the recent ubiquity of belief in market forces in the South as well as the North, the final pair of types may be increasingly endangered: the only choice for Africa in the 1990s and after is likely to be between state capitalism on the one hand and capitalism on the other. The latter is most likely for those (larger?) political economies most dependent on Bank/Fund advice and assistance; the former is most likely in those (smaller?) regimes more able to articulate and negotiate national interests.

In *capitalist* systems, the state continues to shrink in terms of fiscal, physical and political size: under conditionalities, its income, interventions and involvements are diminished; a truly 'weak' state, dominated by the informal sector. By contrast, in *state capitalist* situations, the state resists some of its own demise by insisting on limited public ownership and welfare, including personnel and monies for BHN and infrastructure: a relatively 'strong' state with a resilient formal sector. As the NICs have generally been distinguished by the presence of such strong states, those political economies in Africa able to articulate and advance their collective interests may be better able to develop than the others. Hence the importance of the minority of more nationally-designed and -effected adjustments, notably Nigeria and Zimbabwe. To a lesser extent, those regimes able to insist on some attention to social dimensions – Ghana and Tanzania in particular – may also mitigate some of the high costs, but without sustaining strong states. Those leaderships which have accepted conditionalities and then reneged on some or many of their terms are the most vulnerable – Kaunda's Zambia or Beshir's Sudan, for example. Only very few have thrived without any formal adjustments: Botswana and Mauritius, two very small and special 'success stories'. To date, most of the more democratically-elected successor regimes have chosen to inherit the adjustment terms negotiated by their less open predecessors.

The continuing adjustment project of Bank and Fund has generated not only multiple policies, consultancies and evaluations but also a new sub-field of 'comparative structural adjustment studies' (see especially Campbell and Loxley, 1989; Cornia, van der Hoeven and Mkandawire, 1992; Mosley, Harrigan and Toye, 1991; Nelson, 1989, 1990), particularly in Africa but also elsewhere in the Third World. At the turn of the decade these are both multiplying and diverging:

alternative modes and criteria of analysis and *praxis* produce different conclusions, there being something of a trend, paralleling official discourse, from economic to economic *and* political liberalisation, from bargaining and games to organisational and international politics (e.g. Burdette, 1992; Martin, 1991). Whilst some official evaluations may be positive – conditionalities were both necessary and effective to transcend distortions and declines and so repay debts – the majority tend to be sceptical or critical – either alter or abandon adjustment (Bernstein, 1990). Unhappily, both of these competing positions tend to be derived from largely economistic criteria of shorter- and longer-term factors. All too little extra-economic data are used in evaluations.

At least to date, analyses of impacts on BHN, democracy, ecology and gender have tended to be marginal to the burgeoning sub-field, which is still determined by Bank/Fund priorities. Yet critical, interdisciplinary analysis and discourse is crucial in this as other areas, particularly given the contexts of NIDL and NIDP.

Considerable amounts of myth and ambiguity surround the protracted processes of structural adjustment reforms and conditionalities. The official version is that World Bank and African state negotiate and agree terms, now on an annual basis. But in fact the 'pre-negotiation' phase is fraught and significant, with Washington officials usually drafting the document 'on behalf' of the client. Moreover, Bank and bilaterals' interests are concentrated on sizeable and symbolic regimes, such as those of Ghana, Nigeria and Sudan, respectively: the imperatives of 'success' and dangers of precedent. Furthermore, the strategic salience of African governments varies over time so that 'political' factors shift in importance. The sequence of negotiation–implementation–evaluation–redirection is rarely so straightforward in fact because of external shocks, whether of energy or weather or technology, and internal shifts of regime or ideology or personality, the latter set now being encouraged by pressures for democracy.

In general, neither IFIs nor African states meet all the contracted terms on time; according to Mosley, Harrigan and Toye (1991: 136 and 153) no African case exceeded a 60% implementation rate. In any case, towards the end of the 1980s, many Policy Framework Papers were moderated by mutual agreement to ameliorate some of the mounting human costs of such adjustments: from Structural Adjustment Facility (SAF) to Enhanced SAF and from national to sectoral foci.

In general, the most favourable contracts have been agreed for larger, better-organised or -argued recipients, aside from 'special cases' or 'special relationships' such as those between the US and both Sudan and Zaire for most of the 1980s (Brown, 1992; Martin, 1991). Moreover, Mosley, Harrigan and Toye (1991: 105) assert, Policy Framework Papers impose 'the tightest conditions . . . on small countries in Sub-Saharan Africa which lack the economic strength, the alternative borrowing sources or the importance within the Bank's own portfolio which would enable them to dictate terms to the Bank'. By contrast, NICs, near-NICs and selected OPEC members, which have the capacity to borrow elsewhere, enjoy the easiest, loosest conditions. The mix always includes the familiar range of elements – from liberalisation and devaluation to deregulation and desubsidisation – but the degrees and sequences vary as do the compensatory elements such as finance for targeted services or communities. The readiness of the Bank to 'pay' for reform conditionalities depends on the recipient's salience, importance of precedence, and political-cum-negotiation pressure. Mosley, Harrigan and Toye (1991: 128–9) contrast Kenya 1980 with Ghana 1985 and conclude that the politics of adjustment in terms of both Bank and bilateral talks has led to 'shorter lists of conditions, more tightly policed with 'key conditions' identified and a higher down-payment' at least in theory if not in practice: new varieties of 'distortion'. 'Slippage' is common, indeed pervasive, but its causes and consequences are problematic, unrelated to Bank insistence or recipient dependence.

Indeed, it is important to remember that adjustment is a continuous, essentially bilateral, process which even continues, albeit indirectly, when breakdown has occurred as there then tends to be an orchestrated tango back to the dance floor. Some African regimes have now stretched the slow waltz to ten or twelve years of endless economic footwork.

In general, national adjustment terms, sequences and renegotiations are a function of a selective, technocratic group concentrated in Central Banks and Treasuries rather than an accountable, political community. Overall, according to Mosley, Harrigan and Toye (1991: 177), the financial captains can readily effect exchange and interest changes but are less able to implement other aspects of agreed reform schedules because other individuals, institutions and interests control them.

The 'lost decade' of structural adjustment in Africa begun in the early 1990s to be analysed through several comparative evaluations, aside from those of Bank and Fund themselves: from the UN's ECA,

UNICEF and WIDER projects to the more comprehensive, academic studies of Burdette (1992), Campbell and Loxley (1989), Mosley, Harrigan and Toye (1991), and Nelson (1989, 1990) (see Figure 8–10). These vary somewhat amongst themselves in terms of theory and method, although none are extreme in their ideological predispositions and all are moderate in their claims to reliability and policy.

The two-volume Mosley, Harrigan and Toye (1991) study is perhaps the most comprehensive and rigorous to date, contrasting reformers with non-adjusters, and African with non-African reformers. In general they conclude that the Bank has been trying to achieve too much with the single mechanism of quick-disbursing finance for the enforcement of policy reform. They also confirm that because of the comprehensiveness of the agreed Policy Framework Papers, slippage on implementing conditions is inevitable: 40% on average. And they distinguish impacts according to sectors: favourable to export growth and the external account but negative on

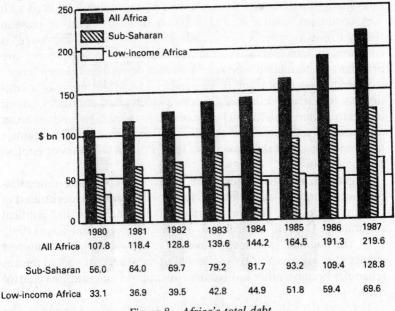

	1980	1981	1982	1983	1984	1985	1986	1987
All Africa	107.8	118.4	128.8	139.6	144.2	164.5	191.3	219.6
Sub-Saharan	56.0	64.0	69.7	79.2	81.7	93.2	109.4	128.8
Low-income Africa	33.1	36.9	39.5	42.8	44.9	51.8	59.4	69.6

Figure 8   Africa's total debt

SOURCE: United Nations (1991).

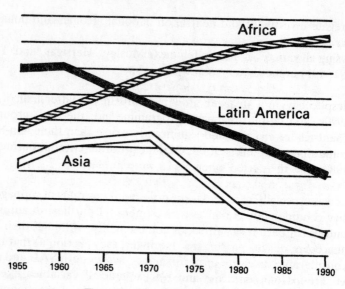

Figure 9   Population growth rates
(annual percentage change)

SOURCE: United Nations (1991).

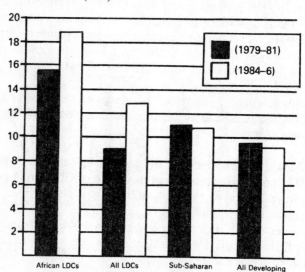

Figure 10   LDC food dependency
(ratio of food imports to food available for internal consumption)

SOURCE: United Nations (1991).

aggregate investment and neutral on national incomes and financial flows.

Using a variety of methodologies, Mosley, Harrigan and Toye (1991: 191) argue that

> despite having a stronger growth record in the latter half of the 1970s, and despite receiving programme aid, the SAL group of countries have performed significantly worse than their non-SAL counterparts, in terms of the GDP growth rate criteria, during the 1980s; i.e. the period when SALs were in place.

This was especially so for SAL countries with *low* rates of slippage on policy conditionality. Likewise, investment fell furthest in adjusting countries, in part as an aspect of conditionality, although their current account deficits moderated. However, they caution a) that there is considerable diversity of performance *within* both SAL and non-SAL groups of countries; and b) 'exogenous' variables like the weather and terms of trade remain important determinants of growth. Adjusting countries record a negative effect on export growth and foreign finance, particularly in the short term.

In brief, Mosley, Harrigan and Toye (1991: 229) conclude that 'the effect of the adjustment programmes of the Bretton Woods institutions has been very different from that which was planned'. And they argue that adjustment-lending has been least appropriate for the poorest, least industrialised states (299 and 303–4):

> economic theory . . . provided no guideline on how much liberalisation, if any, would be appropriate in a 'distorted' developing economy.

> the Bank's chosen package of reforms has more relevance to Thailand and Turkey, say, than to Ghana or Guyana. A policy of trade liberalisation works better if industry is already competitive; price incentives to commercial farmers work better if those farmers have access to credit, fertiliser and good roads; privatisation works better if there exists a private sector able and willing to take over the public sector's assets.

In short, the Bank's reform conditionalities overlook history and inequality for adjustment expectations are really premised on NIC-type success being possible for all simultaneously: the modernisation myth replayed. Given the inappropriateness of many of its terms, slippage or non-compliance may be the only means to realise even minimal rates of development for the Fourth if not Third World in the 1990s. Certainly the pay-offs for compliance with unpleasant even unacceptable and certainly unpredictable terms are minimal other than achieving cross-conditionality; i.e. the continued flow of official bilateral assistance so crucial to regime survival and life-style and the possibility but not certainty of renewed foreign private investment.

Africa's experience with *privatisation* has been very mixed in terms of implementation and impacts. This reversal of stance from the heady post-independence days of Africanisation/indigenisation/ nationalisation marks an apparent turning-point. Yet the results have been minimal to date, in part because regimes are reluctant to dispense with the levers of patronage and in part because national as well as international capital is disinterested in buying unprofitable enterprises. Notwithstanding a plethora of consultations and investigations, both national and international, few states have progressed far towards privatising the heights of parastatal empires. To be sure a few marginal enterprises have been sold at bargain-basement prices; but more have been downsized, commercialised, partially-privatised and/or abandoned. In general, according to Ralph Young (1991), smaller, typically francophone states have been in the vanguard, especially in West and Central Africa, with sell-offs concentrated in manufacturing and rural sectors rather than services or mining, typically through private or public sales, joint ventures, or via management contracts.

Unlike neo-conservative agendas in the North, those in Africa are more externally-encouraged or -imposed and take place in a period of economic contraction rather than expansion. Such strategies serve to confirm the pervasiveness of adjustment and to enhance the viability of local stock exchanges, but they have been more for appearance than effect. They are still controversial when the likely winners are either foreign and local non-Africans, such as the Lebanese in West Africa, Asians in East, and whites in Southern Africa, or indigenous communities not favoured by current regimes, such as the Kikuyu or Luo in Kenya or Ibo in Nigeria. And in South Africa, preemptive moves to sell-off some 'Afrikaner' state capital, such as ISCOR, ESCOM and Transnet, were opposed and so halted by the ANC as being premature given the imminent political transition towards majority if not socialist rule.

In fact, then, the adjustment problematic has affected strong, weak, non- and ex-reformers alike given its pervasive paradigmatic status at present. There is thus 'informal' adjustment – economic as well as political – underway in South Africa as elsewhere. Transitional talks about a post-apartheid dispensation there take place in a policy context in which national debt, deregulation and privatisation had already become dominant, with profound implications for the dismantling of Afrikaner state capitalism and the implementation of African state socialism.

In this context, we should also note the tension between 'second generation' or 'second wave' African regimes, notably Museveni's Uganda, but also successor governments in Ethiopia, Liberia and Somalia, which have come to power through the 'barrel of the gun', not by coups or elections. The degree to which they can successfully rebuild shattered infrastructures and institutions and at the same time implement adjustment conditionalities is quite problematic: Marshall Plan without Marshall Aid?

Finally, there is a significant set of mainly lusophone states which have moved rapidly but belatedly to not only policy reforms but also peace talks. Angola and Mozambique, plus Ethiopia and Namibia, have had to make serious political decisions before getting to the economic negotiations: how to scale down civil wars to release financial and social energies for reform and reconstruction? In general, this parallel process has been advanced by profound changes in the NIDP: the end of the Cold War has compelled reassessments on both sides, including *de facto* 'proxies' like Cuba and South Africa. But the political as well as economic caution and courage required given the intransigence of incumbent regimes, resilient oppositions and calculating supporters have been considerable: neither *glasnost* nor *perestroika* came readily in Addis Ababa, Luanda, Maputo or Windhoek. Given the high coincidence of drought and famine with such long running wars, peace as well as reform in such theatres may moderate much of the 'African' crisis before the end of the century. Certainly the prevailing climate of international opinion about the demise of bipolarity and rise of democracy has reinforced such tendencies as well as circumscribing the range of options of hitherto 'nonaligned' regimes (see Conclusion).

REVISIONIST RADICALISM

The remarkable appearance and acceptance of revisionism in East and West, North and South apparent at the end of the 1980s – from *glasnost* and 'greens' to structural adjustment with or without a more 'human face' – deserves and demands an echo in Africa. The continent has already begun to discard worn out notions of one-party states and adopted selected elements in policy regimes. This new mood of realism and pragmatism demands a positive, creative intellectual as well as policy response: theoretical or analytic correlates or conditionalities. The Monrovia Symposium at the end of the 1970s and the Lagos Economic Summit at the start of the 1980s inaugurated such a debate. Now, at the start of the 1990s, old assumptions and assertions are being discarded to be replaced by *revisionist radicalism*. Confidence in decolonisation and liberation is being superceded by scepticism about socialism and advocacy of accountability, democracy, informality, responsibility etc. Yet reformism should not be defined by external institutions and interests only; popular indigenous demands must also be articulated and heeded if development is to be revived and rendered sustainable. In short, if orthodox adjustment measures become increasingly unworkable, what alternative strategies might be devised to recapture more acceptable levels of development, especially popular participation and optimism?

In a period of revisionism a well as adjustment in Africa, then, some *basic questions* need to be reconsidered, even if they are answered in contemporary ways. For example, given the decline in state resources and responsibilities, how central has it become now in reformed political economies? At a time of deindustrialisation, what is the place of the working class? As the last colony – Namibia – has been decolonised and negotiations for majority rule have finally commenced in South Africa, will the role of liberation movements in Southern Africa evolve away from confrontation and towards dialogue? And, given the appearance of a range of new interest groups – for environment, informal sectors and women (see Table 7), along with the continent's equivalent of greens and grays, if not yet gays outside of South Africa – are new inclusive coalitions possible to supercede old exclusive alignments? In short, both left and right are being compelled to rethink strategy in a period of flux – a rather pre- or non-industrial continent in a post-industrial world. Given this *emerging agenda for African development studies and policies*, I turn to some of the more external or transnational aspects of reformism and revisionism in the next chapter.

Table 7　Women in Development

		Female percentage of population, 1985			Life expectancy at birth, 1987 (years)		Maternal mortality, 1980 (per 100,000 live births)
		Total	Under age 15	Over age 64	Female	Male	
Low-income Sub-Saharan Africa							
1	Ethiopia	50	49	53	48	45	2,000
2	Chad	51	50	55	46	44	700
3	Zaire	51	50	55	54	50	800
4	Guinea-Bissau	52	48	52	40	38	400
5	Malawi	51	51	49	47	44	250
6	Mozambique	51	50	55	49	46	479
7	Tanzania	51	50	56	55	51	370
8	Burkina Faso	54	56	42	49	45	600
9	Madagascar	50	49	48	55	52	300
10	Mali	52	49	51	48	45	–
11	Gambia, The	50	50	50	44	42	–
12	Burundi	51	49	54	50	47	–
13	Zambia	51	50	53	54	51	110
14	Niger	51	50	54	46	43	420
15	Uganda	50	48	53	49	46	300
16	São Tomé and Principe	50	49	52	67	63	–
17	Somalia	50	49	50	48	45	1,100
18	Togo	52	51	45	54	51	476
19	Rwanda	51	50	52	50	47	210
20	Sierra Leone	50	49	55	42	40	450
21	Benin	52	50	46	52	48	1,680
22	Central African Republic	52	50	51	51	48	600
23	Kenya	50	49	49	59	56	510
24	Sudan	49	49	53	51	48	607
25	Comoros	50	49	61	57	54	–
26	Lesotho	51	50	53	57	53	–
27	Nigeria	50	49	55	52	49	1,500
28	Ghana	50	49	50	55	52	70
29	Mauritania	51	51	54	47	44	119
30	Liberia	50	49	53	56	53	173
31	Equatorial Guinea	51	50	55	46	44	–
32	Guinea	52	50	53	43	40	–
Middle-income Sub-Saharan Africa							
33	Cape Verde	54	50	57	67	63	–
34	Senegal	50	49	54	49	46	530
35	Zimbabwe	50	49	44	60	56	150

continued on page 128

Reformism and Revisionism

Table 7   continued

		Female percentage of population, 1985			Life expectancy at birth, 1987 (years)		Maternal mortality, 1980 (per 100,000 live births)
		Total	Under age 15	Over age 64	Female	Male	
36	Swaziland	49	45	63	57	53	–
37	Côte d'Ivoire	48	49	53	54	50	–
38	Congo, People's Republic	51	49	56	60	56	–
39	Cameroon	51	49	55	58	54	303
40	Botswana	53	49	54	62	56	300
41	Mauritius	50	48	62	70	63	99
42	Gabon	55	58	50	54	50	124
43	Seychelles	50	50	57	73	67	–
44	Angola	51	49	55	–	–	–
45	Djibouti	49	48	54	48	45	–

Source: World Bank (1991b).

4 Into the Twenty-first Century: Marginal or Central?

The crisis that swept through the continent during the 1983–1985 drought disaster will not be forgotten for perhaps a generation. The *historical trends* . . . are in many ways pointing to a similar scare for Africa . . . of Africa permanently retarded, of an Africa desperately in search of an elusive development and of an Africa that is chronically in economic difficulties. . . .

The *normative scenario* . . . illustrates the possibilities of Africa's future . . . a viable and equal partner in world development.

ECA (1989d: ii–iii; emphasis added)

The fact is that there is not the remotest chance that Sub-Saharan Africa could meet its old debt obligations and carry large new loans, rebuild its infrastructure, and shore up declining welfare levels and bring its industries back into operation all on the basis of the increases in agricultural production that 'deregulation' might achieve. . . .

The fact that the prices of most of Africa's primary exports have collapsed and have little prospect of long-term recovery merely makes an utterly impossible situation unthinkable.

Bienefeld (1989: 41)

The development of an effective alliance in the South is hampered by differences of ideology, culture, degree of industrialisation, interest in specific commodities and size. These differences are exacerbated by border disagreements and regional imbalances.

Gill & Law (1988: 289)

Development in Africa is unlikely to be either reliable or rapid as the twenty-first century dawns. Indeed, trends in both global economics and global politics do not point in positive, propitious directions. Rather, the combination of New International Division of Labour (NIDL) and great-power diplomatic convergence – a New International Division of Power (NIDP)? – undermine established continental assumptions of economic opportunity and diplomatic centrality. Neither commodity exports nor diplomatic nonalignment point towards promising economic or political contexts. Moreover, internal and continental pressures are likely to push towards further inequalities within and between states leading to a dialectic of opposition and repression. Such revisionist scenarios and sentiments have begun to inform African academics and activists as well as advisors. Yet the pessimism should not be unrelieved as there are reasons for cautious optimism.

If extrapolation from historical trends yields unpropitious predictions, the political economy of the continent does contain some elements which may yet generate more optimistic normative scenarios. These centre essentially on the creativity of Africa's civil society by contrast to the moribund quality of the African state, whether it be party or military: informal sectors, female labours, indigenous technologies, ecological consciousness etc. But whether such popular, survival strategies can capture sufficient power and property to sustain themselves remains problematic. Liberalisation at the peripheries of polity and economy is quite a different proposition from democratisation at their centres. The possibilities of political and economic 'graduation' by more informal groups into more formal sectors and spheres remain problematic given established interests. Thus the dynamic potential of popular forces may remain forever at the margins unless they can turn new and unstable international divisions of labour and power to their advantage.

As noted already, scepticism about the dominant structural adjustment 'project' spread throughout Africa as the 1980s drew to a close and in official as well as non-official circles. Recognition of the pervasiveness of the imperatives of reform has since yielded to reservations about the consequences and costs. In particular, excessive criticism of the state and equally excessive confidence in the marketplace have given way to concerns about an appropriate *balance* between them. As viewpoints as different as Manfred Bienefeld (1989) and Arno Tausch (1993) have recently reminded us, based on Karl Polanyi's earlier cautions, the market is never really self-regulating; rather, the containment of the state merely permits established interests to manage the market more readily. This is especially so in most of Africa where the market is small, familiar and manipulable, typically monopolistic or oligopolistic. Hence the need for a new balance in Africa in the 1990s in the interest of *sustainable development*; at least such development redefined to go beyond superficial 'light green' concerns towards structural 'deep ecology' or substructural questions. This chapter highlights four salient sets of related issues, from security to economy, all of which have inter- or trans-national elements.

Africa is the only Southern region with neither NICs nor sparsely populated OPEC members yet it is becoming more unequal than ever, with profound implications for continental cohesion and direction, in part because reform conditionalities mistakenly assume or imply that all Third World states can and should become like NICs. At independence, most African states were at best colonial commodity producers. During the decades of the African state socialist problematic, the distinctions were largely superstructural: how socialist? how statist? even how African? Now, in addition to macro-differentiations between big and small, Third and Fourth World economies, the Bank project has introduced a hierarchy based on adjustment: 'strong' versus 'weak' and non-reformers, plus ex- or occasional reformers? Such externally-determined rankings would be relatively unimportant except for cross-conditionalities which affect the decisions of bilateral donors and private investors as well as some other multilaterals and NGOs. Moreover, even before the diversions of Eastern Europe and the Middle East, the international community was unable to meet its side of the adjustment compact, as indicated by a series of UN reports and debates. And with recurrent emergency needs in Ethiopia, Somalia and Sudan and in Angola and Mozambique, the resource flow for satisfying adjustment criteria is insufficient. Hence the continued 'high politics' of adjustment and debt negotiations, especially given the relatively high level of foreign exchange provided for so-called 'success stories' like Ghana. As Herbst (1990a: 10) cautions:

> The World Bank and the IMF do not have the funds for 25 or 30 more Ghanas, but they do have the money for five or six as long as one of them is not Nigeria. The lesson for African countries is that it is important to be the second or third fastest reformer rather than the twentieth.

Hence the divide-and-rule impact of adjustment arrangements and the rhetorics of reform commitments rather than the realities of reform implementation: Ghana may be rewarded for its performance on a range of conditionalities, but Egypt, Nigeria and the Sudan have at various times been acknowledged for diplomatic or strategic roles (Martin, 1991).

Although Western aid agencies cooperate with each other in Paris and London Clubs and over cross-conditionalities, reinforced by ubiquitous 'donor dialogue', they also compete for projects, influence and access, especially given the new generosity and activity of Japan. Traditional ex-colonial ties still bind within the Commonwealth and *la francophonie*, and the EC reinforces its North–South regional 'bloc' via the ACP (Stevens, 1992) parallel to the US's role in Latin America and that of Japan in Southeast Asia. But the balance of power has changed in the NIDL and NIDP (Swatuk and Shaw, 1991). African regimes can no longer play the 'nonaligned card'; instead, conditionalities and cross-conditionalities restrain their diplomatic and political as well as economic policies. In reality, they have few alternatives in terms of developmental directions or partners; hence the spread of adjustment programmes by the start of the 1990s to embrace almost all African political economies to one degree or another.

Aside from the problems of the modernisation paradigm, even in its adjustment reformulation and rehabilitation, the marginality of Africa in the global economy and polity poses particular challenges to established dependency perspectives. In particular, it raises the dilemma of why extra-continental interests remain active at all: because intervention is relatively easy and effective notwithstanding targets' relative unimportance? If Africa is the most peripheral continent, consisting of more Fourth World countries than any other, why does it still attract international attention, from aid agencies if not strategic or economic institutions? With the demise of the Cold War, military even diplomatic interest has waned, yet Western governments maintain their aid flows and now claim the right to insist on political – even strategic: i.e. military expenditures (UNDP, 1991: 83) – as well as economic conditionalities. Is such ODA and NGO interventiveness merely a function of bureaucratic politics – without Africa's needs such agencies would be more vulnerable at home? – and/or is it a long-term investment in the future – towards a new, sustainable economic and ecological order? Yet notwithstanding the demise of bipolarity, security issues still affect economic flows and political images, albeit in less intense ways.

SECURITY REDEFINED

Orthodox analysis of security in Africa and elsewhere in the Third World has continued to be based largely on orthodox realist as well as statist assumptions which emphasise great powers and Cold War on the one hand and national resources and capabilities on the other (Laidi, 1990; Somerville, 1990). Such a strategic perspective is quite uncritical and conservative, tending towards dependence: Africa as target and arena for extra-continental power. It is also static and ahistoric, downplaying shifts in both global and continental hierarchies.

However, such a traditional approach in the 1980s had already begun to be revised by a few analysts at the frontiers of the school to incorporate novel factors such as economy, ecology and food; i.e. security expanded to include new conceptions of non-lethal or -violent 'high' politics. Thus, from such a revisionist perspective, derived nonetheless from realist roots, conflict in Africa is no longer treated as only a function of strategic issues but also of new concerns such as development, environment and nutrition; in short, BHN (see Box 11). This reflects a global trend towards treating issues of economy and ecology as crucial, symbolised by the Brandt and Brundtland Commissions, at the beginning and end of the last decade, respectively. This in turn has led to the reconceptualisation of related phenomena, such as economic or environmental rather than merely strategic or political 'refugees'. So regional conflicts in Africa may have distinctive indigenous roots unrelated to extra-continental factors; except that the context of underdevelopment may be a function of global history and serve as an invitation to foreign involvement even intervention (Ravenhill, 1991b; Shaw and Inegbedion, 1991, 1992).

By contrast to such a revisionist extension of orthodox strategic studies for and in Africa – in which symptoms are treated rather than structures and social aggregates rather than classes or fractions – a more radical reformulation has been advanced from a neo-materialist perspective. In the African case, strategy would thereby be redefined as 'state' or 'regime' or 'presidential' rather than 'national' security. And threats would be reconceived as internal – from excluded or impoverished classes – as well as external – from corporate or collective interests challenged by a particular fraction in power. This more fundamental reformulation thus treats security issues as being defined normally by the positions and perceptions of the particular class in power which claims to articulate 'national security' concerns but in

Box 11
Fertility and Food: Malthusian Nightmare

Population and reproduction are controversial issues in Africa, as elsewhere, especially for regimes and for women. Patriarchal prejudices still claim that there is excess land on the continent, yet land-alienation and -hunger are increasingly apparent in, say, Kenya, Nigeria, Senegal and Zimbabwe as well as in the over-populated mini-states of Burundi, Lesotho and Rwanda (see tables 1 and 3). The combination of economic and ecological crises in the 1980s has led to a new policy and political context: many governments have moved towards acceptance and advocacy of child-spacing if not family planning. And 'user-pay' arrangements for education and health are increasing the costs of raising children.

Despite orthodox customs and religions, African women are insisting on their rights over reproduction, in part because they suffer the highest rates of maternal death in the world – officially, 700 per 100,000 live births. Meanwhile, unsanitary illegal abortions and baby-dumping continue to increase in the absence of effective, pro-choice legal rights. And fertility rates remain higher in Africa than any other region, with Gabon, *Côte d'Ivoire* and Kenya heading the list of continental and global population growth rates at 4.4, 4.2 and 4.1%, respectively (see tables 5 and 6). The next pair of boxes treats new factors, especially AIDS, which may moderate the land-labour equation quite dramatically in some parts of Africa in the immediate future.

fact advances fractional if not individual interests; i.e. there is a distinct gap between rhetoric and reality.

By extension, then, a neo-materialist approach to security treats 'foreign policy' as but the external expression of the interests of the ruling class or fraction whereas a more orthodox perspective assumes that such policy is on behalf of the community. The latter may have come to incorporate into its orthodox framework notions of the foreign policy of debt and of environment yet it still declines to focus on the central, sometimes personal or presidential, interests thereby advanced. By contrast, a more radical approach takes it to be axiomatic that both inherited and innovative issues are decided from a distinctive class or fractional viewpoint. In short, a radical rather than merely revisionist perspective would treat production and accumulation as well as distribution and consumption and relate foreign policy to questions of state autonomy (Shaw and Inegbedion, 1991, 1992).

Strategic issues from a traditional perspective were always taken to be 'high' politics whereas economic ones were assumed to be 'low', or less salient. With the incidence of economic shocks and slow-downs, combined with moves towards global detente if not disarmament, this artificial dichotomy has had to be transcended even within the orthodox realist school. However, the latter still adopts a state-centric approach which usually ranks strategic higher than economic factors. And it is disinterested in questions of class and capital: the internal and transnational bases of production and accumulation rather than exchange and technology.

If the state in Africa is shrinking then increasingly foreign relations will be amongst non-state actors, from informal financial exchanges to bourgeois professional associations. Governments may still go to war over boundaries and booty, as diversion or aggrandisement, but most cross-border interactions will be amongst companies and communities. Thus, in the late- or post-adjustment period, foreign policy will be increasingly 'transnational'; i.e. involving non-official actors in a routine manner outside the purview of the diminished state. This will pose challenges for both diplomats and students of diplomacy, leading away from realism over diplomacy and security and towards revisionism about economy and ecology.

FOREIGN POLICY REFORMULATED

The analysis as well as *praxis* of foreign policy has tended to be cautious and conservative everywhere; as 'national interests' are said to be at stake so democratic decision-making tends to be precluded. In Africa, the sub-field is not only conservative but also relatively underdeveloped; relative that is to comparative foreign policy outside the continent and to other fields of enquiry inside the continent. This is particularly unfortunate as African foreign policy is in a stage of transition, as already indicated, for two reasons. First, its *content* is being redefined in a period of adjustment away from diplomacy and security towards an endless series of negotiations over reform conditionalities, particularly debt. And second, as noted above, its hitherto exclusive *status* is being undermined as non-state, trans-national relations multiply outside the purview of official structures: non-governmental and informal sector relations as well as those of multinational corporations and religious missions. And such transi-tions will intensify as adjustment conditionalities come to include political liberalisation, embracing international as well as internal relationships.

Unhappily, notwithstanding the legacy of the 'adjustment decade' of the 1980s, the analysis of comparative foreign policy has remained rather underdeveloped in Africa, especially in regard to its many small, Fourth World states. There are debates about Nigerian (Shaw and Aluko, 1983; Shaw and Okolo, 1993) or South African (Barber and Barratt, 1990; Geldenhuys, 1984; Shaw, 1991b) foreign policy, for example. In the sub-field in general there has been an overcon-centration on diplomacy, ideology and personality and on the great powers, particularly among North Atlantic Africanist scholars, reflec-tive of realist hegemony. By contrast, traditional 'socialist' analyses have overconcentrated on economic factors and non-capitalist strategies. However, an early-1980s collection from the USSR Insti-tute of African Studies constituted something of an exception, em-phasising that 'Differentiation – on a class not a national basis – is becoming increasingly typical of African foreign policy' (Gromyko, 1983: 197). It also nicely captured the dialectic between aspirations of continental integration and the actualities of national divergencies and global marginalisation:

> Any analysis of the foreign policy pursued by independent African countries should take into consideration two simultaneous pro-cesses in inter-African affairs. First, the trend toward unity, con-certed action and comprehensive cooperation on the continental scale. Second, the socio-economic and political polarisation of these countries. . . . These centrifugal and centripetal trends affect the policies of each independent African country. . . . The dialec-tical contradiction between consolidation and differentiation . . . (Gromyko, 1983: 75)

The ensuing decade has been characterised by a dialectic between centrifugal tendencies in terms of policy – spreading structural adjust-ment programmes – and centripetal trends in terms of economy – disparate performances in terms of adjustment conditionalities, environmental conditions, and economic outputs. The continent is

becoming more unequal despite similar economic and political conditionalities and liberalisation because of uneven amounts of external
assistance and exchange. In short, the new interventiveness of IFIs
has created homogeneity in economic policy but heterogeneity in
political economy (see Tables 4, 5 and 6).

Such revisionist international positions and relations are in part a
function of super-power detente and in part a function of structural
adjustment; i.e. NIDP as well as NIDL. First, the decline in antagon-
ism between the US and USSR as well as amongst their allies,
particularly their tacit agreement not to export their conflicts into
regional arenas, has served to reduce the area for and appeal of
nonalignment. And second, the new orthodoxy of market forces in
Africa as well as in both East and West has moderated ideological
competition between 'socialism' and 'capitalism'; Bank/Fund conditionalities mean that most African regimes have now abandoned
state socialism and instead are implementing some type of mixed
economy or state capitalism (Utting, 1992).

This is not to imply that structural adjustment represents some
form of Western conspiracy – it does in association with parallel
moves in West and East add up to a comprehensive restructuring of
the post-war economy – although the socialist bloc had never really
proposed any viable alternative project, even when COMECON was
in a reasonable state of health at the start of the 1980s. Rather, it is to
suggest that the combination of moderating Cold War conflicts along
with declining ideological competition has transformed the context
for both national development and international relations in Africa.
Indeed, the only old-fashioned, purist state socialist regimes are to be
found in the South at the start of the 1990s, and then outside Africa –
Cuba, North Korea and Vietnam – but definitely not either Angola or
Mozambique and probably not Ethiopia given its belated acceptance
of adjustment conditionalities and subsequent change of regime in
1990/1.

Neither global strategic nor global economic contexts at the present time or conducive to orthodox state-centric definitions of 'socialist' or non-capitalist development. Liberalisation in both economy
and polity points towards convergence rather than contradiction:
state capitalism is everywhere, albeit with varying proportions of
capitalism and regulation. Meanwhile, the analysis of transitions
away from state socialism, in Africa as well as Eastern Europe, is an
expanding area of intellectual and political interest, although it has
been developed more in the case of the latter than of the former. And

in both, regression is possible still along with liberalisation, as indicated in the next and final chapter. In short, there are considerable dangers of premature 'triumphalism' in both intellectual and existential worlds over the irreversibility of capitalism and democracy: the global political economy is too extensive and diverse for any world order to be singular and stable over time.

CONTINENTAL CRISES AND REGIONAL CONFLICTS

Africa's developmental difficulties since independence are inseparable from and have been exacerbated by the intensification of social and strategic conflicts in many parts of the continent although the orthodox paradigm fails to recognise this. It has already begun to be argued in revisionist scholarship and admitted by many concerned that most of the apparently 'ecological' challenges have in fact been either caused or increased by such conflicts. Likewise, the imperative of structural adjustment, which has never been directed at the military, has been intensified by ongoing internal and regional conflicts, from the Maghreb and the Horn to Southern Africa. Similarly, the need to compromise with extra- (e.g. great powers) and with intra-African (e.g. Libya, Nigeria and South Africa) threats is in large measure a function of regime, food and ecological imperatives. The balance of causality in this range of factors changes over time, notably in recent years in the direction of less external salience.

The intensification of inequalities on the continent both within and between states, now in part because of the uneven impact of adjustment, has provided some of the causes of conflicts. Thus the range of 'foreign' interventions includes African (e.g. Libya and South Africa), middle (e.g. Cuba and France), and super-power regimes (i.e. US and USSR, at least historically). Together they have reinforced and undermined, not to say diverted, many African governments either directly or through the use of associates or puppets, including in the contemporary period cross-conditionalities. Moreover, the role of the military in the accumulation of African debt has hardly been investigated, although their competitive, acquisitive and spendthrift tendencies cannot be denied, with especial implications for scarce foreign exchange. And notwithstanding down-sizing in most budget lines, expenditure on coercive equipment and proliferating security forces – from secret police to paramilitaries – increase almost exponentially.

In the post-Cold War period, it is possible that African armies will be *less* necessary; i.e. assuming that a major cause sustaining them was extra-continental involvements. Conversely, given widespread opposition to adjustment conditionalities, they may become *more* necessary in internal affairs, maintaining order for isolated and unpopular regimes which have few resources other than coercion through which to maintain control. So the caution of UNDP's *Human Development Report 1991* (82) is justified: 'A peace dividend (in the South) is some way off because peace there is more elusive. The Third World has not been involved in the recent East–West negotiations, or in disarmament talks or in the design for a new framework for world peace. Nor does the Third World have any of its own institutionalized forums for a discussion of military expenditure.' Thus, notwithstanding current superficial moves towards multi-party democracy, there is likely to be a proliferation of unorthodox, nonformal threats to incumbents from alienated and impoverished groups. Thus, the continent is likely to experience a tension between democratic pressures and conditionalities reinforced by novel guerrilla formations on the one hand and discredited and diminished yet not yet defeated or deflated regimes on the other; hence the ambiguities of the debates over 'African democracy'.

Regionalism in Africa is also likely to be characterised by two contradictory tendencies in the 1990s: imperative of economic cooperation and incidence of political dominance. The former is ever more essential for development, given the fragmentation of the continent, and may be rendered compatible with adjustment programmes if liberalisation is directed towards regional rather than global exchange; it is also likely to become more informal in character as communities respond to adjustment conditions. And the second is a function of both continental inequalities and declining global constraints: less super- or great-power interventions but more disinterest, facilitating regional hegemons, whether 'sub-imperial' or not. The roles of, say, Nigeria in Liberia, Senegal in the Gambia, or Zimbabwe in Mozambique may, then, become more commonplace in the post-bipolar era. To be sure, regional cooperation and regional domination are not always compatible, although both are present in typical regional arrangements. Given the global trend towards economic and, to a lesser extent, political regionalisation, Africa *must* become more integrated in the 1990s than before, otherwise it will be ever more marginalised.

AFRICA IN THE GLOBAL POLITICAL ECONOMY

Africa's place at the periphery of the global economy and polity is likely to become more apparent in the 1990s than ever before given NIDL and NIDP. Its marginality was masked in previous decades for essentially superficial or superstructural reasons – independence in the 1960s, NIEO claims and OPEC crises in the 1970s, and economic and ecological traumas in the 1980s. At the start of the new decade, its vulnerability was apparent not only in the spread of structural adjustment conditions throughout the continent but also in terms of super-power detente. Given the decline in Cold War antagonisms, the Non-Aligned Movement (NAM) will have to further redefine itself away from balancing or equidistance: from strategic then economic priorities onto, say ecological or democratic ones, as indicated in the 1990 South Commission report. This imperative is reinforced by the imminent disappearance of *apartheid* as the continent's preoccupation.

The impact of US–USSR coexistence, if not yet collaboration or condominium, on world affairs is likely to be felt particularly in Africa, which has both exploited as well as been exploited by super-power competition over the last 20 or 25 years: regional conflicts, but also leverage or blackmail over aid and trade as well as approval and materiel. If the Cold War rationale has disappeared along with the Warsaw Pact and COMECON then both sides of the disappearing iron curtain will have to develop new criteria – the threat of AIDS (see Boxes 12 and 13), drugs, migration or pollution – or withdraw. Hence the timeliness of adjustment conditionalities, including the new one of military expenditures, for African regimes and Africanist interests.

In the event, given the preoccupations of Eastern Europe and the Middle East, the *withdrawal* option is likely to be preferred. Indeed, its presumed benefits were one of the pressures for the policy of detente in the first place: neither side could afford to intervene everywhere in response to each other given their respective economic difficulties, especially competition with the EC, Japan and the NICs, let alone near-NICs and leading OPEC states. And in a post-industrial world order, Africa's resources were in any case less saleable or lucrative, as revealed by declining levels of foreign investment as well as trade (UN, 1988a; Bennell, 1990). Indeed, given declining levels of trade and profits, the only growing factors, other than food aid, refugee flows and health challenges, are assistance and debt flows (see Tables 3–6 and Figures 11–13).

Box 12
'New' and Old Diseases: AIDS, Hypertension and Malnutrition

Africans are not immune from new infections and stresses in the 'modern' world. AIDS has spread rapidly, particularly in East and Central Africa, where hospital care has become horrendous and trade routes serve to spread viruses. Hypertension has become common as people worry about the future of themselves and their families under adjustment conditions. But most African children still die of diseases of underdevelopment and malnutrition – kwashiorkor syndrome – cholera, diarrhea, malaria, measles, respiratory infections, smallpox etc. Despite global immunisation schemes and oral rehydration therapy, both programmes have lower coverage in Africa than other continents.

By the early 1990s, Africa had over one million cases of AIDS, with increasing proportions falling into the crucial fifteen to fifty year old working age group, particularly the more educated and urban males. Moreover, UNICEF estimates that growing numbers of children will be born HIV positive – up to 30% in some urban areas (e.g. Lusaka) and some high-density rural countries (e.g. Rwanda) – so retarding prospects of 'Health for All by the Year 2000' as well as deterring tourism in forex-dependent states like Kenya and Tanzania. In some African countries, 25% of young males are already HIV positive and 10%–40% hospitalised people have AIDS-related diseases. The high incidence of AIDS in African armies and crucial industries (e.g. mining complexes) will affect security, productivity and profitability; and hence the adjustment project, as Charles Becker (1990: 1599) has suggested:

AIDS will emerge in the 1990s as one of Africa's most serious diseases. The pandemic is presently surging with limited control, especially in Eastern and Central Africa. . . . Structural adjustment policies adopted in response to economic crises (also) contain steps that assist in AIDS containment.

AIDS in Africa was a major feature of the mid-1989 Montreal Conference. WHO data then indicated that the continental total of victims had already passed 50,000, with an incidence of over

continued on page 142

Box 12 *continued*
'New' and Old Diseases: AIDS, Hypertension and Malnutrition

1,000 cases per 100,000 population in Kenya (which had twice as many cases as then West Germany), Uganda (more cases than France), Tanzania (more than Spain), and Zambia. These countries plus Burundi, Congo, Rwanda and Malawi (more cases than Britain) have high concentrations of HIV positive populations, correlating with the more middle-aged, educated, urban communities, especially individuals with multiple partners and sexually-transmitted diseases. But AIDS remains hard to diagnose and harder to treat given financial difficulties and female dependencies (Zaluondo, 1989).

Box 13
AIDS in Central Africa: the Disease of the Rich

The incidence and impact of AIDS in Africa may have been over-dramatised for political and racial reasons; yet current information and projections are profoundly disturbing. More educated, urban, bourgeois and promiscuous populations have a higher incidence of HIV positive and AIDS infections, particularly in Burundi, Kenya, Malawi, Rwanda, Tanzania, Uganda, Zaire, Zambia and Zimbabwe. AIDS in Africa is primarily a scourge of heterosexuals, particularly those in the bureaucracy, diplomacy, industry and military; as Becker (1990: 1605) argues, 'AIDS is . . . a "disease of development"'.

Given the incubation period of the AIDS virus, the epidemic is likely to peak in the mid-1990s, before the impact of prevention measures now being slowly adopted. Until then, the growing populations of young and old will have to be supported by a shrinking work force. The implications of this for political and social stability are profound, threatening momentum in the democracy movement. Meanwhile, male chauvinism and traditional cultures make monogamy and contraception problematic even amongst the most 'vulnerable groups' in Central Africa.

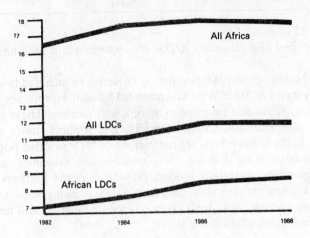

Figure 11 Net ODA to LDCs
($bn at constant 1988 dollars and prices)

SOURCE: *UN Africa Recovery* from OECD data.

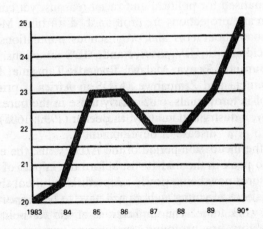

Figure 12 African debt service payments
($bn)

SOURCE: *UN Africa Recovery* based on World Bank data.
* Projected.

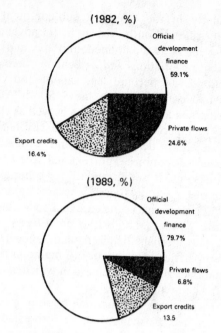

Figure 13   Growing importance for Africa of official flows

SOURCE: United Nations (1991).

However, Africa's new and overt marginality is likely to affect its
abilities to exert leverage and attract official assistance, even if NGOs
have some stake in its adversities. This is particularly so for the more
vulnerable and less attractive 'Fourth World' political economies; the
new majority given the ravages of the devaluation nexus. National
structural adjustment has encouraged divide-and-rule on the continent so the latter's diplomatic cohesion has declined, even on issues
such as the ivory trade, where 'middle powers' like Kenya and
Zimbabwe have been on opposite sides of the ban. Notwithstanding
adjustment conditionalities and compacts, as the salience and visibility of the continent decline in response to global directions so its
ability to attract official assistance and private investment may erode
despite UN and other demands for increasing not decreasing flows of
both: few external 'national interests' are thereby advanced any more
(see Tables 4 and 5).

This trend towards further peripheralisation is likely to be reinforced, particularly in the Southern sub-continent, by progress towards majority rule in South Africa. If the advance of the Mass Democratic Movement is maintained into the mid 1990s through ANC–government negotiations and agreements then external pressures and sanctions will become less salient and comprehensive. Internal terms and conflicts in the 'new' South Africa, including issues of ethnicity, gender and generation as well as class and colour, will then come to supercede and submerge any regional or global concern as the demise of destabilisation and recognition of distance respectively reduce attentions. The regional role of post-apartheid South Africa may come to set a standard for other aspiring regional powers in the post-bipolar continent, whether diplomatic, economic or strategic. It may also serve as the core of a post-Cold War grouping of African middle powers (along with *Côte d'Ivoire*, Kenya, Nigeria and Zimbabwe plus, perhaps, Ethiopia and Senegal, and Egypt and Morocco if North Africa is included?) to maintain continental stability and international visibility in an era in which anti-apartheid sentiment no longer guarantees cohesion.

Particular African states will continue to be of greater importance than others, of course, particularly those with established claims to being located at the continent's semi-periphery, such as *Côte d'Ivoire*, Egypt, Kenya, Morocco, Nigeria, Senegal and Zimbabwe. And major states other than the US and USSR will maintain an interest, especially if the super-powers themselves are irrevocably disinterested, even if only for historical or sentimental reasons: notably a sub-set of EC members, Belgium, Britain, France, Germany, Italy and Portugal (Stevens, 1992). Moreover, during the 1990s both Japan and the NICs may come to play a more activist or interventive role, limited to economic relations, along the lines of Brazil in Angola and Nigeria; i.e. a distinctive and unequal form of South–South exchange (Carlsson and Shaw, 1988). But unless major energy or mineral discoveries are made, involving either new reserves or technologies, Africa is unlikely to be the magnet in the twenty-first century that it was in the nineteenth and first half of the twentieth centuries. In short, continental decline is secular rather than cyclical, structural rather than superficial; hence the intensity of the fallacy of externalisation still insisted upon by orthodox adjustment programmes.

This exponential marginality will impact upon not only Africa's macro-economics but also its micro-politics. If most states attract less investment then over time they will decline, at least in terms of growth; in which case, their regimes will have to discover new forms of political maintenance. Simultaneously, the pressures on them to sustain adjustment reforms, now including democratic ones, will continue, leading to an overall shrinkage in the size of and more transparency in the role of the state. Together, these conditions are likely to produce a dramatically different continental political economy, one characterised by enforced, enhanced *self-reliance*, induced by necessity rather than choice. It is quite problematic whether this can at the same time be democratic, given the continent's tradition of rather authoritarian or hierarchical political cultures; the conditionality of political liberalisation may contradict with the reality of centralisation or coercion.

In short, as the adjustment 'compact' can and will not be met on either the internal or external sides, partially reformed economies will be left to their own devices. To be sure, they will be better able to cope, given all the shocks of the last decade which have reduced popular expectations as well as living standards. And the semi-periphery will still attract relatively greater responses and resources because of its communications, diplomatic and/or economic roles: *Côte d'Ivoire*, Egypt, Kenya, Morocco, Nigeria, Senegal and Zimbabwe plus, of course, post-apartheid South Africa. But most African states will come to down-size their official developmental and foreign policy goals in response to external realities and opportunities.

Given global economic and ecological preoccupations apparent at the start of the 1990s, it is probable that few foreign policies anywhere will be dominated exclusively by strategic concerns and contents, except perhaps at particular regional levels, such as China in Southeast Asia or Iraq in the Middle East (Korany, Brynen and Noble, 1992; Wurfel and Burton, 1990). Conversely, most international policies will be determined by internal adjustments defined by external conditionalities, whether of a formal (e.g. Ghana or Malawi) or informal (e.g. South Africa or Zimbabwe) variety. As incumbent regimes lose effective control of much of their territory and economy to a mixture of informal sectors and insurgent groups so they will come to redefine state–society relations at global and local as well as national levels, a feature overlooked in much of the burgeoning orthodox 'governance' literature (Diamond, 1988; Joseph, 1989) (see Boxes 14 and 15).

The quest for new role definitions given the changing global political economy poses a challenge for super- and major-powers as well as for medium- and small-states. The over-extended post-war superpowers have both had to moderate their global reach in response to internal demands and external difficulties. Likewise, ex-colonial

Box 14
Security of Polity and Property: Africa's Growth Industry

Underdevelopment reinforced by economic crises and political instability has engendered a climate of insecurity particularly amongst more bourgeois and visible communities such as bureaucrats, directors, politicians and other professionals. In turn, such pervasive instability has led to measures to recapture a measure of *security for person and property*, largely outside the under-funded and ineffective state structures of police and military. These include ubiquitous car and house alarms along with the marking and locking of equipment, especially electronic. They also extend to window bars and high fences or walls, along with multiple gates and locks. The vulnerable rich increasingly employ private guards, either directly or through companies such as Securicor, now equipped not only with dogs and vehicles but also with guns and two-way radios. As unemployment and inequalities have increased so job-creation in the private security sector has flourished, a bourgeoning business for an insecure indigenous bourgeoisie. And middle-class vigilante groups now work with the police in patrolling and securing neighbourhoods at night.

The other side of personal property protection is *political security* for regimes and functionaries. In a period of structural adjustment this has led not just to expansion of armies and materiel but also to the spread of special forces and intelligence operations. The former are increasingly used to harass or repress perceived opponents of ruling interests while the latter are employed to inform and intimidate either personal or political detractors. Together, such oppressive organisations have served to contain some of the moves towards more open, democratic processes (see Table 3 and Chapter 5). The climate of fear in states like Kenya, Malawi and Zaire has eroded rights of expression and organisation for many, not just the intelligentsia. Paranoia about secret police and informers has reduced cultural expression unless sanctioned by the regimes. The growing incidence of torture and disappearance has aroused concern and opposition amongst national and global human rights and development groups such as Amnesty International, Africa Watch and Oxfam.

Box 15
*'Prince, Autocrat, Prophet, Tyrant': Personalities in
African Politics*

Politics in Africa as elsewhere are not just about 'who gets what,
when and how'; it is also about larger-than-life personalities and
presidential idiosyncracies. Any such treatment of individuality
needs to be situated in historical and social contexts as Jackson
and Rosberg (1982a) tend not to do in their *Personal Rule in
Black Africa*, the sub-title of which constitutes the heading for
this box.

The 'idiosyncratic variable' may be marginal in any analysis of
political economy but it should not be discounted or excluded
altogether. The characters of continental leaders have mattered
to political and economic developments: from the besuited presence of Banda, Houphouet-Boigny and Moi to the fatigues of
'JJ' Rawlings and 'African' suits of 'KK' Kaunda, Mengistu,
Mobutu and 'Mwalimu' Nyerere. Jomo Kenyatta in old colonial
style always sported a rose in his lapel and a fly-whisk or walking-
stick in his hand; KK waved his white handkerchief; Mobutu
sports a leopard-skin hat; and most military men boast lots of
braid and medals. African presidents are typically jealous of
their prerogatives – presidential palaces, motorcades and jets –
but few are as personally violent or vindictive as Amin, Bokassa,
Mengistu, Nguema or Obote.

Any focus on personality and longevity alone, even within the
established modernisation mode, leads to trivial, almost laughable, 'results'. Thus in a rigorous yet superficial empirical analysis, Bienen and Walle (1989: 31) come up with an unremarkable
conclusion, that presidents who are in power for some time tend
to remain in power: 'The best predictor of whether a leader will
lose power in any given period is the length of rule up to that
point'! Such an ahistorical approach ignores state of the political
economy and tendency towards institutionalisation and repression, as exhibited by Kaunda in his second decade in power (see
Table 2 and Map 3).

powers have had to retreat from the extravagant and elusive pursuit of grandeur and glory, with important implications for the character of post-1992 EC external relations (Stevens, 1992). Only a pair of ex-fascist and economically expansive states – Germany and Japan – are likely to be able and willing to sustain outward-looking policies as they revalue and redistribute, albeit primarily in their own regions of Central Europe and Southeast Asia, respectively (Graf, 1991; Wurfel and Burton, 1990). And regional powers on the continent itself continue to be constrained by adjustment conditions in terms of their economic instabilities and forex scarcities. It is symptomatic, for instance, that Nigeria as an honorary or associated Southern African Front Line State (FLS) should at the end of the 1970s have been so active over Zimbabwe whereas at the end of the 1980s it was quite inactive over Namibia (Swatuk and Shaw, 1991): largely a function of the price of oil.

If the great powers are searching for post-Cold War roles – policies based on human rights and needs rather than resources and force? – then African states will have to move towards post-Non-Aligned or post-nationalist stances. The old rhetoric about imperialism and dependence had already worn rather thin; now it is quite threadbare. But the old habits die hard and reform conditionalities are quite unattractive. Yet if the downside of strategic and economic adjustments is uncertainty, the upside is opportunity: how to redefine foreign policy away from old rhetorics and towards new realities.

This new economic and strategic conjuncture – NIDL now joined by NIDP – provides an alternative, indeed compelling, occasion for redirecting foreign policy away from global chimeras and towards regional communities. Such reorientation would reinforce OAU (1980 and 1991) and ECA (1989b) inclinations and precedents – from *Lagos Plan* and *African Alternative Framework* to *African Economic Community* (see Appendix) – but would also serve to recognise informal economies and encourage informal polities: civil societies at a regional level. The dynamic of regional exchange given economic crises and conditionalities is already a reality which sustains many local political economies whether through the transnational movement of capital, commodities, currencies, drugs or labour (Shaw, 1989b, 1990b).

Whether even diminished regimes can come to accept a more modest international posture in which non-state relations are facilitated even encouraged remains to be seen. But the decade of the 1990s, in theory the run-up to a continental economic community (see Appendix), at least offers an occasion for reconsideration and reevaluation: 'second wave' regionalist initiatives, especially? As such, African, like extra-African, foreign policies may come to be both revisionist and realist before the end of the century, with promising possibilities in terms of revived and sustainable development: onto new forms of integration and industrialisation for the next century appropriate for diminished states and expanded markets and civil societies?

5 Conclusion: African Studies and African States

> the state in the periphery has assumed a progressively more precarious and outrightly repressive character, with frequent violent overthrow and rearrangement of ruling coalitions.
>
> Hutchful (1988: 48)

> the central issues concerning the development of the global economy in the coming decades will relate to the complex interaction between the forces making for transnationalisation, militarisation and the ecological crisis.
>
> Gill & Law (1988: 377)

> structural adjustment policies of the Bank's chosen variety constitute in very poor countries a gratuitous obstruction, just as in the NICs they constitute a welcome acceleration, of the policy evolution . . . in very poor countries, privatisation and removal of infant-industry protective structures are at best an irrelevance. True structural adjustment requires the building up of the country's export sectors and associated infrastructure, which in the short term may require more rather than less state intervention.
>
> Mosley, Harrigan & Toye (1991: 304)

The transformed political economy of Africa – a function of a mixture of adjustments, conflicts, continuities and constraints – has served to both revise and revive the study of Africa. Established orthodoxies of both modernisation and materialism, right and left, have been undermined as new issues and institutions have appeared: the syndrome of NIDL and NIDP. The challenge of the 1990s and beyond lies in working towards innovative analyses and policies which make sense in and for the era: approaches and *praxis* which incorporate and

151

encourage development compatible with hitherto overlooked interests in gender (see Tables 7 and 8), informal sector (see Boxes 4–8)
and environment (see Table 3). To date, some statespersons have
been more creative and positive about this range of new issues than
many scholars. Progress towards synthesis has been advanced more
by the UN system, especially the ECA, UNDP, UNICEF and UN-
RISD and the South Commission, than by academics, individually or
institutionally. The conservatism of the academy stands in contrast to
revisionism in the economy and polity, especially to the new activism
apparent among other elements in civil society. As noted in the
opening chapter and in an opening citation to Chapter Three, the
prevailing paradigm comes from the World Bank and the donor
community rather than from indigenous discourses, experiences, investigations or pressures. The first section of this conclusion laments
this and anticipates alternative agendas and animators.

AFRICA'S CRISES AND ACADEMIC RESPONSES

The potential capacity for creativity among Africa's intelligentsias
and institutions was perhaps best revealed at the turn of the decade
by the discussion and production through the ECA of the *African
Alternative Framework to Structural Adjustment Programmes* (1989)
and *African Charter for Popular Participation* (1990). To be sure,
these were not sustained works of original research; neither did they
concur with the prevailing development *problématique*. But rather,
together they do summarise and symbolise the African agenda which
has emerged since the equally path-breaking Monrovia symposium
and *Lagos Plan of Action* at the start of the 1980s (Adedeji and Shaw,
1985). They constitute responses not only to changing contexts but
also to alternative prescriptions (e.g. from the World Bank) and
academic perspectives (e.g. Bade Onimode). Although other Pan-
African institutions play a role in preparing and popularising revisionist analyses (e.g. CODESRIA), the ECA emerged over the
decade of the eighties, under the guidance of Adebayo Adedeji, as
the centre for indigenous researches and responses (Shaw, 1989a),
preparing the way for the mid-1991 Abuja Declaration of an African
Economic Community (see appendix). More established and eminent
organisations on the continent have yet to catch up with the transformed existential and intellectual conditions at the start of the 1990s.

Indeed, as the African Hunger Foundation (Achebe *et al.*, 1990) (NB *not* the Hunger Project!) suggests, there remains a danger that the most original research about Africa will continue to emanate from outside rather than inside the continent in the 1990s as in previous post-independence decades. This is particularly so because (a) *political conditions* are not yet conducive to debate and disagreement, especially when these detract from the pretentions of presidents and parties, and (b) *economic diversions* which prevent scholars from concentrating on professional pursuits; instead, devaluation of national currencies and professional incomes compel academics and others in related fields like the media to be active in informal sectors, such as agriculture and trade, or in international consultancies for forex (see Boxes 4 and 6). The advent of economic and political liberalisation has yet to facilitate innovative indigenous analysis or activism in a sustainable way.

In such unconducive conditions, there is every prospect that external authors will have superior opportunities both to research and to publish, local book and journal publishers and markets being what they are. Given recession and repression within Africa, a growing proportion of these extra-African researchers have their roots in the continent but cannot afford for economic and/or political reasons to remain in indigenous universities or institutes. There is, therefore, a growing critical community from Africa in the diaspora, particularly within Europe and North America, which focuses on issues of African development but which cannot return on a continuous basis until political and/or economic conditions improve; from Julius Ihonvbere, Sam Nolutshungu and Nzongola-Ntalaja in North America to Yusuf Bangura, Ngugi Wa Thiong'o and Ben Turok in Europe. Such African–Americans or African–Europeans reinforce the established dominance of Africanists whose role was so controversial in previous decades. Given the shrinking of the globe in terms of communications amongst scholars in major centres – fax and electronic mail in addition to airlines, couriers, phones and telex – location is no longer so crucial: commitment and relevance are. If intra-African criticism continues to be repressed – witness a further category of intra-African exiles, such as Thandika Mkandawire and Okello Oculli (see Box 5) – then extra-continental comment and input are crucial, particularly in terms of vulnerable indigenous groups; vulnerable that is for political and ecological as well as economic reasons. Such vulnerability may decline as political conditionalities become more effective, but repression continues in many states despite internal and external pressures for liberalisation (see regular 'Africa Watch' and Amnesty International reports as well as 'Africa Rights Monitor' in each quarterly issue of *Africa Today* (Denver) and 'Afric Demos' from the African Governance Program of the Carter Center). I look first at academic responses both within and outside Africa before turning to internal and international reactions: the state of the African state and the global political economy in the last decade of the twentieth-century (see Sandbrook, 1988, 1990).

The continuing continental crisis and orthodox stabilisation reactions pose enormous, exponential challenges to the academy in Africa in its institutional, intellectual and national or international roles. As elsewhere in the educational, financial and technological worlds of the 1990s, the university in Africa confronts a new set of challenges to its authority and integrity. These are symbolised on the one hand by the World Bank's (1988) comprehensive and threatening report on *Education in Sub-Saharan Africa* and on the other hand by the visible decay of hitherto prestigious institutions such as Ibadan University in Nigeria, the University of Ghana at Legon, Makerere University in Uganda and the University of Zambia in Lusaka. These harsh times are unlikely to be relieved soon either in the North or in Africa, where many tertiary institutions have been compelled to take hard decisions which involve some combination of user-pay, privatisation, commercialisation, rationalisation, consultations, corporate or donor finance, and debt. As Thandika Mkandawire, head of CODESRIA, has recently lamented, 'African countries are witnessing the worst economic crisis since independence and this crisis has a dramatic impact on educational institutions. . . . Perhaps the most strikingly visible feature of the crisis of social sciences in Africa is the disintegration of the research infrastructure' (*CODESRIA Bulletin*, 4, 1988: 1). Likewise, the World University Service (WUS) (1990: 1–12 and 185–90) has cautioned about growing threats to academic freedom and institutional autonomy, particularly in the South, expressed in its 1988 'Lima Declaration on Academic Freedom and Autonomy'.

First, the *institutional* challenge to the African university lies in the combination of reduced real funding and increased demands. As elsewhere in the world of the late twentieth century, more students but fewer faculty and other facilities; often dramatically eroded library, equipment, materials and other resources; expanded expectations of national, regional and continental contributions from consultancies to secondments; and relentless dependence on, as well as accompanying ambiguity about, external finances, prescriptions, evaluations and skills. The incidence of national fiscal deficits and external forex shortages has served seriously to undermine the capacity of tertiary institutions – universities, technical and teachers' colleges, national training and research institutes etc. – to survive let alone develop. Hence the lament in CODESRIA's 'Dakar Declaration' about 'the increasing deterioration of the infrastructure for the practice of social science' (*CODESRIA Bulletin*, 7). In only a few states have such institutions thrived in terms of (reasonable) financial inputs and (relative) academic freedom – Algeria, Botswana, Senegal and Zimbabwe (and perhaps South Africa in transition). Elsewhere, frustrated faculties seek greener pastures, usually through appointments to international agencies, especially in the North, or regional institutions in the South, or to academic posts in the few relatively forex-rich countries, including the Black 'Bantustan' universities in South Africa (WUS, 1990).

Responses to this unsatisfactory and unacceptable situation have ranged from sentimental laments for bygone days to neo-classical advocacy of user-pay. Notwithstanding all the rhetoric about market forces, the World Bank (1991a) has belatedly come around to recognising the necessity of at least some residual tertiary training facilities on the continent. But its African Capacity Building Initiative (ACBI) is intended to reinforce structural adjustment measures through socialising a new administrative elite to effect reforms. In association with the established macro-economic and positivist African Economic Research Consortium and bilaterally supported 'networks', such as those spawned by IDRC and SAREC, ACBI is instructed to create regional graduate networks compatible with current conditionalities: a return to post-independence support for education but with contemporary adjustment preoccupations.

Second, the *intellectual* challenge in an era of not only existential adjustment but also conceptual 'counter-revolution' involves creative resistance and alternatives to the spread of *laisser-faire* ideology. The prevalent paradigm in Africa in the 1970s had become *dependencia* with the then ubiquitous one-party state and still pervasive nationalist inclinations: African state socialism. But despite the unique attempt to implement and institutionalise self-reliance, especially in its collective guise, in the Monrovia Declaration and *Lagos Plan of Action*, the displacement of the modernisation mode was short-lived and consideration of the alternative materialist mode fleeting. The doctrine of 'market forces' advocated by the *Berg Report* has since superceded *dependencia* as the acceptable approach – its dominance reflected in the recognition of its hegemony – reinforced by national conditionalities and consultancies. The elusiveness of the NIEO has since been superceded by the harsh realities of the NIDL and now NIDP. This paradigmatic conjuncture and its policy correlates – the adjustment project of devaluation, deregulation, deficit reduction, deindustrialisation etc. – concluded the continent's brief moment of self-confidence and has revived reliance on externally determined concepts and criteria. As Mkandawire has commented, it is ironic that when Africa lacked social scientists it was under pressure to provide local contributions to the series of post-colonial national plans (see Box 3) yet, now that such resources are more readily available, planning is *passé* so that external inputs once again largely determine the definition of national reforms or market forces (Martin, 1991; Mosley, 1992)!

The 'de-Africanisation' of research has coincided with the 'privatisation' and 'commercialisation' of education (see Box 10 and Table 3) – from private schools such as Daystar (Nairobi) and Africa (Mutare) universities to ODA and NGO projects to informal sectors – so that international agencies mainly set the agenda and approach. Such external bodies have expressed their own concern about the evaporation of capabilities on the continent through attempts to overcome the 'book famine' to the creation of regional 'centres of excellence'. Yet these all tend to be rather short term and superficial reactions to essentially long term, structural problems. Reforms and reconstruction are not enough when curricula are outmoded and political economies in continuing decline. Creative pedagogy and institutional redirection are urgently needed, reflective of social needs not market forces. Hopefully, by the mid 1990s, the African academy will be able to draw strength from the renaissance in civil society to respond creatively and critically to the prevalent yet deficient adjustment hegemony. Both scholars and/or radicals need creative concepts and coalitions to confront the flawed yet forceful developmentalist hegemony (cf. Gulhati, 1990; Nelson, 1989).

However, Mkandawire has also cautioned against 'alternative' NGO and quasi-governmental domination of higher education agendas, criticising both 'action-oriented' research and research 'networks' as further intrusions by foreign interests and ideologies which divert attention away from indigenously defined theoretical and methodological priorities (*CODESRIA Bulletin*, 2–4). To rectify this imbalance, the continent needs to define its own processes and paradigms through professional and research networks which build on indigenous impulses from official, private, NGO and 'informal' sectors; i.e. the research, policy, publication and dissemination aspects of revived and regionalised civil societies (Clark, 1991).

Third, then, in terms of *national and international roles*, particularly regional and continental, African scholars and schools now are subject to greater pressures than ever. Undergraduate and graduate instruction and supervision are no longer enough. Rather, indigenous advisors and researchers are expected to assist in the continent's redirection and reconstruction, even if they lack basic amenities and resources at their so-called 'universities'. The definition of 'relevance' has always been problematic in Africa as elsewhere. Yet in a period of personal and national deprivation, many scholars are turning, as noticed already, to either 'moonlighting' and/or consulting as imperatives for personal and familial survival given the high social costs of adjustment (see Boxes 5–7 and 15 and 16).

Both these survival strategies divert attention away from orthodox scholarship. And the consultancy syndrome poses acute personal, ethical and professional dilemmas. In particular, it not only forces practitioners away from research committed to longer term, more sustainable development, it also encourages them to be atheoretical, pragmatic and 'practical'. Academe as a whole was everywhere always intended to reinforce established structures despite some radical faculty and student opinion to the contrary. The contemporary necessity for institutional 'relevance' and personal 'excellence' let alone 'international' professional 'standards' and occasional national police supervision all serve to reinforce this conservative role and responsibility, notwithstanding recent opportunities for democratic activity. Indeed, quasi- and extra-academic NGOs have been more in the vanguard of popular pressures, sometimes establishing 'research institutes' to advance their activities on, say, democracy, gender and human rights. Only a few courageous academic groups have taken a similar stand such as faculty unions in Nigeria, Tanzania and Zimbabwe and non-racial educational groups in South Africa.

Resistance to state-defined functions has always been hazardous in Africa and has not (yet?) become markedly easier despite debates about political conditionalities. Advocates of African nationalism in colonial and settler states, including South Africa in the 1980s, along with critics of indigenous repression, such as that practised in Ethiopia, Kenya, Malawi, Somalia, Zaire etc., have all faced dangers. Opposition to policies and practices which are contrary to human rights and needs, from structural adjustment to preventive detention

---

Box 16
Political Wives and Social Corruption

As post-colonial Africa has yet to experience a female head-of-state, all presidential spouses thus far have been female. Occasionally such wives have been non-indigenous (e.g. Mrs Khama (British), Mugabe (Ghanaian), Nkrumah (Egyptian), and Senghor (French)); a few presidents have been polygamous; and a few leaders have been officially single yet required social partners (e.g. Banda). Political wives in Africa have been the source of considerable social and financial speculation because of their close connection with sometimes politically and economically omnipotent and corrupt partners. Rumours of their influence and affluence are legion but hard to verify, and may be exaggerated by chauvinist male commentators: companies in finance, foreign trade, housing, land, transportation etc. Clearly their ability to get licences, contracts and favours is privileged. Likewise, their capacity to avoid detection from national and international supervision of informal and illegal trade in, say, drugs or forex, is superior. This is not to allege that all presidential spouses are so involved, but that the possibility and temptation do exist. In addition, they often get cast in gender-stereotypical roles, such as setting role models for other females and being involved in orthodox women and development and family planning activities. Indeed, the position of several of them as heads of national and/or party women's movements has been controversial, a particular aspect of both democratic and feminist demands (see Tables 5 and 6).

---

and arbitrary regime repression, has if anything become increasingly dangerous (Africa Watch, Amnesty International and UNDP, 1991). Notwithstanding continuous discourse about political liberalisation, especially of the formal multi-party variety, the state has been reduced to repression to maintain (its) stability and security; less overt forms of coercion or cooptation have tended to disappear with adjustment conditionalities and constraints (see Box 17). As the head of CODESRIA (*CODESRIA Bulletin*, 4, 1988: 1) warned as the turn of the decade approached:

Box 17
Military Roles and Debts: Costs of Coups or Equipment

The military has always been visible and interventive in both the pre- and post-colonial continent, as well as in imperial administrations and wars. It has rarely been excluded from direct or indirect power in African regimes for long, being responsible for scores of successful coups since independence and innumerable unsuccessful attempts, at least until the contemporary 'democratic' period and mood. Even when supposedly civil governments hold power, the soldiers typically constitute the primary threat – the leading force in any corporatist or praetorian arrangement – although they are rarely cohesive or homogenous. Aside from traditional service distinctions – army, air-force, navy – there are other distinctive units in many African states – presidential, paramilitary and secret armies in addition to several police units, again from orthodox to secret and intelligence operatives. Moreover, there are fundamental distinctions between officers and men (there being very few female soldiers on the continent) and among generations; i.e. pluralism or proliferation of coercive capabilities.

The military as institution rather than administration is responsible for a considerable proportion of Africa's debt load. To keep presidents and regimes in power, they have been able to consume scarce foreign exchange and national income on sophisticated imports of materiel: from jet fighters, short-range missiles, small tanks and armoured personnel carriers to ammunition and vehicles (Mercedes-Benz jeeps and trucks as well as automobiles!). The continent has very few military-industrial complexes outside Egypt, Nigeria and South Africa just as it has no NICs, so national or regional sourcing is limited. Given unstable regimes as well as uncertain borders and ambitious neighbours, presidential or party control over military profligacy has usually been minimal.

This is the one sector which structural adjustment conditionalities have rarely reached, in part because many bilateral donors have also been arms suppliers and military trainers, at least until the more self-conscious post-Gulf War period. Military-related

continued on page 160

Box 17 *continued*
Military Roles and Debts: Costs of Coups or Equipment

deficits and debts are likely to continue to escalate if corporatist rather than democratic control is used to effect policy reforms. In association with police units, military forces in Africa remain a threat to both popular participation and financial regulation. Their ambiguous role will likely continue, however, especially as, in a post-bipolar period, 'unconventional' threats will tend to predominate over the more orthodox to regime and presidential, let alone party, security; that is unless current propositions for a military-related form of conditionality is implemented (see Table 3 and Chapters 4 and 5).

The African environment has hardened. Confronted with dwindling legitimacy in the eyes of their own people and persuaded that foreign capital requires the 'political will' to impose unpopular adjustment policies, law and order, and a docile civil society, most African governments have resorted to direct repression. The effects on the social sciences are familiar enough – closure of universities, detentions, prohibition of publications, expulsion from countries, loss of jobs etc.

Or, as Diamond (1988: 20 and 21) has argued from different, more orthodox theoretical premises:

The typical African state may be described as 'swollen' in that it is at once both too large and too weak. . . . The swollen nature of the African state has had diffuse and profound consequences for democracy.

One final implication of the adjustment context is that, aside from transnational networks and Africans in the diaspora, a new and worrisome intellectual division of labour has tended to emerge, undermining the integrity of social science in the continent. According to Mkandawire, it is one in which,

the tedious basic data gathering is left to the Africans and the theoretical digestion and elaboration is left to 'Africanists'. . . . On the one hand, it leads to a kind of mindless empiricism in which Africans are contracted to churn out meaningless data while, on the other hand, it leads the 'Africanists' towards faddish theorisation of the African reality and pursuit of often exclusively expatriate and ephemeral 'debates' that vanish as mysteriously as they emerged. (*CODESRIA Bulletin*, 1988: 3)

Happily, a few African intellectuals and institutions have both recognised and puzzled over such dilemmas, notably CODESRIA, ECA and IFAA, plus scholars and groups associated with the more radical schools, both inside and outside the continent. The critical nationalist perspective – revisionist forms of dependency and materialism – is not yet moribund but, hopefully, is awaiting an appropriate occasion for its reappearance and rehabilitation; post-triumphalism in Africa as well as in Eastern Europe and Middle East? The mid-1991 OAU agreement on an African Economic Community symbolises the potential for creative, realistic responses to the NIDL which includes regionalisation (see Appendix and Boxes 18 and 19); hopefully, the proposed 'Pan-African Parliament' plus links with other regional groups and NGOs will be institutionalised and influential.

Meanwhile, the ECA's Abuja, Khartoum and Arusha conferences reflect the ongoing synthesis of enlightened African and developmental opinion with the new focus on democratisation of both production and distribution (if not yet accumulation!). CODESRIA, for example, advocates the integration of theoretical and applied aspects of the social sciences within an interdisciplinary context. Consistent with the approach of this text, CODESRIA insists (*CODESRIA Bulletin*, 4, 1988: 8) in its own programmes that:

Research themes must give rise to projects leading to the promotion of alternatives at the theoretical, conceptual, and even political levels. Both methodological and epistemological efforts at rethinking all the categories and concepts currently in use must be encouraged.

I conclude with one such dichotomy – that between the now-fashionable 'democratic development' and the new threat of 'corporatism' or other forms of authoritarianism – which raises a set of issues which are threaded throughout this text, especially its boxes, yet which are all too easily overlooked by the prevailing adjustment paradigm.

Box 18
Deindustrialisation and Perpetual Underdevelopment

Africa is already by far the least industrialised of the Southern continents, contributing less than 4% of global trade in manufactures. Given the incidence and impact of structural adjustment it has experienced *deindustrialisation* rather than industrialisation in the 1980s. Its limited industrial production was always highly uneven – Algeria, *Côte d'Ivoire*, Egypt, Kenya, Mauritius, Nigeria and Zimbabwe as well as South Africa (Riddell, 1990) – as well as inefficient, because of its high-cost import-substitution origins. Given the conditionalities of privatisation and liberalisation, unless the continent's industrialists can find international market niches – e.g. Zimbabwean cotton goods and chrome products – they will suffer further decline. The NIDL is founded on highly efficient producers of high-tech and basic goods, from micro-computers to fashion garments. Except for a few specific comparative advantages – e.g. Kenya's tropical flowers, fruits and vegetables – Africa has yet to find niches for its products in such an internationalised but competitive global market-place. In particular, it has not been incorporated into new patterns of international 'just-in-time' production in which no state produces all the parts for any final product (see Tables 1 and 3).

In short, ironically, the UN's 1980s Industrial Development Decade for Africa was characterised by deindustrialisation and un- and under-employment. And as the UN (1988a) report on *Financing Africa's Recovery* indicated, the continent is unlikely to attract much non-concessional capital in the foreseeable future. Internal investment in industries integrated into restructured national and regional economies is the only feasible direction, yet one which stabilisation and adjustment criterion disfavour and discourage. As Mkandawire (1988: 31) cautions in his careful overview of the continent's deindustrialisation, the adjustment era 'will once again leave Africa unprepared to capture whatever new opportunities an upturn in the world economy may have'. Finally, despite the rhetorical claims of orthodox materialists and populists, the working class in Africa is in no condition to challenge capital as it is being numerically reduced and politically marginalised almost everywhere outside South Africa. Realistic analysis of deindustrialisation contradicts the claims of, say, Sender and Smith (1986: 133) that there is a 'rapidly growing African working class' whose 'organised labour' African 'regimes have most to fear'.

Symptomatic of the difficulties of industrialisation under conditions of contraction and devaluation has been a series of disastrous fires which indicate inadequate maintenance and security, from oil-refinery blazes in Nigeria and Zambia to a major hydro-electric installation in Zambia and TV studio in Ghana. Some fires at banks and ministries have been deliberately set to hide evidence of forex or drug deals such as at the Central Bank in Tanzania and in Nigeria at the Ministry of Foreign Affairs, External Telecommunications and Cocoa Marketing Board.

Box 19
African Multinational Corporations

Despite the stereotypical images still presented of Africa by orthodox and outdated dependency analysts, the continent is no longer a passive victim of multinational corporate manipulation, if it ever was so. Colonial trading companies' influence in Africa has declined over the last decade or so for four interrelated reasons:

a) *technological change* means that only a few commodities attract external investment any longer – petroleum and gas rather than copper, cotton or gold – so, as the UN (1988) reported in *Financing Africa's Recovery*, direct foreign investment has been in decline for over a decade (see Table 4);

b) *political decisions* after independence within an African 'state socialist' problematic favoured state or joint ventures which led to regime-dominated economies with all their attendant disadvantages; only a few well-established British (e.g. Lonrho), Dutch (Shell and Unilever), or French (CFAO) companies remained active in such an unattractive policy environment;

continued on page 164

Box 19 *continued*
African Multinational Corporations

c) *economic crises* meant restrictions on production and profit, especially overseas remittances, so foreign companies reduced both their output and expectations, down-scaling which was reinforced by a series of devaluations, droughts and debt renegotiations; and

d) *policy reforms* have after a decade begun to encourage some indigenous in addition to international capital as privatisation has proceeded and external interests have shrunk, particularly in Nigeria (e.g. Ibru Group) and Zimbabwe (e.g. TA Holdings). Informal sectors and corruption may advance such domestic investment and accumulation, which do not include the well-known but unrecorded entrepreneurial pursuits and profits of some presidential circles, such as *Côte d'Ivoire*'s Boigny, Kenya's Moi, Malawi's Banda, Zaire's Mobutu and Zambia's Kaunda family 'trusts'.

The transformed political and economic contexts at the end of the 1980s under the combined pressures of NIDL/NIDP and adjustment conditionalities will continue to advance the ideological and institutional rehabilitation of private companies in Africa, especially those which are partially or fully locally-owned, particularly those which now trade throughout their regions if not the continent as a whole (see listing of 'Africa 300' in *South* 101, March 1989: 63–74). Yet extra-continental foreign investment continued to decline through the 1980s, from $8 billion in 1981 to under $1 billion in 1985, without taking inflation into account (see Table 4). Hence the almost indecent rush towards 'liberalisation' and incentives like tax holidays and export processing zones to attract new investors rather than familiar traditional African companies such as Anglo American, CFAO and Lonrho. Yet *South*'s 1990 listing of the 'Africa 300' contains very few manufacturers let alone high-technology enterprises. The top 30 companies are still concentrated in colonial commodities like cocoa, copper, cotton, diamonds, tea, tobacco, and oil, with the only service sectors being airlines and tourism. And such corporations are still heavily state-owned and concentrated in a few countries: Egypt and the Maghreb, Kenya and Zimbabwe.

DEMOCRATIC DEVELOPMENT AND CORPORATIST COALITIONS

Africa at the start of the 1990s confronts a contradictory set of options or conditions: liberalisation and/or contraction in both economics and politics. Given its wide range of political economies and political cultures, some of it may move in several of these directions at once. The primary tension which is emerging is between *economic contraction* and *political liberalisation*, a combination which is rather ominous for incumbent regimes, which might prefer the alternative mix of economic expansion and political contraction; indeed, that was the underlying basis of the post-colonial African socialist model. The contrary condition of economic contraction is quite familiar by now, induced by a mix of external, ecological and internal realities and policies. But the political correlates are more elusive and problematic: regime inclinations to dominate and external pressures to democratise. Meanwhile, the international concern with 'human rights' as well as human needs, women and development, and sustainable development, has grown since the US presidency of Jimmy Carter; and it has also developed away from notions of formal democracy towards those of democratic development or popular participation (contrast Table 2 with Bratton, 1989a and b; Clark, 1991).

By contrast, given the state–society dialectic, many regimes' natural inclination is to look for arrangements which ensure their longevity. The adjustment project is permissive, even supportive, of the rise of a *national bourgeoisie* – as suggested above, a crucial yet tenuous (see Boxes 6, 7, 15 and 16) element in any process of sustainable democracy – alongside more bureaucratic, comprador, military, political and technocratic fractions. Therefore, incumbent leaders have sought, in a period of declining, if not shrinking, resources, to replace the corruptive tendencies of cooption with those of *corporatism*. They can no longer afford the expansive (and expensive!) gestures of patronage; instead, they have begun to rely on the less predictable but also less expensive arrangements of corporatism. Corporatism consists merely of a set of structured social relations which both include and exclude major groups in the political economy. Normally it revolves around some understanding among state and economy, particularly labour and both national and international capitals; but it may also include connections with other major social institutions in civil society already identified, such as religions and universities, media and interest groups, professional associations and NGOs, women's and youth groups (Nyang'oro and Shaw, 1989).

Corporatism as analysis and *praxis* has its roots in Europe and Latin America of the 1930s. It has since spread to embrace non-fascist and Catholic regions and regimes. Particular arrangements at different times among state, capital and labour in, for example, Australia, Britain, Canada and France in the post-war period have been so characterised; i.e. corporatist elements or periods within the Keynesian welfare state. Most post-war attention within this *genre* has focused on Latin America, particularly Peronist Argentina, where a useful variety of sub-categories has been isolated, such as authoritarian or bureaucratic corporatisms, often including the military and regular and secret police units as salient components.

Surprisingly, corporatism as perspective or practice has received minimal attention in Africa to date. There has been some recognition that it helps to explain settler and post-settler states in, say, Zimbabwe (Stoneman and Cliffe, 1989). But, in general, a concern for trilateral or triangular relations among state, capital and labour has not been apparent, despite parallel, even compatible, notions of authoritarianism or exclusion, Bonapartism and commandism (Hutchful, 1988). Nyang'oro and Shaw (1989) have attempted to rectify this oversight by encouraging comparative analysis of a variety of corporatisms in contemporary Africa. And the continuing unfolding of myriad social implications of adjustment facilitates such analytic direction.

Moreover, corporatism at the level of the *state* may not be incompatible with limited pluralism at the level of *society* or market forces at the level of the *economy* – formal and informal forms of political economy – particularly in a period of adjustment. More formal national-level arrangements amongst state, capital and labour may be compatible with more informal sub-national activities of cooperatives, ethnic communities, interest groups, religions, NGOs etc. But such an understanding would require maturity on both sides – the state doesn't need to monopolise *all* social relations and, conversely, social groups don't automatically threaten the state; i.e. *a new internal division of labour and powers internally*, compatible with international changes and contexts. All too few African leaders have been prepared to countenance such real devolution and decentralisation, at least until the second decade of adjustments. So state–society relations are likely, in general, to be undermined by regime insecurity or social irrepressibility. Hence the ongoing and unstable state–society stand-off – problematic rather than 'precarious' (Rothchild and Chazan, 1988) – which is likely to extend into the next century, when social restructuring will be even more apparent than today (see Chapter 2).

The enhanced space for popular participation is not uncontroversial in either its size or content. The state will continue to try to make occasional inroads before retreating given its self-defined prerogatives and its jealousy about alternative structures. And a variety of both old and new 'interest groups' will expand to fill the vacuum, from established ethnic, professional, regional and religious institutions to innovative ecological, female, informal and survival communities. The latter set will itself be divided between more national and more transnational NGOs or Private Voluntary Organisations (PVOs) whose roles are expanding in response to adjustment conditionalities. Over time, as in Eastern Europe at the end of the 1980s, it will become harder for centralised regimes to exert control or coordination over such myriad groups in civil society. But there will be no simple, unilineal advance throughout the continent to either democracy or development given Africa's heterogeneity and inequalities.

The corporatism–democratisation dialectic is something of a contemporary successor to that between authoritarianism–militarisation and participation–pluralism. It incorporates some of the distinctive elements which are beginning, belatedly, to be recognised and treated in contemporary Africa, such as bourgeois fractions and informal sectors, along with gender and ecology. But such neo-materialism is still tentative given the interrelated challenges of intellectual and empirical changes. Moreover, as suggested above, there is no single trend but, rather, several tendencies related to the diversity of inheritances and institutions in Africa's political economies. Happily, most of the discourse over Africa has yet to be polluted or paralysed by the diversion of 'post-modernism' so prevalent across the North Atlantic in non- (anti-?) materialist circles; one intellectual fad the continent could readily miss (see Boxes 20 and 21).

The combination of economic contraction and political challenge has not always led to a benign state. Indeed, in a rather contrary manner, the weakened state has come to rely on coercion rather than cooptation as resources for the latter shrink; witness the extreme 'distortions' in Liberia and Somalia, for example. So, despite some tendencies towards political as well as economic liberalisation, African regimes maintained, even expanded, their repressive capabilities in the 1980s (see Boxes 14, 15, 17; and UNDP, 1991: 81–3). To be sure, there is a wide spectrum of behaviours on the continent, which

Box 20
Fate Worse than Debt?

Africa is not the most indebted continent *in toto* but it is so in *per capita* terms and debt-service ratios. Its debt, unlike that of Latin America, is essentially official rather than private and rose faster than that of any other continent in the 1980s. With the write-off of some of it by the majority of major bilateral donors, most is now with the IFIs (see Table 4); so, by the mid 1980s, net resources began to flow *from* rather than *to* Africa. By the end of the decade, continental debt exceeded US$240 billion, of which some $30 billion was Nigeria's: less than 20% of the Third World total. Africa had but three of the world's score of 'Highly Indebted Countries' – *Côte d'Ivoire* and Morocco in addition to Nigeria – but did contain some 30 'Debt-Distressed' states. The delicacy of Africa's debt crisis, with its historical and structural roots, has been well-summarised by Tony Killick and Matthew Martin (1989: 5):

> Much of the economic case for special assistance to Africa is derived from the structural weaknesses of most such economies. . . . If there is to be any prospect of economic recovery, there can be no question of attempting to require Sub-Saharan Africa to generate trading surpluses in the manner which some of the major Latin American debtors have done.

The continent's debt service ratio of some US$30 billion p.a. approaches 30% GNP while interest payments despite rescheduling have increased to almost 15% of exports (see Table 4). Africa is already the most rescheduled continent, with almost 100 in 1980–82 before the intensification of the crisis. Without further write-offs and defaults, as debated at the OAU's Cairo conference in debt in mid 1989, servicing will reach US$45 billion by 1995. By the mid 1980s, aid *to* Africa was only slightly greater than service payments *from* it (see Table 5). The top recipients are concentrated in Eastern Africa: Kenya, Tanzania, Mozambique, Sudan and Ethiopia in order of magnitude (just over to just under $1 billion each p.a.), with Mozambique (65%) and Tanzania (30%) receiving the highest proportion of GNP.

Yet debt, however accumulated and calculated, is not an unmitigated disaster (Herbst, 1990b). Not only is it forcing African states to adjust in realistic directions, it is also leading to new forms of investment: debt-equity as well as -ecology swaps and debt-discounting (up to 75%), especially for export-oriented projects, such as agricultural commodities, value-added processing and tourism. Nowadays, such package deals typically involve a consortium consisting of investment insurance agencies (e.g. OPIC and ECGD), development agencies (e.g. CDC), multilateral banks (e.g. IBRD and ADB), national private and state capitals, NGOs (e.g. WWF and OXFAM) and international banks as well as resilient multinational companies. The only fate worse than exploitation is not receiving any interest, assistance or investment from outside!

Box 21
Gold Rush: Minerals in the Informal Sector

The continent has a long history of small-scale mining, from the bronze of Benin to the copper of Central Africa. But contemporary economic pressures have encouraged the revival and popularisation of diamond and gold mining and panning by individuals or cooperatives, the former concentrated around Sierra Leone, the latter in Zimbabwe. Considerable incomes, networks and risks are involved as this 'currency' passes hands and crosses borders, in addition to cave-ins or floodings of poorly engineered and maintained mines. In Zimbabwe in the late 1980s, for example, it was estimated that Z$45 million of gold was being informally mined annually by some 50,000 people, 80% of whom were women and children. They have even organised themselves into a Small-Scale Miners' Association to change perceptions and treatment of small-scale miners and panners. Yet, despite adjustment conditionalities, governments and corporations remain ambivalent about such informal mining, seeing it as threatening to their revenue bases and oligopoly rents, respectively. Nevertheless, some elements of the 'wild west' prevail in such Africanised pioneer mining ventures.

also vary among presidencies and periods. But, in general, the tendency towards intolerance remains substantial, exacerbating debt as well as repression because of the high forex content in security expenditures other than labour. Despite Bank/Fund advocacy of accountablility, democracy, transparency etc. for the continent, in most individual cases they have turned a blind eye to repression, hiding behind 'non-interference' in members' national affairs, notwithstanding the structural 'intervention' of adjustment conditionalities, which may now be extended to include the criterion of declining military expenditures (UNDP, 1991: 83).

Indeed, there have been relatively few African states which have encouraged participation of either a traditional-formal democracy or a non-traditional-informal kind: Botswana, the Gambia, Mauritius and Senegal have been notable exceptions to the rule (see Map 3 and Table 2). Conversely, unlike other parts of the Third World, there have been relatively few truly authoritarian and arbitrary regimes: Ethiopia under Mengistu, Somalia under Barre, Uganda under Obote II, Zaire under Mobutu (Jackson and Rosberg, 1982a and b). In the mid 1970s, the continent suffered Amin in Uganda, Bokasa in the Central African 'Empire' and Nguema in Equatorial Guinea, but these have all been removed, bequeathing to successor regimes unenviable challenges of reconstruction and reconciliation as well as adjustment. Paternalistic dictatorships like those of Banda in Malawi and Kenyatta and now Moi in Kenya maintain themselves through institutionalised repression which only occasionally leads to physical elimination. Yet, in the majority of African political economies, arbitrary arrest and customary censorship prevail with intelligence operatives always curious about conversations and organisations. Few political cultures on the continent exhibit the resilience even independence of that in Nigeria, in which occasional imprisonment and harassment fail to suppress media or intelligentsia (see Box 1).

The expansion of informal, popular participation may come to limit the scope of official supervision. But regular and continuing reports on the confinement of academics, activists, analysts, ministers, students and unionists by Africa Watch, Amnesty International and Index on Censorship (1989) are indicative of state preoccupations. Regimes have been particularly sensitive to any criticism about their adjustment programmes, conditionalities and performances despite the new linkage being made by the IFIs and bilaterals between economic and political liberalisation, and now demilitarisation. Until the role of law – especially freedom to organise and articulate and fearlessness of arbitrary arrest or assassination – and regular elections prevail, as a minimum, Africa will be neither democratic nor developed. And its capitalism as well as pluralism will be less productive and sustainable.

The apparent trend towards official, national 'multipartyism' should not be exaggerated, then. Economic liberalisation does indeed have profound political and social implications, well beyond the purview of the Bank and Fund (Campbell and Loxley, 1989; Mosley, Harrigan and Toye, 1991; Nelson, 1989, 1990). Symbolic of the dangers and delusions of superficial approaches to and acceptance of Africa's leaders' commitment to democracy was Mobutu's continued oppression through the initial years of the 1990s despite his apparent commitment to a multi-party regime. Some 60 opposition parties may have been established yet their leaderships were harassed and the incumbent regime resisted allowing a national conference to facilitate the transition despite extreme economic difficulties. Thus most human rights groups still accuse the Mobutu security apparatus of arbitrary arrests, torture, banishment etc. So the seeming change of heart of hitherto oppressive one-party or -person states is in large measure a function of transformations in Eastern Europe and increasingly explicit political as well as economic conditionalities of multi- and bi-lateral donors: a novel form of 'counter-revolutionary' preemptive action. To be sure, in many parts of the continent, civil societies have come to feel more empowered because of the new transnational legitimacy of human rights and NGOs. But even formal pluralism would not mean sustainable democracy throughout Africa's fifty-odd territories in the foreseeable future (see Map 2).

Related to domestic and developmental pressures is the possible revival of *self-reliance*, by default if not design, for post- or late-adjustment Africa. Collective as well as national forms of self-reliance are likely to become attractive once again in the 1990s to compensate for difficulties in South–North exchange. Notwithstanding the diversions of national adjustments which encourage global rather than regional externalisation, South–South trade – informal as well as formal – has become more important in the 1980s as the South has become less homogeneous. There are now greater complementarities to be exploited, particularly by the NICs of the South in sectors like manufactures, technology and services (Carlsson and Shaw, 1988). Encouraged by the South Commission (1990) and Group of 15, South–South potentials are once again being considered. This is so in particular because of a) the relative success of

Box 22
Uganda: Rehabilitation Despite Conditionalities

The 'pearl of Africa' has gone through twenty troubled years following the Amin coup of 1971 and the Obote II holocaust in the early 1980s. Uganda constitutes a cautionary tale of unworkable colonial legacy and unstable authoritarian rule. It may yet represent an optimistic story of indigenous transition and transformation. Given its range of natural resources, it may come by the mid 1990s to achieve national and personal standards of living approaching those of the late 1970s, 25 years earlier; that is, if intense devaluations and deflations do not destroy both economy and polity meanwhile.

Uganda is a mixed lesson of oppressive, genocidal regimes, notoriously those of Idi Amin, (1971–9) and Milton Obote (1980–5) in which a viable, relatively integrated and self-sufficient political economy with an extensive physical and administrative infrastructure was run down to a survival, informal economy in which saving was negative. But it is also the first and most unequivocal instance thus far of an indigenous guerrilla army undermining and overthrowing an unacceptable regime with minimal external assistance – from the Tanzania People's Defence Force only – the first of a 'second wave' of truly postcolonial states? The Museveni government is populist, democratic and determined, yet the beneficiary of minimal foreign assistance and investment, despite the domestic war and structural adjustment. The rehabilitation of roads, hospitals, industries, plantations and administration proceeds, but despite satisfying adjustment terms – political as well as economic – little ODA or NGO aid has been committed to date. Uganda could yet become a pearl again, but foreign capital, exchange and recognition would facilitate and accelerate the process: its unique indigenous political transformation and democratic development deserve better, especially as it may represent one path towards a sustainable political economy (see Table 2 and Chapters 3 and 4).

new forms of such regionalism in, say, ASEAN and SAARC; and b) the constraints on South–North exchange given NIDL and NIDP, particularly the recession and disorganisation on the OECD, diversions first to the Pacific Rim and now to Eastern Europe and the Middle East, setbacks to GATT's 'Uruguay Round' of global trade liberalisation negotiations, and the disappointments of structural adjustment contracts and promises (Hardy, 1990: 2–5).

Self-reliance in the 1990s draws ideological and political strength from the latest reformulation of the dependency perspective – the South Commission's *Challenge to the South* (1990) – as well as from compatible ECA, UNDP and UNICEF reports. In a period in which the terms of trade continue exponentially to worsen for the South – according to *The Economist* (13 April 1991: 85) the commodity-price index had fallen to 50% below its recent 1988 peak – dependency and self-reliance may yet have another day, particularly if they can be appropriately revisionist. *Collective self-reliance* is clearly essential in a world dominated by issues arising from the NIDL and NIDP which largely exclude Africa: the potentials of South–South given the deficiencies and disappointments of South–North and the pressures of regionalisation in the world economy, such as the North American (trilateral?) free trade area and the EC (of the 12, 14, or 18?) 1992, which necessitate initiatives like the belated and statist African Economic Community (see Appendix). *National self-reliance* is likewise an imperative if some development is to be achieved and sustained because orthodox packages are overly economistic and standardised. Finally, and more controversially, *local self-reliance* is inevitable, particularly in the larger countries, given the declining resources and reach of most African states because of both adjustment conditionalities and the realities of recession: if urban and rural communities and NGOs do not fill the space vacated then BHN will be further retarded. Whether these three levels of self-reliance can be rendered compatible in policy, political and programmatic terms is still problematic; one of the challenges confronting the continent as the twenty-first century approaches (see Table 8).

In short, reflective of the revisionist period and mood, *who, what and why will define civil society, democracy and development in Africa at the start of the next century?* I am encouraged that such a question can at least be posed when in previous decades responses were taken for granted: the African ('socialist') project. In particular, given the resilience of the state, its subjection and reaction to continuous

Box 23
Africa's Last Colony: the Independence of Namibia, 1990

The turn of the decade marked the formal 'independence' of the continent's final colony – the distinctive case of Namibia – which had been *de facto* a South African ward or province since the First World War. Its accession to and the incidence of independence are largely a function of diplomatic and strategic coincidence: South Africa's defeats in Southern Angola and debt conditionalities combined with shifts in super-power leaders and relations in the late 1980s; i.e. NIDL and NIDP. Thus this 'side-show' of South African struggles became something of a show-piece for UN involvement ten years after Resolution 435 had been first approved. Yet Namibia is a classic case of dependence on South Africa (for imports and transit) and the global political economy (for exports and, now, assistance); it has minimal manufacturing and exists on revenues from uranium, diamonds and tourism. Although relatively underpopulated (1.5 million people in over 800,000 square kms) and affluent ($1,500 GNP p.a. but very unevenly distributed), Namibia is most vulnerable ecologically as well as politically and economically: its land, water and oceans have been exploited by others rather than by indigenous populations. Although it did receive some external assistance at independence to substitute for South African support and presence, it has immediately become overshadowed again by the protracted progress of negotiation and transition to a 'new' South Africa (Swatuk and Shaw, 1991).

Namibia, like Botswana, may become one of Africa's few success stories, based on mineral resources and conservative decisions, reinforced by immediate adjustment conditionalities; or it could become another Lesotho or Zambia, with depleted mineral or natural resources. It can hardly become another Zimbabwe as it lacks the range of resources, both natural and technical, and did not have an extended period either of external economic sanctions or of internal guerrilla struggles. And its 40,000 returnees were not as educated or skilled as Zimbabwe's.

Table 8 Women's Comparative Rank According to Alternative Indexes

Country	Index of Women's Advancement (IWA) Rank	Human Development Index (HDI) Rank	Under 5 Mortality Rate (U5MR) Rank	Purchasing Power Parity (PPP$) Rank	Composite[a] Rank
Mauritius	38	34	26	40	34
Lesotho	39	59	69	54	55
Botswana	42	54	50	43	50
South Africa	43	44	54	24	38
Tanzania	45	76	83	87	75
Tunisia	46	52	43	37	45
Gabon	47	64	81	46	61
Cameroon	48	70	75	56	64
Zimbabwe	56	60	52	59	58
Kenya	61	69	62	66	67
Mozambique	63	96	106	–	92
Congo, Peoples Rep	64	77	63	68	69
Côte d'Ivoire	66	78	71	60	71
Senegal	68	91	87	62	78
Burundi	69	98	91	86	90
Algeria	70	55	60	39	57
Rwanda	72	88	92	78	86
Liberia	74	84	93	72	82
Madagascar	75	73	85	76	79
Egypt, Arab Rep.	77	66	56	58	66
Benin	78	99	76	75	84
Morocco	79	67	64	51	68
Libya	80	45	65	–	65
Togo	82	83	74	73	80
Uganda	83	82	80	80	83
Zaire	84	89	68	88	85
Ghana	85	80	72	81	81
Zambia	86	68	67	71	76
Burkina Faso	88	106	100	–	104
Nigeria	89	86	82	74	87
Central Afr. Rep	91	93	97	77	93
Sudan	92	94	84	69	89
Niger	94	108	98	85	100
Malawi	95	95	102	83	99
Somalia	96	102	95	–	103
Ethiopia	98	90	99	84	97
Guinea	99	103	101	–	106
Sierra Leone	100	105	103	82	102
Mauritania	101	101	94	65	95
Mali	103	107	104	79	105
Chad	105	104	96	–	107

Source: Krishna Ahooja-Patel, 'Gender Distance among Countries', Halifax (August 1991).

[a] Based on the four indices in this table.

democratic pressures are crucial: the democratic processes of accountability, responsibility, transparency etc. I have suggested that unless
ecological, gender, and informal sector elements are recognised and
prioritised in any foreseeable democratic formulation then sustainable development will remain elusive because the paradigm of adjustment will otherwise prevail as it did throughout the lost decade of the
1980s (cf. Box 24). Hence the imperative of truly popular and radical
intellectual and political struggles and alternatives – revisionist radicalism – which democratic pressures facilitate and require, but which
authoritarian and corporatist regime machinations are still always
ready to repress: *the ongoing dialectics of African adjustment into the
next century*.

Box 24
Success Stories: For Whom? For How Long?

Notwithstanding the prevalence of 'Afro-pessimism', the state of
the continent is not just unmitigated disaster or depression.
'Success stories' like Botswana, established economies like Zimbabwe, export enclaves like Mauritius, and peasant societies like
Malawi stand in stark contrast to conflict and crisis in neighbouring states like Angola, Mozambique, Zaire and Zambia (see
Tables 1 and 3). Yet the cyclical nature of the global economy
does provide cautionary tales. In the 1950s, Ghana was richer
than South Korea, now a NIC; and, also in the 1950s, Angola
and Zambia both had per capita incomes higher than those in
Zimbabwe. Then Zimbabweans went north to shop; now Zam-
bians travel to Harare or Francistown to buy goods which are
scarce and expensive in Lusaka or Ndola. Botswana's current
booming diamond (and copper and soda ash) economy might
reflect on Zambia's brief copper booms in the mid 1950s and
early 1970s, or Nigeria's oil boom in the late 1970s: construction
and financial companies and employees move readily from boom
to boom, from Nigeria to Botswana, for example, and onto
post-war Kuwait. Similarly, as indicated in Boxes 6 and 7, many
African(ist) academics moved in the 1980s southwards from
Central and West Africa down to Zimbabwe and South Africa;
but in the 1990s they may have to move on, to Europe and North
America: the ultimate 'exit' option.

In Africa as elsewhere, infrastructural investment should be built to last and must be well maintained given the relentless environment. And opportunities to diversify have to be seized; sage advisors *did* caution against over-reliance on one, declining commodity, such as Ghana's cocoa and Zambia's copper. Informal exchange invariably moves in opposite directions once a boom has passed, whether the Bank so recognises shifting economic fortunes or not; i.e. popular appreciation of local effects of NIDL as well as adjustment conditionalities . . . and opportunities!

Box 25
Eritrea, 1993: protracted struggle to recapture independence

The Eritrean People's Liberation Front finally won the 30-year independence war for its 3.5 million people in May 1991 when it captured the capital, Asmara, coinciding with the overthrow of Mengistu in the 'imperial' Ethiopian capital of Addis Ababa. The Provisional Government anticipates a referendum by April 1993, followed by formal independence involving some economic and transit arrangements with any post-Amarhic regimes in the rest of Ethiopia. Thus the shame of four decades of Abyssinian/African 'colonial' rule will be eliminated in the Horn. Given Eritrea's distinct history, ecology and society, the post-independence regime is likely to be multi-ethnic and social democratic, encouraging private enterprise by both local and diasporic Eritreans: reflections of political pluralism and economic liberalisation. The careful Eritrean approach to autonomy constitutes something of a model for other aspiring states in post-Cold War Africa, where the old taboo on not altering inherited boundaries set by the Berlin Conference of the mid-1880s seems finally to be being transcended. Certainly the admission of such a new regime as Eritrea into the OAU will set something of a precedent. Regional economic relations should be facilitated by peace providing some political understandings and arrangements are made. Given judicious policies, Eritrea has considerable agricultural, coastal, ecological and entrepreneurial resources and promise if initial physical and psychological reconstruction is rapid and sustained.

Appendix

Organisation of African Unity

Treaty Establishing the African Economic Community (June 1991)

TABLE OF CONTENTS

Articles

179

182   *Appendix*

Chapter II

Establishment, Principles, Objectives, General Undertaking and Modalities

Article 2

Establishment of the Community

The High Contracting Parties *hereby establish among themselves an African Economic Community. . . .*

Article 3

Principles

The High Contracting Parties, *in pursuit of the objectives stated in Article 4, of this Treaty solemnly affirm and declare their adherence to the following principles:*

(a) *equality and inter-dependence of Member States;*
(b) *solidarity and collective self-reliance;*
(c) *inter-State cooperation, harmonisation of policies and integration of programmes;*
(d) *promotion of harmonious development of economic activities among Member States;*
(e) *observance of the legal system of the Community;*
(f) *peaceful settlement of disputes among Member States, active cooperation between neighbouring countries and promotion of a peaceful environment as a pre-requisite for economic development;*
(g) *recognition, promotion and protection of human and peoples' rights in accordance with the provisions of the African Charter on Human and Peoples' Rights; and*
(h) *accountability, economic justice and popular participation in development.*

Article 4

Objectives

1. *The objectives of the Community shall be:*

(a) *to promote economic, social and cultural development and the integration of African economies in order to increase economic self-reliance and promote an endogenous and self-sustained development;*

(b) to establish, on a continental scale, a framework for the development, mobilisation and utilisation of the human and material resources of Africa in order to achieve a self-reliant development;

(c) to promote cooperation in all fields of human endeavour in order to raise the standard of living of African peoples, and maintain and enhance economic stability, foster close and peaceful relations among Member States and contribute to the progress, development and the economic integration of the Continent; and

(d) to coordinate and harmonise policies among existing and future economic communities in order to foster the gradual establishment of the Community.

2. *In order to promote the attainment of the objectives of the Community as set out in paragraph I of this Article, and in accordance with the relevant provisions of this Treaty, the Community shall, by stages, ensure:*

(a) the strengthening of existing regional economic communities and the establishment of other communities where they do not exist;

(b) the conclusion of agreements aimed at harmonising and coordinating policies among existing and future sub-regional and regional economic communities;

(c) the promotion and strengthening of joint investment programmes in the production and trade of major products and inputs within the framework of collective self-reliance;

(d) the liberalisation of trade through the abolition, among Member States, of Customs Duties levied on imports and exports and the abolition, among Member States, of Non-Tariff Barriers in order to establish a free trade area at the level of each regional economic community;

(e) the harmonisation of national policies in order to promote Community activities, particularly in the fields of agriculture, industry, transport and communications, energy, natural resources, trade, money and finance, human resources, education, culture, science and technology;

(f) the adoption of a common trade policy vis-à-vis third States;

(g) the establishment and maintenance of a common external tariff;

(h) the establishment of a common market;

(i) the gradual removal, among Member States, of obstacles to the free movement of persons, goods, services and capital and the right of residence and establishment;

(j) the establishment of a Community Solidarity, Development and Compensation Fund;

(k) the granting of special treatment to Member States classified as least developed countries and the adoption of special measures in favour of land-locked, semi-land-locked and island countries;

(l) the harmonisation and rationalisation of the activities of existing African multi-national institutions and the establishment of such institutions, as and when necessary, with a view to their possible transformation into organs of the Community;

(m) the establishment of appropriate organs for trade in agricultural and cultural products, minerals, metals, and manufactured and semi-manufactured goods within the Community;

(n) the establishment of contacts and the promotion of information flow among trading organizations such as State commercial enterprises, export promotion and marketing bodies, chambers of commerce, associations of businessmen, and business and advertising agencies;

(o) the harmonisation and coordination of environmental protection policies; and

(p) any other activity that Member States may decide to undertake jointly with a view to attaining the objectives of the Community.

Article 5

General Undertakings

1. Member States undertake to create favourable conditions for the development of the Community and the attainment of its objectives, particularly by harmonising their strategies and policies. They shall refrain from any unilateral action that may hinder the attainment of the said objectives.

2. Each Member State shall, in accordance with its constitutional procedures, take all necessary measures to ensure the enactment and dissemination of such legislation as may be necessary for the implementation of the provisions of this Treaty.

3. Any Member State which persistently fails to honour its general undertakings under this Treaty or fails to abide by the decisions or regulations of the Community may be subjected to sanctions by the Assembly upon the recommendation of the Council. Such sanctions may include the suspension of the rights and privileges of membership and may be lifted by the Assembly upon the recommendation of the Council.

Article 6

Modalities for the Establishment of the Community

1. The Community shall be established gradually in six (6) stages of variable duration over a transitional period not exceeding thirty-four (34) years.

2. At each such stage, specific activities shall be assigned and implemented concurrently as follows:

(a) First Stage:
Strengthening of existing regional economic communities and, within a period not exceeding five (5) years from the date of entry into force of this Treaty, establishing economic communities in regions where they do not exist;

(b) Second Stage:
  (i) *at the level of each regional economic community and within a period not exceeding eight (8) years, stabilising Tariff Barriers and Non-Tariff Barriers, Customs Duties and internal taxes existing at the date of entry into force of this Treaty; there shall also be prepared and adopted studies to determine the time-table for the gradual removal of Tariff Barriers and Non-Tariff Barriers to regional and intra-Community trade and for the gradual harmonisation of Customs Duties in relation to third States;*
  (ii) *strengthening of sectoral integration at the regional and continental levels in all areas of activity particularly in the fields of trade, agriculture, money and finance, transport and communications, industry and energy; and*
  (iii) *coordination and harmonisation of activities among the existing and future economic communities.*

(c) Third Stage:
  At the level of each regional economic community and within a period not exceeding ten (10) years, establishment of a Free Trade Area through the observance of the time-table for the gradual removal of Tariff Barriers and Non-Tariff Barriers to intra-community trade and the establishment of a Customs Union by means of adopting a common external tariff.

(d) Fourth Stage:
  Within a period not exceeding two (2) years, coordination and harmonisation of tariff and non-tariff systems among the various regional economic communities with a view to establishing a Customs Union at the continental level by means of adopting a common external tariff.

(e) Fifth Stage:
  Within a period not exceeding four (4) years, establishment of an African Common Market through:
  (i) *the adoption of a common policy in several areas such as agriculture, transport and communications, industry, energy and scientific research;*
  (ii) *the harmonisation of monetary, financial and fiscal policies;*
  (iii) *the application of the principle of free movement of persons as well as the provisions herein regarding the rights of residence and establishment; and*
  (iv) *constituting the proper resources of the Community as provided for in paragraph 2 of Article 82 of this Treaty.*

(f) Sixth Stage:
  Within a period not exceeding five (5) years:
  (i) *consolidating and strengthening of the structure of the African Common Market, through including the free movement of people, goods, capital and services, as well as, the provisions herein regarding the rights of residence and establishment;*
  (ii) *integration of all the sectors namely economic, political, social and cultural; establishment of a single domestic market and a Pan-African Economic and Monetary Union;*
  (iii) *implementation of the final stage for the setting up of an African*

Monetary Union, the establishment of a single African Central Bank and the creation of a single African Currency;

(iv) *implementation of the final stage for the setting up of the structure of the Pan-African Parliament and election of its members by continental universal suffrage;*

(v) *implementation of the final stage for the harmonisation and coordination process of the activities of regional economic communities;*

(vi) *implementation of the final stage for the setting up of the structures of African multi-national enterprises in all sectors; and*

(vii) *implementation of the final stage for the setting up of the structures of the executive organs of the Community.*

3. *All measures envisaged under this Treaty for the promotion of a harmonious and balanced development among Member States, particularly, those relating to the formulation of multi-national projects and programmes, shall be implemented concurrently within the time period specified for the attainment of the objectives of the various stages outlined in paragraph 2 of this Article.*

4. *The transition from one stage to another shall be determined when the specific objectives set in this Treaty or pronounced by the Assembly for a particular stage, are implemented and all commitments fulfilled. The Assembly, on the recommendation of the Council, shall confirm that the objectives to a particular stage have been attained and shall approve the transition to the next stage.*

5. *Notwithstanding the provisions of the preceding paragraph, the cumulative transitional period shall not exceed forty (40) years from the date of entry into force of this Treaty.*

Chapter III

Organs of the Community

Article 7

Organs

1. *The organs of the Community shall be:*

(a) *the Assembly of Heads of State and Government;*
(b) *the Council of Ministers;*
(c) *the Pan-African Parliament;*
(d) *the Economic and Social Commission;*

(e) *the Court of Justice;*
(f) *the General Secretariat; and*
(g) *the Specialised Technical Committees.*

2. *The Organs of the Community shall perform their duties and act within the limits of the powers conferred on them by this Treaty.*

Chapter IV

Regional Economic Communities

Article 28

Strengthening of Regional Economic Communities

1. *During the first stage, Member States undertake to strengthen the existing regional economic communities and to establish new communities where they do not exist in order to ensure the gradual establishment of the Community.*

2. *Member States shall take all necessary measures aimed at progressively promoting increasingly closer cooperation among the communities, particularly through coordination and harmonisation of their activities in all fields or sectors in order to ensure the realisation of the objectives of the Community.*

Chapter V

Customs Union and Liberalisation of Trade

Article 29

Customs Union

Member States of each regional economic community agree to progressively establish among them during a transitional period specified in Article 6 of this Treaty, a Customs Union involving:

(a) *the elimination, among Member States of each regional economic community, of customs duties, quota restrictions, other restrictions or prohibitions and administrative trade barriers, as well as all other non-tariff barriers; and*
(b) *the adoption by Member States of a common external customs tariff.*

Article 30

Elimination of Customs Duties among Member States of Regional Economic Communities

1. *During the second stage, Member States of each regional economic community shall refrain from establishing among themselves any new customs duties and from increasing those that apply in their mutual trade relations.*

2. *During the third stage, Member States shall progressively reduce and eliminate finally among themselves, at the level of each regional economic community, customs duties in accordance with such programme and modalities as shall be determined by each regional economic community.*

3. *During each stage, the Assembly, on the recommendation of the Council, shall take the necessary measures with a view to coordinating and harmonising the activities of the regional economic communities relating to the elimination of customs duties among Member States.*

Article 31

Elimination of Non-Tariff Barriers to Intra-Community Trade

1. *At the level of each regional economic community and subject to the provisions of the Treaty, each Member State shall, upon the entry into force of this Treaty, progressively relax and ultimately remove quota restrictions, and all other non-tariff barriers and prohibitions which apply to exports to that State, of goods originating in the other Member States, at the latest, by the end of the third stage and in accordance with paragraph 2 of this Article. Except as otherwise provided or permitted by this Treaty, each Member State shall thereafter refrain from imposing any further restrictions or prohibitions on such goods.*

2. *Subject to the provisions of this Treaty, each regional economic community shall adopt a programme for the progressive relaxation and ultimate elimination, at the latest by the end of the third stage, of all quota restrictions and prohibitions and all other non-tariff barriers that apply in a Member State, to imports originating in the other Member States; it being understood that each regional economic community may subsequently decide that all quota restrictions, other restrictions and prohibitions be relaxed or removed within a shorter period than that prescribed in this paragraph.*

3. *The arrangements governing restrictions, prohibitions, quota restrictions, dumping subsidies and discriminatory practices shall be the subject of a Protocol concerning Non-Tariff Trade Barriers.*

Article 32

Establishment of a Common External Customs Tariff

1. *During the third stage, Member States shall, at the level of each regional economic community, agree to the gradual establishment of a common external customs tariff applicable to goods originating from third States and imported into Member States.*

2. *During the fourth stage, regional economic communities shall, in accordance with a programme drawn up by them, eliminate differences between their respective external customs tariffs.*

3. *During the fourth stage the Council shall propose to the Assembly the adoption, at Community level, of a common customs and statistical nomenclature for all Member States.*

Article 33

System of Intra-Community Trade

1. *At the end of the third stage, no Member State shall, at the level of each regional economic community, levy customs duties on goods originating in one Member State and imported into another Member State. The same prohibition shall apply to goods originating from third States which are in free circulation in Member States and are imported from one Member State into another.*

2. *The definition of the notion of products originating in Member States and the rules governing goods originating in a third States and which are in free circulation in Member States shall be governed by a Protocol concerning the Rules of Origin.*

3. *Goods originating from third States shall be considered to be in free circulation in a Member State if (i) the import formalities relating thereto have been complied with, (ii) customs duties have been paid thereon in that Member State, and (iii) they have not benefitted from a partial or total exemption from such customs duties.*

4. *Member States undertake not to adopt legislation implying direct or indirect discrimination against identical or similar products originating from another Member State.*

Article 34

Internal Taxes

1. *During the third stage, Member States shall not levy, directly or indirectly on goods originating from Member State and imported into any Member State, internal taxes in excess of those levied on similar domestic products.*

2. *Member States, at the level of each regional economic community, shall progressively eliminate any internal taxes levied for the protection of domestic products. Whereby virtue of obligations assumed under a prior agreement signed by a Member State, that Member State is unable to comply with this Article, it shall notify the Council of this fact and shall not extend or renew such agreement when it expires.*

Article 35

Exceptions and Safeguard Clauses

1. *Notwithstanding the provisions of Articles 30 and 31 of this Treaty, any Member State. having made its intention known to the Secretariat of the Community which shall inform Member States thereof, may impose or continue to impose restrictions or prohibitions affecting:*

(a) *the application of security laws and regulations;*
(b) *the control of arms, ammunitions and other military items and equipment;*
(c) *the protection of human, animal or plant health or life, or the protection of public morality;*
(d) *export of strategic minerals and precious stones;*
(e) *the protection of national treasures of artistic or archaeological value or the protection of industrial, commercial and intellectual property;*
(f) *the control of hazardous wastes, nuclear materials, radioactive products or any other material used in the development or exploitation of nuclear energy;*
(g) *protection of infant industries;*
(h) *the control of strategic product; and*
(i) *goods imported from a third country to which a Member State applies total prohibition relating to country of origin.*

2. *The prohibitions or restrictions referred to in paragraph 1 of this Article shall in no case be used as a means of arbitrary discrimination or a disguised restriction on trade between Member States.*

3. *Where a Member State encounters balance-of-payments difficulties arising from the application of the provisions of this Chapter, that Member State may be allowed by the competent organ of the Community, provided that it has taken all appropriate reasonable steps to overcome the difficulties, to impose,*

for the sole purpose of overcoming such difficulties, quantitative or similar restrictions or prohibitions on goods originating in the other Member States for such period as shall be determined by the competent organ of the Community.

4. *For the purpose of protecting an infant or strategic industry, a Member State may be allowed by the competent organ of the Community, provided it has taken all appropriate reasonable steps to protect such industry, to impose, for the sole purpose of protecting such industry, quantitative or similar restrictions or prohibitions, on similar goods originating in the other Member States for such period as shall be determined by the competent organ of the Community.*

5. *Where the imports of a particular product by a Member State from another Member State increase in a way that causes, or is likely to cause, serious damage to the economy of the importing states, the latter may be allowed by the competent organ of the Community to apply safeguard measures for a specified period.*

6. *The Council shall keep under regular review the operation of any quantitative or similar restrictions or prohibitions imposed pursuant to paragraphs 1, 3, and 4 of this Article and shall take appropriate action in this connection. It shall submit, each year, to the Assembly, a report on the aforementioned matters.*

Article 36

Dumping

1. *Member States shall prohibit the practice of 'dumping' within the Community.*

2. *For the purposes of this Article, 'dumping' shall mean the transfer of goods originating from a Member State to another Member State for them to be sold:*

   (a) *at a price lower than the usual price offered for similar goods in the Member State from which those goods originate, due account being taken of the difference in conditions of sale, taxation, transport expenses and any other factor affecting the comparison of prices;*
   (b) *in conditions likely to prejudice the manufacture of similar goods in the Member State.*

Article 37

Most Favoured Nation Treatment

1. *Member States shall accord one another, in relation to intra-community trade, the most-favoured-nation treatment. In no case shall tariff concessions*

*granted to a third State pursuant to an agreement with a Member State be more
favourable than those applicable pursuant of this Treaty.*

2. *The text of the agreements referred to in paragraph 1 of this Article shall be
forwarded by the Member States parties thereto, through the Secretary-
General, to all the other Member States for their information.*

3. *No agreement between a Member State and a third State, under which tariff
concessions are granted, shall be incompatible with the obligations arising out
of this Treaty.*

Article 38

Re-export of Goods and Intra-Community Transit Facilities

1. *During the third stage, Member States shall facilitate the re-export of goods
among them in accordance with the Protocol concerning the Re-export of
Goods.*

2. *Member States shall grant one another freedom of transit through their
territories to goods proceeding to or coming from another Member State in
accordance with the Protocol concerning Intra-Community Transit and Transit Facilities and in accordance with the provisions of any Intra-Community
Agreements to be concluded.*

Article 39

Customs Cooperation and Administration

*Member States shall, in accordance with the Protocol concerning Customs
Cooperation, take all necessary measures for harmonising and standardising
their customs regulations and procedures in such a manner as shall be
appropriate for ensuring the effective implementation of the provisions of this
Chapter and facilitating the movement of goods and services across their
frontiers.*

Article 40

Trade Documents and Procedures

*For the purpose of facilitating intra-community trade in goods and services,
Member States shall simplify and harmonise their trade documents and proce-
dures in accordance with the Protocol concerning the Simplification and
Harmonisation of Trade Documents and Procedures.*

Article 41

Diversion of Trade arising from Barter or Compensatory Exchange Agreement

1. *If, as a result of a barter or compensatory exchange agreement relating to a specific category of goods concluded between a Member State or a person of the said Member State, on the one hand, and a third State or person of the said third State, on the other, there is substantial diversion of trade in favour of goods imported under such agreement and to the detriment of similar goods of the same category imported from and manufactured in any Member State, the Member State importing such goods shall take effective steps to correct the diversion.*

2. *In order to determine whether a diversion of trade has occurred in a specific category of goods within the meaning of this Article, consideration shall be given to all the relevant trade statistics and other data available on such category of goods for the six-month period preceding a complaint from an affected Member State concerning diversion of trade, and for an average of two comparable six-month periods during the twenty-four (24) months preceding the first importation of goods under the barter agreement or compensatory exchange agreement.*

3. *The Secretary-General shall refer the matter to the Council for consideration and submission to the Assembly for decision.*

Article 42

Trade Promotion

1. *In order to attain the objectives of the Community set out in sub-paragraph 2 (m) Article 4 of this Treaty, Member States agree to undertake the trade promotion activities stated below in the following areas:*

(a) **Intra-Community Trade**
   (i) *promote the use of the Community's local materials, intermediate goods and inputs, as well as finished products originating within the Community;*
   (ii) *adopt the 'All-Africa Trade Fair of the OAU', as an instrument of the Community trade promotion;*
   (iii) *participate in the periodic fairs organised under the auspices of the 'All-Africa Trade Fair of the OAU', sectoral trade fairs, regional trade fairs and other trade promotion activities of the Community;*
   (iv) *develop an intra-community trade information network, linking the computerised trade information systems of existing and future regional economic communities and individual Member States of the Community; and*

    (v) *with the assistance of the Secretariat, study the supply and demand patterns in Member States and disseminate the findings thereon with the Community.*

  (b) **South–South Trade**
    (i) *promote the diversification of Africa's markets, and the marketing of Community products;*
    (ii) *participate in extra-community trade fairs, in particular, within the context of South–South Cooperation; and*
    (iii) *participate in extra-community trade and investment fora.*

  (c) **North–South Trade**
    (i) *promote better terms of trade for African commodities and improve market access for Community products;*
    (ii) *participate as a group in international negotiations within the framework of GATT and UNCTAD and other trade-related negotiating fora.*

2. *The modalities of organising trade promotion activities and trade information systems of the Community shall be governed by a Protocol concerning Trade Promotion.*

Chapter VI

Free Movement of Persons, Rights of Residence and Establishment

Article 43

General Provisions

1. *Member States agree to adopt, individually, at bilateral or regional levels, the necessary measures, in order to achieve progressively the free movement of persons, and to ensure the enjoyment of the right of residence and the right of establishment by their nationals within the Community.*

2. *For this purpose, Member States agree to conclude a Protocol on the Free Movement of Persons, Right of Residence and Right of Establishment.*

Chapter VII

Money, Finance and Payments

Article 44

Monetary, Financial and Payment Policies

1. *In accordance with the relevant Protocols, Member States shall, within a time-table to be determined by the Assembly, harmonise their monetary, financial and payments policies, in order to boost intra-Community trade in goods and services, to further the attainment of objectives of the Community and to enhance monetary and financial cooperation among Member States.*

2. *To this end, Member States shall:*

  (a) *use their national currencies in the settlement of commercial and financial transactions in order to reduce the use of external currencies in such transactions;*
  (b) *establish appropriate mechanisms for setting up multilateral payments systems;*
  (c) *consult regularly among themselves on monetary and financial matters;*
  (d) *promote the creation of national, regional and sub-regional money markets, through the coordinated establishment of stock exchanges and harmonising legal texts regulating existing stock exchanges with a view to making them more effective;*
  (e) *cooperate in an effective manner in the fields of insurance and banking;*
  (f) *further the liberalisation of payments and the elimination of payment restrictions, if any, among them and promote the integration of all existing payments and clearing mechanisms among the different regions into an African Clearing and Payments House; and*
  (g) *establish an African Monetary Union through the harmonisation of regional monetary zones.*

Article 45

Movement of Capital

1. *Member States shall ensure the free movement of capital within the Community through the elimination of restrictions on the transfer of capital funds between Member States in accordance with a time-table to be determined by the Council.*

2. *The capital referred to in paragraph I of this Article is that of Member States or persons of Member States.*

3. *The Assembly, having regard to the development objectives of national, regional and continental plans, and upon the recommendation of the Commission and after the approval of the Council acting on the recommendation of the Commission, shall prescribe the conditions for the movement within the Community of the capital funds other than those referred to in paragraph (2) of this Article.*

4. *For the purpose of regulating the movement of capital between Member States and Third States, the Assembly, upon the approval of the Council, acting on the recommendation of the Commission, shall take steps aimed at coordinating progressively the national and regional exchange control policies.*

References

Achebe, Chinua *et al.* (1990), *Beyond Hunger in Africa: Conventional Wisdom and an African Vision* (London: James Currey).

Adedeji, Adebeyo (1990), 'The African Challenges in the 1990s: New Perspectives for Development', *Indian Journal of Social Science*, 3: 255–69.

—— and Timothy M. Shaw (eds) (1985), *Economic Crisis in Africa* (Boulder, Col.: Lynne Rienner).

'Africa in a New World Order' (1991), *Review of African Political Economy*, 50, March.

African Development Perspectives Yearbook 1989, volume 1: *Human Dimensions of Adjustment* (1990) (Berlin: Schelzky & Jeep).

African Review 1991/2 (1991) (Saffron Walden: World of Information).

Africa South of the Sahara, 1991 (1991) (London: Europa) 20th edn.

Ake, Claude (1981), *A Political Economy of Africa* (London: Longman).

Almond, Gabriel A. and James S. Coleman (eds) (1960), *The Politics of the Developing Areas* (Princeton, N.J.: Princeton University Press).

Amin, Samir (1975), 'Underdevelopment and Dependence in Black Africa: Origins and Contemporary Forms', *Journal of Modern African Studies*, 10(4), December: 503–24.

Anyang' Nyong'o, Peter (ed.) (1987), *Popular Struggles for Democracy in Africa* (London: Zed for UNU).

Bangura, Yusuf (1991), 'Authoritarian Rule and Democracy in Africa: a Theoretical Discourse' (Geneva: UNRISD) March, Discussion Paper Number 18.

Barber, James and John Barratt (1990), *South Africa's Foreign Policy: The Search for Status and Security, 1945–1988* (Cambridge: Cambridge University Press).

Barkan, Joel D. and Frank Holmquist (1989), 'Peasant–State Relations and the Social Base of Self-Help in Kenya', *World Politics*, 41(3): 359–80.

Becker, Charles M. (1990), 'The Demo-Economic Impact of the AIDS Pandemic in Sub-Saharan Africa', *World Development*, 18(12), December: 1599–619.

Beckman, Bjorn (1981), 'Imperialism and the "National Bourgeoisie"', *Review of African Political Economy*, 22, October–December: 5–19.

—— (1988), 'The Post-Colonial State: Crisis and Reconstruction', *IDS Bulletin*, 19(4): 26–34.

—— (1989), 'Whose Democracy? Bourgeois vs Popular Democracy', *Review of African Political Economy*, 45/46: 84–97.

Bennell, Paul (1990), 'British Industrial Investment in Sub-Saharan Africa: Corporate Responses to Economic Crisis in the 1980s', *Development Policy Review*, 8(2), June: 155–77.

Berg, Robert J. and Jennifer Seymour Whitaker (eds) (1986), *Strategies for African Development* (Berkeley, Cal.: University of California Press).

Bernstein, Henry (1990), 'Agricultural "Modernisation" and the Era of

Structural Adjustment: Observations on Sub-Sahara Africa', *Journal of Peasant Studies*, 18(1), October: 3–35.

Bienefeld, Manfred (1988), 'Dependency Theory and the Political Economy of Africa's Crisis', *Review of African Political Economy*, 43: 68–87.

—— (1989), 'Lessons of History and the Developing World', *Monthly Review*, 41(3), July–August: 9–41.

Bienen, Henry and Nicholas van de Walle (1989), 'Time and Power in Africa', *American Political Science Review*, 83(1), March: 19–34.

Bratton, Michael (1989a), 'Beyond the State: Civil Society and Associational Life in Africa', *World Politics* 41(3): 407–30.

—— (1989b), 'The Politics of Government–NGO Relations in Africa', *World Development*, 17(4), April: 569–87.

Bread for the World Institute (1990), *Hunger 1990: Report on the State of World Hunger* (Washington).

Brent, R. S. (1990), 'Aiding Africa', *Foreign Policy*, 80: 121–40.

Brown, Richard (1992), *Public Debt and Private Wealth: Debt, Capital Flight and the IMF in Sudan* (London: Macmillan for ISS).

Burdette, Marcia (ed.) (1992), *Rethinking Structural Adjustment in the 1990s* (London: Macmillan).

Burkett, Paul (1990), 'Poverty Crisis in the Third World: the Contradictions of World Bank Policy', *Monthly Review*, 34(7), December: 20–32.

Callaghy, Thomas M. (1990) 'Lost between State and Market: the Politics of Economic Adjustment in Ghana, Zambia and Nigeria', in Joan M. Nelson (ed.), *The Politics of Economic Adjustment in Developing Nations* (Princeton, NJ: Princeton University Press) 257–319.

—— and John Ravenhill (eds) (1992), *Hemmed In: Responses to Africa's Economic Decline* (New York: Columbia University Press).

Cammack, John, David Pool and William Tordoff (1988), *Third World Politics: A Comparative Introduction* (London: Macmillan).

Campbell, Bonnie K. (ed.) (1989), *Political Dimensions of the International Debt Crisis: Africa and Mexico* (London: Macmillan).

—— and John Loxley (eds) (1989), *Structural Adjustment in Africa* (London: Macmillan).

Carlsson, Jerker (ed.) (1983), *Recession in Africa* (Uppsala: Scandinavian Institute of African Studies).

—— and Timothy M. Shaw (eds) (1988), *Newly Industrialising Countries and the Political Economy of South–South Relations* (London: Macmillan).

Chabal, Patrick (ed.) (1986), *Political Domination in Africa: Reflections on the Limits of Power* (Cambridge: Cambridge University Press).

—— (1992), *Power in Africa: An Essay in Political Interpretation* (London: Macmillan).

Chazan, Naomi (1988), 'Ideology, Policy and the Crisis of Poverty: the African Case', *Jerusalem Journal of International Relations*, 10: 1–30.

—— et al. (1988), *Politics and Society in Contemporary Africa* (Boulder, Col.: Lynne Rienner).

—— and Timothy M. Shaw (eds) (1988), *Coping with Africa's Food Crisis* (Boulder, Col.: Lynne Rienner).

Clark, John (1991), *Democratizing Development: The Role of Voluntary Organizations* (London: Earthscan).

Clapham, Christopher (1985), *Third World Politics: An Introduction* (London: Croom Helm).

Cobbe, James (1990), 'Africa's Economic Crisis: Review Article', *Journal of Modern African Studies* 28(2), June: 351–8.

CODESRIA Bulletin, 4 (1988).

Coleman, James S. and Carl G. Rosberg (eds) (1964), *Political Parties and National Integration in Tropical Africa* (Berkeley, Cal.: University of California Press).

Commander, Simon (ed.) (1989), *Structural Adjustment and Agriculture* (London: James Currey for Overseas Development Institute).

Committee on Africa (1942), *The Atlantic Charter and Africa from an American Standpoint: A Study by the Committee on Africa, the War and Peace Aims* (New York).

Corbo, Vittorio, Morris Goldstein and Mohsin Khan (eds) (1987), *Growth-Oriented Adjustment Programs* (Washington, D.C.: IMF and World Bank).

Cornia, Giovanni Andrea *et al.* (eds) (1987), *Adjustment with a Human Face: Protecting the Vulnerable and Promoting Growth* (Oxford: OUP for UNICEF).

—— (1988), *Adjustment with a Human Face: Ten Country Case-Studies* (Oxford: OUP for UNICEF).

Cornia, Giovanni Andrea, Rolph van der Hoeven and Thandika Mkandawire (eds) (1992), *Africa Recovery in the 1990s: From Stagnation and Adjustment to Development* (London: Macmillan for UNICEF).

Crook, Richard (1990), 'State, Society and Political Institutions in Côte d'Ivoire and Ghana' and Christopher Clapham, 'State, Society and Political Institutions in Revolutionary Ethiopia', *IDS Bulletin*, 21(4), October: 20–45.

Davies, Rob, David Sanders and Timothy M. Shaw (1991), 'Liberalisation for Development: Zimbabwe's Adjustment without the Fund', Florence: UNICEF, May; Innocenti Occasional Paper Number 16.

—— (1992), 'Liberalisation for Development: Zimbabwe's Adjustment without the Fund', in Giovanni Andrea Cornia, Rolph van der Hoeven and Thandika Mkandawire (eds), *Africa Recovery in the 1990s: From Stagnation and Adjustment to Development* (London: Macmillan for UNICEF).

'Democracy & Development' (1990), *Review of African Political Economy*, 49, Winter: 3–110.

de Soto, Hernando (1989), *The Other Path: The Invisible Revolution in the Third World* (New York: Harper & Row).

de Zalduondo, Barbara O. *et al.* (1989), 'AIDS in Africa: Diversity in the Global Pandemic', *Daedalus*, 118(3), Summer: 165–204.

Diamond, Larry *et al.* (eds) (1988), *Democracy in Developing Countries*, volume 2: *Africa* (Boulder, Col.: Lynne Rienner).

Doornbos, Martin (1990), 'The African State in Academic Debate: Retrospect and Prospect', *Journal of Modern African Studies*, 28(2), June: 179–98.

Drabek, Anne Gordon (ed.) (1987), 'Development Alternatives: The Challenge for NGOs', *World Development*, 15 (special issue), Autumn: 1–261.

Duncan, Alex and John Howell (eds) (1991), *Structural Adjustment and the African Farmer* (London: Zed for ODI).

Economic Commission for Africa (1983), *ECA and Africa's Development, 1983–2008: A Preliminary Perspective Study* (Addis Ababa, April).

—— (1989a), *Economic Report on Africa 1989* (Addis Ababa, April).

—— (1989b), *African Alternative Framework to Structural Adjustment Programmes for Socio-Economic Recovery and Transformation* (Addis Ababa, July).

—— (1989c), *Statistics and Policies: ECA Preliminary Observations on the World Bank Report 'Africa's Adjustment and Growth in the 1980s'* (Addis Ababa).

—— (1989d), *Beyond Recovery: ECA's Revised Perspectives on Africa's Development, 1990–2008* (Addis Ababa).

—— (1990) *African Charter for Popular Participation in Development and Transformation, Arusha, February 1990* (Addis Ababa).

Edwards, Michael (1989), 'The Irrelevance of Development Studies', *Third World Quarterly*, 11(1), January: 116–35.

Elson, Diane (ed.) (1991), *Male Bias in the Development Process* (Manchester: Manchester University Press).

Fatton, Robert (1990), 'Liberal Democracy in Africa', *Political Science Quarterly*, 105(3), Fall: 455–73.

Fowler, Alan (1991), 'The Role of NGOs in Changing State–Society Relations: Perspectives from Eastern and Southern Africa', *Development Policy Review*, 9(1), March: 53–84.

Frank, André Gunder (1979), *Dependent Accumulation and Underdevelopment* (London: Macmillan).

Frimpong-Ansah, Jonathan *et al.* (eds) (1991), *Trade and Development in Sub-Saharan Africa* (Manchester: Manchester University Press for CEPR).

Geldenhuys, Deon (1984), *The Diplomacy of Isolation: South African Foreign Policy Making* (London: Macmillan).

Ghai, Dharam (ed.) (1991), *The IMF and the South: Social Impact of Crisis and Adjustment* (London: Zed).

Gill, Stephen and David Law (1988), *The Global Political Economy* (Hemel Hempstead: Harvester-Wheatsheaf).

Glantz, Michael (ed.) (1987), *Drought and Hunger in Africa* (Cambridge: Cambridge University Press).

Graf, William (1991), *The Internationalization of the German Economy* (London: Macmillan).

Gromyko, Anatoly (ed.) (1983), *African Countries' Foreign Policy* (Moscow: Progress).

Gulhati, Ravi (1990), *The Making of Economic Policy in Africa* (Washington, DC: Economic Development Institute of IBRD, April).

Hancock, Graham (1991), *Lords of Poverty* (London: Mandarin).

Hansen, Emmanuel (ed.) (1987), *Africa: Perspectives on Peace and Development* (London: Zed for UNU).

Hardy, Chandra (1990), 'Toward a Self-Reliant South', North–South Institute 'Briefing', Ottawa, B28.

Harris, Nigel (1987), *The End of the Third World: NICs and the Decline of an Ideology* (Harmondsworth: Penguin).

Harrison, Paul (1989), *The Greening of Africa: Breaking Through in the Battle for Land and Food* (London: Paladin).

Havnevik, Kjell J. (ed.) (1987), *The IMF and the World Bank in Africa* (Uppsala: Scandinavian Institute of African Studies).

Haynes, George E. (1950), *Africa: Continent of the Future* (New York: Association Press for YMCA).

Helleiner, Gerald (ed.) (1985), *Africa and the IMF* (Washington, DC: IMF).

—— (1989), 'Lessons for Sub-Saharan Africa from Latin American Experiences', *African Development Review*, 1(1): 3–20.

Herbst, Jeffrey I. (1990a), 'Economic Reform in Africa: Lessons of Ghana', *UFSI Field Staff Reports*, 15(198): 9–90.

—— (1990b), 'Structural Reform and Debt in Africa', in Richard O'Brien and Ingrid Iverson (eds), *Finance and the International Economy*: 3 (Oxford: OUP) 155–68.

Hjort Ornas, A. and M. A. Mohamed Salih (eds) (1989), *Ecology and Politics: Environmental Stress and Security in Africa* (Uppsala: Scandinavian Institute of African Studies).

Hodder-Williams, Richard (1984), *An Introduction to the Politics of Tropical Africa* (London: George Allen & Unwin).

Hutchful, Eboe (1988), 'The Violence of Periphery States', *African Journal of Political Economy*, 2(1): 48–74.

Hyden, Goran (1980), *Beyond Ujamaa in Tanzania: Underdevelopment and an Uncaptured Peasantry* (London: Heinemann).

—— (1983), *No Shortcuts to Progress: African Development Management in Perspective* (London: Heinemann).

——, and Michael Bratton (eds) (1991), *Governance and Politics in Africa* (Boulder, Col.: Lynne Rienner).

IDRC (1987), *Economic Adjustment and Long-Term Development in Uganda* (Ottawa, November).

Index on Censorship (1989), 'Special Issue on Africa', 18(9), October: 7–23.

Jackson, Robert H. and Carl G. Rosberg (1982a), *Personal Rule in Black Africa* (Berkeley, Cal.: University of California Press).

—— (1982b), 'Why Africa's Weak States Persist: The Empirical and the Juridical in Statehood', *World Politics*, 35(1): 1–24.

Joseph, Richard (ed.) (1989), *Beyond Autocracy in Africa* (Atlanta: Carter Center).

—— (1990), *African Governance in the 1990s* (Atlanta: Carter Center).

Kay, Geoffrey (1982), *Development and Underdevelopment: A Marxist Analysis* (London: Macmillan).

Kearney, Richard C. (1990), 'Mauritius and the NIC Model Redux: or, How Many Cases Make a Model?', *Journal of Developing Areas*, 24(1): January: 195–216.

Kennedy, Paul (1988), *African Capitalism* (Cambridge: Cambridge University Press).

Killick, Tony and Matthew Martin (1989), 'African Debt: The Search for Solutions', UN Africa Recovery Programme 'Briefing Paper', 1, June.

Kitching, Gavin (1989), *Development and Underdevelopment in Historical Perspective* (London: Routledge).

Korany, Bahgat, Rex Brynen and Paul Noble (eds) (1992), *The New Face of National Security in the Arab World: Dilemmas of Security and Development* (London: Macmillan).

Laidi, Zaki (1990), *The Superpowers and Africa: The Constraints of a Rivalry, 1960–1990* (Chicago: University of Chicago Press).

Lancaster, Carol (1989), 'Economic Restructuring in Sub-Saharan Africa', *Current History*, 88(538): 213–16 and 244.

Larson, Ann (1990), 'The Social Epidemology of Africa's AIDS Epidemic', *African Affairs*, 89(354), January: 5–25.

Lehman, Howard P. (1990), 'The Politics of Adjustment in Kenya and Zimbabwe: The State as Intermediary', *Studies in Comparative International Development*, 25(3), Fall: 37–72.

—— (1993), *Indebted Development: Strategic Bargaining and Economic Adjustment in the Third World* (London: Macmillan).

Leys, Colin (1991), *The Rise and Fall of Development Theory* (London: James Currey).

Liebenow, J. Gus (1986), *African Politics: Crises and Challenges* (Bloomington: Indiana University Press).

Loxley, John (1988), *Ghana: Economic Crisis and the Long Road to Recovery* (Ottawa: North–South Institute).

Maliyamkono, T. Luta and Mboya S. D. Bagachwa (1990), *The Second Economy in Tanzania* (London: James Currey).

Mandaza, Ibbo (ed.) (1986), *Zimbabwe: The Political Economy of Transition, 1980–86* (Dakar: CODESRIA).

Markovitz, Irving L. (ed.) (1987), *Studies in Power and Class in Africa* (New York: Oxford University Press).

Martin, Matthew (1991), *The Crumbling Façade of African Debt Negotiations: No Winners* (London: Macmillan).

Mengisteab, Kidane and Bernard I. Logan (1990), 'Implications of Liberalization Policies for Agricultural Development in Sub-Saharan Africa', *Comparative Political Studies*, 22(4), January: 437–57.

Mittelman, James H. (1988), *Out from Underdevelopment: Prospects for the Third World* (London: Macmillan).

Mkandawire, Thandika (1988), 'The Road to Crisis, Adjustment and Deindustrialisation: The African Case', *Africa Development*, 13(1): 5–31.

Mosley, Paul (ed.) (1992), *Development Finance and Policy Reform* (London: Macmillan).

—— and L. Smith (1989), 'Structural Adjustment and Agricultural Performance in Sub-Saharan Africa, 1980–1987', *Journal of International Development*, 1(3): 321–55.

—— and John Toye (1988), 'The Design of Structural Adjustment Programmes', *Development Policy Review*, 6(4), December: 395–413.

——, Jane Harrigan and John Toye (1991), *Aid and Power: The World Bank and Policy-based Lending*, 2 vols; vol. 1: *Analysis and Policy Proposals*; vol. 2: *Country Case Studies* (London: Routledge).

Murphy, Craig N. and Roger Tooze (eds) (1991), *The New International Political Economy* (London: Macmillan).

Naylor, R. T. (1987), *Hot Money and the Politics of Debt* (London: Unwin & Hyman).

Nelson, Joan M. *et al.* (1989), *Fragile Coalitions: The Politics of Economic Adjustment* (New Brunswick: Transaction).

—— (ed.) (1990), *The Politics of Economic Adjustment in Developing Nations* (Princeton, NJ: Princeton University Press).

New African Yearbook: 48 African Countries, 1991–1992 (1991) (London: IC Publishers) 8th edn.

Nyang'oro, Julius E. (1989), *The State and Capitalist Development in Africa: Declining Political Economies* (New York: Praeger).

—— and Timothy M. Shaw (eds) (1989), *Corporatism in Africa: Comparative Analysis and Practice* (Boulder, Col.: Westview).

—— and Timothy M. Shaw (eds) (1992), *Beyond Structural Adjustment in Africa: The Political Economy of Sustainable and Democratic Development* (New York: Praeger).

Nzongola-Ntalaja (1987), *Revolution and Counter-Revolution in Africa: Essays in Contemporary Politics* (London: Institute for African Alternatives and Zed).

O'Connor, Anthony (1991), *Poverty in Africa: A Geographical Approach* (London: Bellhaven/Pinter).

Olaniyan, R. Onutayo and Chibuzo N. Nwoke (eds) (1990), *Structural Adjustment in Nigeria: The Impact of SFEM on the Economy* (Lagos: NIIA).

Onimode, Bade (1988), *A Political Economy of the African Crisis* (London: Zed).

Onwuka, Ralph I. and Timothy M. Shaw (eds) (1989), *Africa in World Politics: Into the 1990s* (London: Macmillan).

Organisation of African Unity (1980), *Lagos Plan of Action for the Economic Development of Africa, 1980–2000* (Geneva: International Institute for Labour Studies).

—— (1991), 'Treaty Establishing the African Economic Community', Abuja, June (selections in Appendix).

Parfitt, Trevor W. and Stephen P. Riley (1989), *The African Debt Crisis* (London: Routledge).

Parpart, Jane L. and Kathleen A. Staudt (eds) (1989), *Women and the State in Africa* (Boulder, Col.: Lynne Rienner).

Peet, Richard (1991), *Global Capitalism: Theories of Societal Development* (London: Routledge).

Pickett, James (1989), 'Reflections on the Market and State in Sub-Saharan Africa', *African Development Review*, 1(1), June: 58–86.

—— and Hans Singer (eds) (1990), *Towards Economic Recovery in Sub-Saharan Africa* (London: Routledge).

Pirages, Dennis C. and Christine Sylvester (eds) (1990), *Transformations in the Global Political Economy* (London: Macmillan).

'Price of Economic Reform' (1990), *Review of African Political Economy*, 47.

Quarsoo, Philip K. (1990), 'Structural Adjustment Programmes in Sub-Saharan Africa: Evolution of Approaches', *African Development Review*, 2(1), December: 1–26.

Ravenhill, John (ed.) (1986), *Africa in Economic Crisis* (London: Macmillan).

—— (1988), 'Adjustment with Growth: A Fragile Consensus', *Journal of Modern African Studies*, 26(2), June: 179–210.

—— (1990a), 'Reversing Africa's Economic Decline: No Easy Answers', *World Policy Journal*, 7(4), Fall: 703–32.

—— (1990b), 'The North–South Balance of Power', *International Affairs*, 66(4), October: 731–48.

Ray, Donald I. (1989), *Dictionary of the African Left: Parties, Movements and Groups* (Aldershot: Gower).

Riddell, Roger (ed.) (1990), *Manufacturing Africa* (London: James Currey).

Rodriguez, Ennio and Stephany Griffith-Jones (eds) (1992), *Conditionality, Banking Regulation and Third World Debt* (London: Macmillan).

Rothchild, Donald and Naomi Chazan (eds) (1988), *The Precarious Balance: State and Society in Africa* (Boulder, Col.: Westview).

Roxborough, Ian (1979), *Theories of Underdevelopment* (London: Macmillan).

—— (1988), 'Modernisation Theory Revisited: A Review Article', *Comparative Studies in Society and History*, 30(4), October: 753–61.

Sandbrook, Richard (1985), *The Politics of Africa's Economic Stagnation* (Cambridge: Cambridge University Press).

—— (1988), 'Liberal Democracy in Africa: A Socialist-Revisionist Perspective', *Canadian Journal of African Studies*, 22: 240–67.

—— (1990), 'Taming the African Leviathan: Political Reform and Economic Recovery', *World Policy Journal*, 7(4), Fall: 673–701.

Saul, John (1979), *The State and Revolution in Eastern Africa* (New York: Monthly Review).

Save the Children Fund/Overseas Development Institute (1988), *Prospects for Africa* (London: Hodder & Stoughton).

Schatz, Sayre P. (1987), 'Laissez-Faireism for Africa?', *Journal of Modern African Studies*, 25(1), March: 129–38.

Seers, Dudley (1963), 'The Limitations of the Special Case', *Oxford University Institute of Economics and Statistics Bulletin*, 25(2), May.

—— (1989), 'The Limitations of the Special Cases', *IDS Bulletin*, 20(3).

Sender, John and Sheila Smith (1986), *The Development of Capitalism in Africa* (London: Methuen).

Shaw, Timothy M. (1979), 'The Actors in African International Politics', in Timothy M. Shaw and Kenneth A. Heard (eds), *Politics of Africa: Dependence and Development* (London: Longman) 357–96.

—— (1985), *Towards a Political Economy for Africa: The Dialectics of Dependence* (London: Macmillan).

—— (1987), 'Security Redefined: Unconventional Conflict in Africa', in Steven Wright and Jan Brownfoot (eds), *Africa in World Politics* (London: Macmillan) 17–34.

—— (1988a), 'Africa in the 1990s: from Economic Crisis to Structural Readjustment', *Dalhousie Review*, 68: 37–69.

—— (1988b), 'Africa's Conjuncture: From Structural Adjustment to Self-Reliance', *Third World Affairs, 1988* (London: Third World Foundation) 318–37.

—— (1989a), 'The UN Economic Commission for Africa: Continental Development and Self-reliance', in David P. Forsythe (ed.), *The United Nations in the World Political Economy* (London: Macmillan) 98–111.

—— (1989b), 'The Revival of Regionalism in Africa: Cure for Crisis or Prescription for Conflict?', *Jerusalem Journal of International Relations*, 11: 79–105.

—— (1990a), 'Dependent Development in the New International Division of Labour: Prospects for Africa's Political Economy', in David G. Haglund and Michael K. Hawes (eds), *World Politics: Power, Interdependence and Dependence* (Toronto: Harcourt Brace Jovanovich) 333–60.

—— (1990b), 'Regionalism and the African Crisis', in Julius Emeka Okolo and Steven Wright (eds), *West Africa: Regional Cooperation and Development* (Boulder, Col.: Westview) 115–45.

—— (1990c), 'The Future of the Fourth World: Choices of and Constraints on the Very Poor in the 1980s', in Dennis C. Pirages and Christine Sylvester (eds), *Transformations in the Global Political Economy* (London: Macmillan) 195–229.

—— (1990d), 'Foreign Policy in the New International Division of Labour: The African Dimension', in David Wurfel and Bruce Burton (eds), *The Political Economy of Foreign Policy in Southeast Asia* (London: Macmillan) 38–53.

—— (1990e), 'Dependent Development in the New International Division of Labour: Prospects for Africa's Political Economy', *Indian Journal of Social Science*, 3: 225–54.

—— (1990f), 'Popular Participation in Non-Governmental Structures in Africa: Implications for Democratic Development', *Africa Today*, 37(3), Third Quarter: 5–22.

—— (1991a), 'Reformism, Revisionism and Radicalism in African Political Economy in the 1990s', *Journal of Modern African Studies*, 29.

—— (1991b), 'South and Southern Africa in the New International Division of Labour', in Larry A. Swatuk and Timothy M. Shaw (eds), *Prospects for Development and Peace in Southern Africa in the 1990s: Canadian and Comparative Perspectives* (Lanham: University Press of America).

—— (1991c), 'Overview of African Development: From National Independence to Structural Adjustment', in O. Teriba and J. C. Senghor (eds), *Adebayo Adedeji at Sixty: Issues in African Development and Future Prospects* (forthcoming).

—— (1991d), 'Black Africa and the New International Division of Labour at the Start of the 1990s', in Prosser Gifford and Bogumil Jewsiewicki (eds), *State and Civil Society in Eastern Europe and Africa* (Lanham: University Press of America).

—— (1992a), 'Africa after the Crises of the 1980s: the Dialectics of Adjustment', in Mary Hawkesworth and Maurice Kogan (eds), *Routledge Encyclopaedia of Government and Politics* (London: Routledge).

—— (1992b), 'Beyond Structural Adjustment: Revisionism in African Political Economy in the 1990s', Geneva: UNRISD, Discussion Paper Number xx.

—— and Olajide Aluko (eds), (1983) *Nigerian Foreign Policy: Alternative Perceptions and Projections* (London: Macmillan).

—— and Rob Davies (1992), 'The Political Economy of Adjustment in Zimbabwe: Convergence and Reform' in Marcia Burdette (ed.), *Rethinking Structural Adjustment in the 1990s* (London: Macmillan).

—— and John Inegbedion (1991) 'Alternative Approaches to Peace and Security in Africa', in Jorge Rodriguez Beruff, Peter Figueroa and J. Edward Greene (eds), *Conflict, Peace and Security in the Caribbean* (London: Macmillan) 259–83.

—— and John Inegbedion (1992), 'Africa in the New Global Political Economy', in Bahgat Korany, Rex Brynen and Paul Noble (eds), *The New Face of National Security in the Arab World: Dilemmas of Security and Development* (London: Macmillan).

—— and Julius Emeka Okolo (eds) (1993), *The Political Economy of Foreign Policy in ECOWAS States* (London: Macmillan).

Shivji, Issa (1988), *Fight my Beloved Country: New Democracy in Africa* (Harare: SAPES Trust).

Simon, Roger (1982), *Gramsci's Political Thought: An Introduction* (London: Lawrence & Wishart).

Sklar, Richard L. (1988), 'Beyond Capitalism and Socialism in Africa', *Journal of Modern African Studies*, 26(1), March: 1–21.

—— and C. S. Whitaker (1991), *African Politics and Problems in Development* (Boulder, Col.: Lynne Rienner).

Somerville, Keith (1990), *Foreign Military Intervention in Africa* (London: Pinter).

South Commission (1990), *The Challenge to the South* (New York: OUP).

Spark, D. (1989), 'Review Article: What Chance of Change for Africa?', *Development Policy Review*, 7(2): 193–8.

Stevens, Chris (1992), *Europe and the Third World since Decolonisation* (London: Macmillan).

Stichter, Sharon and Jane L. Parpart (eds) (1988), *Patriarchy and Class:African Women in the Home and Workforce* (Boulder, Col.: Westview).

Stoneman, Colin and Lionel Cliffe (1989), *Zimbabwe: Politics, Economics and Society* (London: Pinter).

Swatuk, Larry A. and Timothy M. Shaw (eds) (1991), *Prospects for Development and Peace in Southern Africa in the 1990s: Canadian and Comparative Perspectives* (Lanham: University Press of America).

Tangri, Roger (1985), *Politics in Sub-Saharan Africa* (London: James Currey).

Tausch, Arno (1993), *Towards a Socio-Liberal Theory of World Development* (London: Macmillan).

Timberlake, Lloyd (1988), *Africa in Crisis: The Causes, the Cures of Environmental Bankruptcy* (London: Earthscan).

Tordoff, William (1984), *Government and Politics in Africa* (London: Macmillan).

Toye, John (1987), *Dilemmas of Development: Reflections on the Counter-revolution in Development Theory and Policy* (Oxford: Basil Blackwell).

Turok, Ben (1987), *Africa: What Can Be Done?* (London: Institute for African Alternatives and Zed).

—— (1989), *Mixed Economy in Focus: Zambia* (London: Institute for African Alternatives).

United Nations (1986), *UN Programme of Action for African Economic*

Recovery and Development, 1986–90 (New York).

—— (1988a), *Financing Africa's Recovery: Report and Recommendations of the Advisory Group on Financial Flows for Africa* (New York).

—— (1988b), *Africa Four Years On: Overview of UN–NGO Conference, Geneva, April 1988* (Geneva, November).

United Nations Africa Recovery Programme, *Briefing Papers* (1989) 'African Debt', 1, June.

—— (1990), 'African LDCs: Among the Most Vulnerable and Least Developed', 2, August.

United Nations Conference on Trade and Development (1990), *Africa's Commodity Problems: Towards a Solution* (Geneva).

United Nations Development Programme (1990), *Human Development Report 1990* (New York: OUP).

—— (1991), *Human Development Report 1991* (New York: OUP).

United Nations Children's Fund (1990), *The State of the World's Children, 1990* (Oxford: OUP).

Utting, Peter (1992), *Economic Reform and Third World Socialism* (London: Macmillan for UNRISD).

van Donge, Jan Kees (1990), 'Review Article: on Democracy in Africa', *Journal of Modern African Studies*, 28(2), June: 351–8.

Vickers, Jeanne (ed.) (1991), *Women and the World Economic Crisis* (London: Zed).

Weissman, Stephen R. (1990), 'Structural Adjustment in Africa: Insights from the Experiences of Ghana and Senegal', *World Development*, 18(12), December: 1621–34.

Werlin, H. (ed.) (1991), 'Special Issue: Bottlenecks to Development', *Public Administration and Development*, 11(3): May–June: 189–302.

Whitaker, Jennifer Seymour (1988), *How Can Africa Survive?* (New York: Harper & Row).

Wiseman, John (1990), *Democracy in Black Africa: Survival and Revival* (New York: Paragon House).

World Bank (1981), *Accelerated Development in Sub-Saharan Africa: An Agenda for Action* (Washington).

—— (1986), *Financing Adjustment with Growth in Sub-Saharan Africa, 1986–1990* (Washington).

—— (1988), *Education in Sub-Saharan Africa* (Washington).

—— (1989a), *World Development Report 1989* (Washington, June).

—— (1989b), *Sub-Saharan Africa: From Crisis to Sustainable Growth. A Long-term Perspective Study* (Washington, November).

—— (1990a), *World Development Report 1990* (Washington, June).

—— (1990b), *Long-Term Perspective Study of Sub-Saharan Africa: Background Papers* (Washington, June).

—— (1990c), *Making Adjustment Work for the Poor: A Framework for Policy Reform in Africa* (Washington, September).

—— (1991a), *The African Capacity-Building Initiative: Toward Improved Policy Analysis and Development Management* (Washington, January).

—— (1991b), *World Development Report 1991* (Washington, June).

World Bank and UNDP (1989), *Africa's Adjustment and Growth in the 1980s* (Washington, March).

World University Service (1990), *Academic Freedom 1990: a human rights report* (London: Zed).

Wurfel, David and Bruce Burton (eds) (1990), *The Political Economy of Foreign Policy in Southeast Asia* (London: Macmillan).

Young, Ralph A. (1991), 'States and Markets in Africa', in Maurice Wright and Michael Moran (eds), *States and Markets* (London: Macmillan).

Young, Roger (1987), *Zambia: Adjusting to Poverty* (Ottawa: North–South Institute).

—— and John Loxley (1990), *Zambia: An Assessment of Zambia's Structural Adjustment Experience* (Ottawa: North–South Institute).

Index